Economic and Managemen
Tourism and Hospitality R

?!ackburn
ollege

Economic and Management Methods for Tourism and Hospitality Research

PROFESSOR THOMAS BAUM
The Scottish Hotel School, University of Strathclyde

and

DR RAM MUDAMBI
ISMA Centre, University of Reading

JOHN WILEY & SONS
Chichester · New York · Weinheim · Brisbane · Singapore · Toronto

National   01243 779777
International (+44) 1243 779777
e-mail (for orders and customer service enquiries): cs-book@wiley.co.uk
Visit our Home Page on http://www.wiley.co.uk
        or http://www.wiley.com

Other Wiley Editorial Offices

John Wiley & Sons, Inc., 605 Third Avenue,
New York, NY 10158-0012, USA

WILEY-VCH Verlag GmbH, Pappelallee 3,
D-69469 Weinheim, Germany

Jacaranda Wiley Ltd, 33 Park Road, Milton,
Queensland 4064, Australia

John Wiley & Sons (Asia) Pte Ltd, 2 Clementi Loop #02-01,
Jin Xing Distripark, Singapore 129809

John Wiley & Sons (Canada) Ltd, 22 Worcester Road,
Rexdale, Ontario M9W 1L1, Canada

Library of Congress Cataloging-in-Publication Data
Baum, Thomas.
   Economic and management methods for tourism and hospitality
research / Thomas Baum, Ram Mudambi.
      p.   cm.
   Includes bibliographical references and index.
   ISBN 0-471-98392-6 (cloth)
   1. Hospitality industry—Management.   2. Hospitality industry—
Economic aspects.   3. Tourist trade—Management.   4. Tourist trade—
Economic aspects.   I. Mudambi, Ram. 1954 .   II. Title.
TX911.3.M27B38   1998
647.94'068—dc21
                                                        98–24166
                                                        CIP

British Library Cataloguing in Publication Data

A catalogue record for this book is available from the British Library

ISBN 0471-98392-6

Typeset in 10/12 pt Palacio from editors' disks by Mathematical Composition Setters Ltd,
Salisbury, Wiltshire.
Printed and bound in Great Britain by Antony Rowe Ltd, Eastbourne
This book is printed on acid-free paper responsibly manufactured from sustainable forestry, in
which at least two trees are planted for each one used for paper production.

For my parents,
Dr (Mrs) Sumati R. Mudambi and Dr Mudambi V. Rajagopal
for their encouragement, support and love

R.M.

For my grandparents Baum and von Gierke

T.B.

Contents

Contributors   ix

Preface   xi

Acknowledgements   xiii

PART I   1

1 Quantitative Methods: Introductory Note   3
  Ram Mudambi
2 Input-Output Models   7
  John Fletcher
3 Portfolio Models of Tourism   25
  M. Thea Sinclair
4 Transactions Cost Analysis of Tourism   39
  Peter J. Buckley
5 Behavioral Models Related to Tourism   47
  Stephen J. Hiemstra and Joseph A. Ismail
6 An Empirical Analysis of Oligopolistic Hotel Pricing:
  The Case of Bermuda Resort Hotels   67
  Tom Baum and Ram Mudambi
7 A Positioning Analysis of Hotel Brands   85
  Chekitan S. Dev, Michael S. Morgan and Stowe Shoemaker
8 A Utility Analysis of Cross-Time Tourism Consumption   99
  Zheng Gu

PART II   117

9 Multidisciplinary Methods: Introductory Note   119
  Tom Baum
10 Assessing Local Income and Employment Effects of Tourism:
   Experience Using the Nordic Model of Tourism   123
   Marja Paajanen
11 Strategic Segmentation: An Empirical Analysis of Tourist
   Expenditure in Turkey   145
   Ram Mudambi and Tom Baum

12 The Economic Aspects of Location Marketing   159
    Stephen Wanhill
13 Package Holiday Pricing: Cause of the IT Industry's
    Success, or Cause for Concern?   197
    Eric Laws
14 Economic Pricing Strategies for Hotels   215
    Stephen J. Hiemstra
15 Environmental Aspects of Tourism: Applications of
    Cost-Benefit Analysis   233
    Michael Stabler

Index   269

Contributors

Tom Baum is Professor of International Hospitality Management at the Scottish Hotel School, University of Strathclyde, Glasgow, UK

Peter J. Buckley is Professor of International Business and Director of the Centre for International Business, University of Leeds (CIBUL) at the Leeds University Business School, UK

Chekitan S. Dev is Associate Professor of Strategic Marketing at the School of Hotel Administration, Cornell University, Ithaca, New York, USA

John Fletcher is Professor in the International Centre for Tourism and Hospitality Research at the School of Service Industries, Bournemouth University, Poole, UK

Zheng Gu is Associate Professor of Finance in the Department of Tourism & Convention Administration at the William F. Harrah College of Hotel Administration, University of Nevada, Las Vegas, Nevada, USA

Stephen J. Hiemstra is Professor of Marketing in the Department of Restaurant, Hotel, Institutional and Tourism Management, Purdue University, West Lafayette, Indiana, USA

Joseph A. Ismail is Assistant Professor of Management in the Department of Restaurant, Hotel, Institutional and Tourism Management, Purdue University, West Lafayette, Indiana, USA

Eric Laws is Senior Lecturer at the School of Marketing and International Business, Queensland University of Technology, Brisbane, Australia

Michael Morgan is a former Assistant Professor of Marketing at the School of Hotel Administration, Cornell University, Ithaca, New York, USA

Ram Mudambi is Reader in International Business at the International Securities Market Association (ISMA) Centre, University of Reading, UK

Marja Paajanen is a Research Associate at the Helsinki School of Economics and Business Administration, Helsinki, Finland

Stowe Shoemaker is Assistant Professor of Hotel Administration at the William F. Harrah College of Hotel Administration, University of Nevada, Las Vegas, Nevada, USA

M. Thea Sinclair is Senior Lecturer in Economics at Keynes College, University of Kent, Canterbury, UK

Michael Stabler is Senior Lecturer in Spatial Economics at the Centre for Spatial and Real Estate Economics (CSPREE), University of Reading, UK

Stephen R. C. Wanhill is Travelbag Professor of Tourism at the School of Service Industries, Bournemouth University, Poole, UK

Preface

The tourism and hospitality sector is, arguably, one of the largest components of the global economy, with a growth rate in consumption that supersedes that of most other goods and services. Mass international tourism, dispersed on a global scale, is also a relatively recent phenomenon, dating from the post-war era and, particularly, the advent of the jet engine within commercial aviation and the freedom of the roads provided by the motor car. The growth in tourism consumption in the developing regions of the world is more recent and is still in its infancy, presenting the prospect of travel on an international scale in the future which far exceeds the 600+ million annual arrivals at the present time. As a consequence of the growth in international (and domestic) travel, the profile of tourists is changing as consumers become more experienced, demanding and likely to treat tourism purchases in very much the same way as they do any other item of consumption.

Tourism and hospitality is also a sector undergoing significant change in its supply side organisation. The role of the public sector has already altered significantly and the role of market facilitation rather than direct development and policing is likely to grow. The private sector, while still dominated by the small operator in many countries, is witnessing considerable consolidation in sectors such as air transportation, accommodation and tour operations, so that the future seems to hold out the prospect of a sector increasingly dominated by large organisations or the alliance of major international suppliers within or across subsectors. Communications and transport technology are, in many respects, the key to this process of global consolidation in tourism and hospitality and there is little evidence of a slow down in the pace of change in these areas.

Anticipating and managing change and development within tourism and hospitality has, therefore, become a challenge which is faced by those in the public as well as the private sector, with a wide range of policy and operational briefs. Recognising the breadth of the information environment within which the tourism and hospitality sector operates is a key starting point for this management responsibility. Tourism and hospitality draw their theoretical and practical inspiration from a wide range of academic disciplines including geography, economics, anthropology and management. In addition, a number of practitioner contexts such as planning, heritage, environmental management, food service, accommodation and transport are relevant as well. Thus, information collection, evaluation and analysis becomes a complex and challenging yet vital task. Understanding the variety of tools and methods available to managers and decision-makers in tourism and hospitality as well as to those engaged in academic and other research in the field is a critical element in overcoming the information challenge in tourism and hospitality.

This book is designed to provide managers and researchers with insights into the practical application of tools for gathering and analysing information. These tools can be used in understanding tourism phenomena and in planning responses. Although quantitative in focus, the methods presented here draw on a variety of disciplinary origins and have application across the range of decision-making contexts that arise in tourism and hospitality.

The book is intended for readers who have mastered basic quantitative and economic concepts and techniques, and who, hopefully, will have the opportunity to apply the techniques in real or simulated contexts. The readership, therefore, is likely to include tourism professionals with policy, planning, research or statistical remits. In addition, the book will be of value to final year undergraduates and postgraduate students with a significant research dissertation requirement. We welcome all comments, suggestions and constructive criticism and look forward to hearing from our readers.

Tom Baum
Scottish Hotel School, University of Strathclyde

and

Ram Mudambi
ISMA Centre, University of Reading

Acknowledgements

This project began while we were both teaching at the University of Buckingham. During the course of teaching graduate courses and supervising research, we found that many students did not have the requisite familiarity with the quantitative tools commonly used in management and economics. We would like to thank many generations of graduate students at the School of Business at the University of Buckingham who took our Research Methods seminar and whose suggestions ultimately influenced the choice of topics in the present volume. We would also like to thank the Dean, Martin Ricketts, for making resources available for us to run the seminar.

Three chapters are developments of work that has appeared earlier. Chapter 6 is based on 'An empirical analysis of oligopolistic hotel pricing: The case of Bermuda resort hotels', *Annals of Tourism Research*, 22 (3), 1995: 501–516. Chapter 7 is a development of 'A positioning analysis of hotel brands – based on travel manager perceptions', *Cornell Hotel and Restaurant Administration Quarterly*, 36, December 1995: 48–55. Chapter 11 is a development of 'Strategic segmentation: an empirical analysis of tourist expenditure in Turkey', *Journal of Travel Research*, 36(1), 1997: 29–34.

We would like to thank Elsevier Science, the School of Hotel Administration at Cornell University and the Travel and Tourism Research Association for cooperation in connection with including these chapters. We would like to extend our thanks to the respective editors, Jafar Jafari at the University of Wisconsin – Stout, Glenn Withiam at Cornell and Chuck Goeldner at the University of Colorado – Boulder.

We would like to acknowledge the more recent support and input of our colleagues at, respectively, Strathclyde and Reading. We would also like to place on record the efforts of our contributors, leaders in their fields, and therefore, busy people who gave of their time and insights in order to make this book what it is. Any shortcomings in the final product, however, must be attributed to us.

No work of this magnitude is accomplished without significant support on the home front. For unstinting support here we would like to acknowledge our wives, Brelda and Susan, as well as our children, Alexander, Rajan and Maya.

Tom Baum, *Glasgow*
Ram Mudambi, *Reading*

PART I

1 Quantitative Methods: Introductory Note

RAM MUDAMBI

The travel, tourism and hospitality (TTH) industry group is generally accepted to be the largest industry group in the world. Further, its component industries are (generally) characterised by relatively low technology and high labour intensity. This makes it particularly suited to the requirements of the developing regions of the world, where technology is often scarce and labour is abundant and cheap. Several such regions have reaped large returns from investments in the tourism infrastructure and some, like Singapore, have achieved developed status (Heng and Low, 1990).

Further, as incomes have risen in developed regions of the world, the demand for customised products in general, and leisure products in particular, has burgeoned (Litteljohn, 1993). This is one of the factors underlying the increase in the share of the service sector in gross world product. Thus, even in mature developed economies, the TTH industry group is one of the fastest growing sectors.

One of the basic and well-known problems associated with the TTH industry group is its diverse nature. It is very difficult to demarcate the boundaries of the group. It includes core industries such as the hotel industry and the package tour industry, but also includes parts of many other industries, which cater to tourists and non-tourists alike. This means that statistics relating to the TTH industry group as a whole tend to be difficult to come by and those that are available tend to be relatively crude estimates. This is the main reason why historically, quantitative work in the area of TTH has lagged behind that in other social sciences.

All this is beginning to change. Statistics relating to TTH are improving as more and more authorities begin to realise the potential of this industry group in fuelling growth. It is therefore particularly important that the newly available data are used to their maximum potential in the crucial decision-making process. A wide variety of sophisticated quantitative techniques

Economic and Management Methods for Tourism and Hospitality Research.
Edited by Thomas Baum and Ram Mudambi © 1999 John Wiley & Sons Ltd.

have been developed for use in economics and management. Many of these are particularly appropriate for use in the area of TTH. It is clearly impossible to deal with the wide variety available within the confines of a single volume. We have necessarily had to be selective. In Part I of this volume, we have selected eight quantitative techniques that we believe will form a useful 'tool-kit' for students, researchers and practitioners in the field.

The broadest quantitative questions in the field concern the development and implementation of government policy. The most crucial policy choices emerge in decisions with regard to public expenditure, much of which is directed towards infrastructural development. Formulation of the most effective policies requires information about the value of alternative investments (Bull, 1991).

The TTH industry group is particularly dependent on infrastructural investment. Airports, ports, roads, reliable supplies of electricity and clean water and many other such facilities are essential to the survival and growth of industries in the group. In virtually all cases, such investments have a large element of public funding in them, as externality and free rider problems ensure that the private sector will invariably lack the incentives to provide them in sufficient quantity.

The two important techniques used in public investment decision-making are multiplier estimation and input-output methods. These are related methodologies and address the question of how much value, in the broadest sense, is generated by particular levels of public expenditure. John Fletcher addresses these questions in chapter 2. The authorities will always be faced with an array of fundable projects and these methods can help them in selecting those with the highest social benefits. It is also possible to factor in concerns about non-pecuniary issues such as environmental concerns.

These questions relate, broadly speaking, to returns on public investments made to support the TTH industry group. An associated question is the volatility of the returns to such investments. Areas or regions which increase their dependency on the TTH industry group also increase their exposure to economic shocks associated with the group (Schulmeister, 1979). These shocks largely emanate from the originating countries or regions of the industry group's customers. Such risks can be systematically analysed using portfolio analysis, a technique commonly used in finance. In chapter 3, Thea Sinclair demonstrates how this technique may be used in the TTH industry group.

Moving down to the level of the individual business firm, a series of quantitative questions arise. The most frequently encountered questions concern issues of firm organisation, demand forecasting, excess demand, branding issues and intertemporal choice. The organisation of the firm, particularly in an industry group characterised by such diversity, requires the reduction of decisions to a common denominator. Transactions cost analysis, which was developed largely in the economics literature (Coase, 1937; Williamson,

1975) is a methodology which can be used to achieve this. Peter Buckley, one of the major contributors to this literature, demonstrates the use of this methodology in chapter 4.

Demand forecasting is a crucial requirement in all industries and at all levels. The key question relates to determining the causal factors associated with the dependent variable of interest. Models focusing on this causal relationship are called behavioural models and are particularly useful in the context of projections over relatively long periods of time. Stephen Hiemstra and Joseph Ismail demonstrate the use of such models in chapter 5.

Associated with demand forecasting and business cycles is the issue of excess demand and excess supply. Seasonality is a big factor in many tourist destinations and this leads to substantial excess capacity during parts of the demand cycle. Periods of excess supply are a particular problem when capacity cannot be readily adjusted, as is the case with many industries in the TTH group. The analysis of this problem is rather more technical than one might suspect. Simple price-led strategies can lead to substantial volatility. In chapter 6, Tom Baum and Ram Mudambi demonstrate the source of the volatility and suggest the basis for creative solutions.

As part of the service sector, branding is particularly important to industries in the TTH group (Aaker, 1996). In building a strong brand, choosing the right position for one's product and service offerings is the most important question. A methodology for quantitatively determining this position is proposed by Chekitan Dev, Michael Morgan and Stowe Shoemaker in Chapter 7.

Finally, the question of intertemporal choice by one's customers is addressed by Zheng Gu in chapter 8. The allocation of consumer expenditure over time is a major issue in the modern literature on investment and finance. Various factors, such as age, the interest rate and the inflation rate affect such decisions. Understanding this decision-making can help a firm to assess the impact of intertemporal demand-shifting programmes like time-limited discounts and peak and off-peak pricing.

This tool-kit does not pretend to be exhaustive. However, it does provide methodologies to deal with a wide variety of problems. Further, in a pedagogical sense, familiarity with this set of tools should develop the abilities of students and practitioners to the extent where they are able to progress to using other tools with much greater ease. Thus, we see the set of techniques in this section as useful for direct application as well as a foundation for the development of further learning.

REFERENCES

Aaker, D.A., 1996, *Building strong brands*, The Free Press, New York
Bull, A., 1991, *The economics of travel and tourism*, Longman Cheshire, Australia
Coase, R.H., 1937, The nature of the firm, *Economica*, NS 4: 386–405

Heng, T.M., Low, L., 1990, Economic impact of tourism in Singapore, *Annals of tourism research*, **17**(2): 246–267

Litteljohn, D., 1993, Western Europe, in Jones, P., Pizam, A., eds, *The international hospitality industry: organizational and operational issues*, John Wiley, New York

Schulmeister, S., 1979, *Tourism and the business cycle*, Austrian Institute for Economic Research, Vienna

Williamson, O.E., 1975, *Markets and hierarchies: analysis and antitrust implications*, The Free Press, New York

2 Input-Output Models

INTRODUCTION

There are a variety of methods that can be used to measure the economic impact and effects associated with tourist expenditure. These methods generally result in the construction of multiplier ratios. This chapter briefly examines the techniques available but focuses upon the use of input-output analysis. The chapter sets out the major assumptions that underpin input-output analysis and examines the structure of the models. Finally, the results of input-output models are examined together with discussions as to how these results should be interpreted. The concluding section leads on to some recent developments that have been made concerning the construction and delivery of input-output models in order to make them indispensable planning tools.

METHODS OF ESTIMATING ECONOMIC IMPACTS

Researchers have been concerned with developing models to estimate the economic impact of changes in final demand for more than a century. However, the most significant advances have taken place within the last 40 years. (For a more comprehensive history of the multiplier see Fletcher and Archer, 1991.) Although the models that have been developed may, at first, appear quite dissimilar, there is a clear development path and the models may all be attributed to the same pedigree. All of the models discussed below use some form of ratio as means of expressing the relationship between an exogenous change in final demand and the resultant change in economic variables, such as income, employment and government revenue. Similarly, all of the models take account of the relationship between the structure of the economy and the level of foreign trade that takes place. However, in some· fundamental aspects the models differ considerably. Some of the models are all-encompassing in the sense that they are *general equilibrium models* whereas others are *partial equilibrium models*. One of the

Economic and Management Methods for Tourism and Hospitality Research.
Edited by Thomas Baum and Ram Mudambi © 1999 John Wiley & Sons Ltd.

models does not take into account the structure of the economy, other than its export content, whereas others are built around the structural relationships that exist between the productive sectors.

There is also the question of impact levels. When measuring the economic impact of changes in tourist spending it is important to recognise that economic impacts occur across a wide range of economic variables and at three different levels.

Economic impact multiplier values can be derived for:

1. Income (all forms of local income)
2. Employment (generally expressed as full-time equivalent jobs)
3. Output (also sales and transactions multipliers which are adjusted for changes in inventories)
4. Government revenue (tax revenues and operational surplus)
5. Imports (including goods, services and repatriated income)

There are three levels of impact that can be estimated for each of the above variables:
(A) direct effects; (B) indirect effects; (C) induced effects.

Direct effects: The direct effects (also known as first-round effects) are those economic impacts derived directly from changes in tourist spending as it occurs in the tourism-related establishments. For example, the direct income effect will include the increase in wages, salaries and profits accruing to hotels as a result of an increase in tourist spending in those hotels.

Indirect effects: The indirect effects (also known as secondary effects) are those effects that occur because of the increased purchases of the tourism-related businesses. For example, if tourist spending in restaurants increases, then the restaurants will need to increase their purchases of food and beverages from their suppliers, their suppliers (perhaps wholesalers) will need to increase their purchases from their suppliers and so on, until the amount of money being respent in this way becomes negligible. All of these consequential changes in expenditure are indirect effects.

Induced effects: During the direct and indirect effects local income will have accrued in the form of wages, salaries, profits, rent and dividends. When this money is respent within the local economy it will generate additional economic impacts. These changes are known as the induced effects.

Because of the multitude of variables that can be analysed using multiplier analysis and the different levels of impact that can be estimated, it is essential that the same concepts are being used if multiplier values for different countries, or the same country at different times, are being compared. Some international agencies, such as the World Bank, do not take the third level of impact (the induced effects) into account when undertaking the worth of a project. This exclusion is justified on the grounds that the induced effects are likely to be the same regardless of the nature of the change in final demand. This is true providing that there are a priori grounds for believing that the consumption patterns of those people whose income is affected by the initial change in tourist spending is not significantly different to the consumption pattern of other members of the economy.

The impact models discussed below may be calculated to show each of the various types of multipliers. In general, output (sales and transactions) multipliers are significantly larger than those of other variables for the same economy. Employment multipliers, because of the relationship between a unit change in tourist spending and the incremental change in employment arising from that unit change, will be relatively small and are often expressed either to 4 decimal places or per \$10 000 of spend rather than per unit of spend.

The first model worthy of brief consideration is the Base Theory Model. Base Theory uses the proportion of an economy's production that is devoted to exports as a yardstick for the ratio of impacts. An early application of base theory was undertaken in 1966 in order to estimate the employment effects associated with tourist spending in Appalachia (Nathan Associates, 1966) and the model was based on the following structure:

$$\frac{Er}{Erx^2} = \frac{1}{1 - Erc/Er} \tag{1}$$

where

Er = the total local employment
Erc = local employment servicing local consumer demand
Erx^2 = the direct change in employment created by changes in tourist spending

Which was further developed to incorporate investment effects to

$$\frac{Er}{Erx^2} = \frac{1 + i^2}{1 - Erc/Er} \tag{2}$$

Where i^2 = a statistically estimated parameter (between 0 and 1) relating changes in investment to changes in tourist spending.

The major problem with base theory models is their lack of sound theoretical underpinning. They are not founded on fundamental economic theory and they are oversimplistic in their approach to tracing the economic impact caused by changes in final demand.

An alternative to base theory models is the Keynesian multiplier approach. This model provides a much sounder basis for studying the changes brought about by a change in final demand but lacks precision because of the level of aggregation used in the model's structure. Keynes' multiplier model may be stated simply in the following expression:

$$k = \frac{1}{1 - c + m} \tag{3}$$

where

   k = the multiplier
   1 = a one unit change in tourist spending
   c = how much out of each unit of additional income consumers will spend
   m = how much out of each additional unit of income consumers will spend on imported goods and services

This model too can be extended to take into account the longer term effects of investment, taxation and government spending. An example of such an extended model is shown below:

$$k = \frac{1 - L}{1 - c(1 - t_i)(1 - t_d - b) + m - i - g} \tag{4}$$

where

   L = the first round of leakages out of the economy
   t_i = indirect taxes created per additional unit of tourist spending
   t_d = direct taxes created per additional unit of tourist spending
   b = additional units of benefits (transfer payments) as a result of one additional unit of tourist spending
   i = additional investments created per additional unit of tourist spending
   g = additional government spending created per additional unit of tourist spending

But even this extended form of Keynesian multiplier model is oversimplistic. It fails to acknowledge the fact that different sectors of the economy will have different propensities to import, consume, pay taxes and so on. Thus, the model's structure is too aggregated to be of practical use. This observation leads to the first fundamental conclusion, that is, to be of practical use models that are used to calculate the economic impact of changes in tourist spending must be constructed within a disaggregated framework to allow for variances in expenditure patterns between the different sectors of the economy.

   The penultimate form of model that could be adopted is the ad hoc multiplier model. This type of model adopts the Keynesian multiplier structure but instead of starting at an aggregate level it is built up from sector data. That is, the researcher collects data from each productive sector assumed to be affected by tourist spending and then the model is aggregated in order to provide an overall picture. Archer and Owen (1971) provided one of the early rigorous attempts at such a model in their study of tourist spending on Anglesey in North Wales.

In matrix algebra, the Archer–Owen model can be shown as:

$$Ax\frac{1}{1-BC} \tag{5}$$

where

A = how much of each unit of additional tourist expenditure remains in the economy after the first round leakages

B = how much out of each additional unit of income local people will spend within the local economy

C = how much each unit of local expenditure will accrue as local income

The Archer–Owen model is vastly superior to the Keynesian model even though it is based upon the same fundamental principles. The superiority comes from the fact that the model is constructed from the bottom upwards, allowing different propensities to import and generate income and tax revenue for each productive sector. The researcher can incorporate all of the sectors that they believe will be influenced, directly and indirectly, by a change in final demand, such as tourist spending.

This flexibility of the ad hoc model is also to some extent its Achilles' heel. A model constructed in this manner is known as a partial equilibrium model in the sense that it need not cover every aspect of the economy being studied. This means that it is quite possible, in fact probable, that the researchers will omit sectors that play a small but nevertheless vital role in the generation of economic activity. The subjective aspect of choosing which sectors should be included means that:

(A) different multipliers may be derived for the same economy if different researchers build the model;

(B) the multiplier values derived from such a model will most likely under-estimate the true impacts.

Finally, input-output analysis can be used to measure economic impacts associated with changes in final demand. This is a *general equilibrium approach* in the sense that it encompasses all of the sectors of the economy and yet it also provides the detail offered by the disaggregated approach developed by Archer and Owen.

INPUT-OUTPUT ANALYSIS

The technique of input-output analysis has a long pedigree stretching back to Quesnay's Tableau Economique in 1758. Quesnay produced a table that demonstrated the economic interdependence that existed between the various productive sectors of the economy. This table, however, is more representative of a set of national accounts rather than an attempt at input-output analysis. It was almost a hundred years later before the notion of sectoral economic dependence became integrated into a general equilibrium model by Walras (see Wright, 1956). A second link in the chain that led to the construction of input-output models was the development of the concept of the multiplier that was first cited in the work of Bagehot (1882). In spite of significant works by such eminent economists as Johannsen (1908, 1925) and Pigou (1929) it was not until Kahn (1931) and Keynes (1933) that the multiplier concept became an accepted notion and was firmly placed on the listing of economic tools.

Leontief undertook input-output analyses, drawing upon the concept of the multiplier, in 1941 and 1953 in his seminal works on the structure of the United States Economy. It was this research that led to Leontief being regarded as the 'father' of input-output analysis. The methodology of input-output analysis may be broken down into two distinct stages. First there is the construction of an input-output table and, secondly, there is the construction of an input-output model.

Input-output tables

Input-output tables are analogous to national account tables for the economy being examined. They can be constructed at national or subnational levels and can even be constructed in such a way as to provide tables of different national or regional economies that show how they interact. The tables are generally easier to assemble at national rather than subnational level because of the availability of key economic statistics such as imports, exports, tax revenues and so on. These statistics are used to provide control totals when assembling the tables. Such data are generally not available at subnational levels, indeed the imports of goods and services into and out of subnational geographical areas can be extremely difficult to estimate.

The form that the input-output table may take is illustrated in Figure 2.1. This diagram shows the four different areas (quadrants) of the table's structure.

Quadrant A: This area of the table registers the sales and purchases made by each sector, from each of the other sectors (including itself) within the local economy. The column entries in this quadrant (A) can be seen as the input of goods and services required by each of the local sectors of production from each other local sector of production.

Quadrant B: This area of the table shows the purchases of primary inputs (income, government revenue and imports) that each sector of the economy

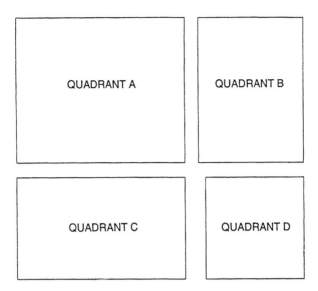

Figure 2.1. The structure of an input-output table

makes. This quadrant (B) will include all forms of income that is paid to factors of production within the economy including wages, salaries, profits, rent, interest and dividends. Similarly, it will include all forms of government revenue including direct and indirect taxes, excise duty and trading surplus.

Quadrant C: This area of the table shows how each productive sector sells its output to final users (final demand) including households, governments, capital formation and exports. Tourist expenditure would be included here with domestic tourist spending being included as a subset of the household expenditure and international tourist expenditure being recorded as a subset of exports.

Quadrant D: Finally, this area of the table shows the direct use of primary inputs for final demand, such as for oil imported for re-export, labour directly employed by households, and so on.

Because the sum total of each column represents all of the inputs of that sector, regardless of the nature or origin of that input, it will be exactly equal to the sum total of the corresponding row. That is, in Figure 2.2 the column total of column 1 (X_1) will be identical to the row total of row 1 (X_1). The same is true for each other column and corresponding row.

Therefore, Figure 2.1 is an input-output table in the sense that it is a set of local accounts that focus upon each sector's inputs and outputs. As such, it is not an operational model but simply an accounting table. Nevertheless it is useful in the sense that it can be used to examine the structure of an economy, its nature and even its bottlenecks where apparent. It shows each sector's relationship with key economic variables such as government revenue and imports. It also shows how each sector relies upon either final or intermediate demand for its sales market and so on. However, as it stands it does not represent an operational model.

Input-output models

To transform the input-output table into an operational model it is necessary to make a distinction between those parts of the table that may be considered to be endogenous and those that are exogenous. The endogenous part of the table is that concerned with the provision and/or purchase of intermediate goods and services whereas the exogenous part is that concerned with final user demand.

For example, in Figure 2.2, industry 1 is shown to be purchasing goods/services from the other sectors of the economy x_{11} to x_{m1} and these purchases are regarded as being endogenous. All remaining purchases W_1, P_1, T_1 and M_1 are regarded as being exogenous. If the table is examined from the point of view of the rows a similar picture may be developed. The endogenous part of the table includes all of the sales from each sector to each other sector within the economy. Thus, for industry 1, the endogenous sales are those from X_{11} to X_{1m} and the exogenous sales are C_1, I_1, G_1 and E_1.

In order to develop an input-output model it is necessary to trace the flow of tourist expenditure as it percolates through the economy. For instance, an additional unit of tourist spending on the output of industry 1 will affect the demand, not only of industry 1 but also of all those industries that supply goods and services to industry 1. Similarly, those industries that supply goods and services to industry 1 will purchase goods and services from other industries within the economy and these too will interact with other sectors. It is possible to trace this flow of tourist spending by incorporating some simple matrix algebra. However, first it is necessary to *normalise* the table by converting it from absolute values to coefficients. This is achieved by dividing the value in each cell by its corresponding row total. Therefore, each column will be made up of cells whose values, when summed, will just equal 1.

Let X be a vector of the total sales of goods/services of each industry of the economy and A be a matrix of the inter-industrial sales/purchases within the economy. Now, let Y be a vector of final demand sales, including tourism. Finally, I is the identity matrix, equivalent to the number 1 in basic algebra.

$$X = AX + Y \qquad (6)$$

SALES TO / PURCHASES FROM	INTERMEDIATE DEMAND — Productive Sectors (Industry)						FINAL DEMAND — Final Demand Sectors				X
	1	2	3	4	......	m	H	I	G	E	
Industry 1	X_{11}	X_{12}	X_{13}	X_{14}	......	X_{1m}	C_1	I_1	G_1	E_1	X_1
Industry 2	X_{21}	X_{22}	X_{23}	X_{24}	......	X_{2m}	C_2	I_2	G_2	E_2	X_2
Industry 3	X_{31}	X_{32}	X_{33}	X_{34}	......	X_{3m}	C_3	I_3	G_3	E_3	X_3
Industry 4	X_{41}	X_{42}	X_{43}	X_{44}	......	X_{4m}	C_4	I_4	G_4	E_4	X_4
Industry m	X_{m1}	X_{m2}	X_{m3}	X_{m4}	......	X_{mm}	C_m	I_m	G_m	E_m	X_m
Wages and Salaries	W_1	W_2	W_3	W_4	......	W_m	W_C	W_I	W_G	W_E	W
Profits/Dividends	P_1	P_2	P_3	P_4	......	P_m	P_C	P_I	P_G	P_E	P
Taxes	T_1	T_2	T_3	T_4	......	T_m	T_C	T_I	T_G	T_E	T
Imports	M_1	M_2	M_3	M_4	......	M_m	M_C	M_I	M_G	M_E	M
TOTAL INPUTS	X_1	X_2	X_3	X_4		X_m	C	I	G	E	X

Productive Sectors
Primary Inputs

Where:
X = output
C = consumption (households)
I = investment (private)
G = government expenditure
E = exports
M = imports
W = wages and salaries
P = profits and dividends
T = taxes

FINAL DEMAND SECTORS
H = household consumption sector
I = investment expenditure sector
G = government expenditure sector
E = exports sectors

Figure 2.2. A basic input-output transaction table

This tells us that the total output of each industry X is equal to the intermediate sales plus the final demand sales. An alternative way of expressing this statement is to say that the total output of each industry, X, less that output used for intermediate production, AX, will just leave the output left for final demand, Y. This is shown below:

$$X - AX = Y \qquad (7)$$

Rearranging this to derive an expression for X,

$$(I - A)X = Y \qquad (8)$$

$$X = (I - A)^{-1}Y$$

Now, in order to trace the impact of a change in final demand, such as tourist spending, let the change in final demand be ΔY. This change in final demand will lead to further changes in the level of output of each of the industries within the economy and can be shown by:

$$\Delta X = (I - A)^{-1} \Delta Y \qquad (9)$$

Thus the change in final demand ΔY will lead to a change in the output of the economy of ΔX.

The basic input-output model shown above can be developed further to provide a much broader range of information. The change in output generated by the change in final demand can be translated into income and government revenue as well as output effects. Making a distinction between competitive and non-competitive imports allows the researcher to assess the accuracy of the model since, by their nature, non-competitive imports are more readily predictable than those that compete with domestic production. This model is shown below:

$$\Delta X = (I - K^*A)^{-1} \Delta Y \qquad (10)$$

where K^* is a matrix that has diagonal values reflecting the level of competitive imports associated with each industry. This allows the A matrix output values to be reduced by the appropriate amount.

The model can be modified to show the economic impacts associated with the tourist expenditure by letting ΔT represent the change in tourist spending and using the following expression:

$$\Delta W = B(I - K^*A)^{-1} \Delta T \qquad (11)$$

and

$$\Delta \Pi = B(I - K^*A)^{-1} \Delta T \qquad (12)$$

$$\Delta T = B(I - K^*A)^{-1} \Delta T$$

where

> ΔW = changes in wages
> $\Delta \Pi$ = changes in profits
> ΔT = changes in taxes
> B = an $m \times n$ matrix of primary inputs

Finally, the model can be expanded to include employment effects associated with any exogenous change in final demand. To do this the employment levels of each industry must be entered into the model as a row vector (E). This will provide the following structure:

$$\Delta E = E(I - K^*A)^{-1} \Delta T \qquad (13)$$

The model can be disaggregated even further to provide a more useful human resource management planning model. Instead of entering the employment data as a row vector it can be entered as a matrix whereby either the skill categories or educational requirements of each industry are used. In this way, any change in final demand, traced through the inverted A matrix, will yield a series of employment coefficients that can be translated into job opportunities based upon either the skill or educational requirements.

The model as described thus far will allow the derivation of the various multipliers at the direct and indirect level of impacts. In order to complete the assessment of impact it is necessary to establish the size of the induced impact. That is the impact generated in the economy as a result of the respending of the additional income accrued as a result of the increase in tourist spending. To achieve this it is necessary to transfer the income rows (wages, profits, rent, interest and dividends) from the exogenous part of the table to the endogenous. That is, from the B matrix to the A matrix. Furthermore, the expenditure of that income, as represented by the household consumption function, must be transferred from the exogenous final demand (C Quadrant) into the A matrix as a column.

If the A matrix is now inverted it will result in the derivation of multiplier values that reflect direct, indirect and induced levels of impact for each of the economic variables set out above.

Assumptions underlying the input-output model

There are a variety of assumptions that are necessary for the input-output model to be operative. However, the key assumptions worthy of discussion include that of the nature of the production and consumption functions, and the static nature of a model that is expressly concerned with estimating the dynamic effects of changes in final demand.

The functioning of the model is based upon the crucial assumption that the money value of goods and services purchased by any one of the local sectors of production is a linear and homogeneous function of the output level of that industry. In other words, an industry that is subject to a change in demand for its output will increase its purchases of inputs in exactly the same proportion as the average expenditure pattern displayed in the appropriate column of the A matrix. Thus, if an hotel spent 5% of its total inputs on, say, communications, then an increase in demand for the hotel sector's output of 100US$ would lead to a direct increase in the purchase of services from the communication sector of 5US$. The problem is founded in the fact that the columns of the A matrix are based on average expenditure patterns taken from a variety of businesses. Some of these businesses may be large multinationals whereas others may be small family-owned establishments, and both may have very different production functions. In an ideal world the input-output table should be formulated on the basis of marginal coefficients rather than average coefficients but the cost of constructing such a table is such that it outweighs the benefits that may be derived from the improvement in accuracy. Secondly, but related to the first issue, is the fact that these production functions, because they are assumed to be linear and homogeneous, by definition exclude the possibility of economies of large-scale production. In many cases, particularly within the tourism and hospitality related sectors, the question of economies of large-scale production may not be too problematic. The vast majority of the businesses in the tourism and hospitality sectors are small and medium-sized enterprises (SMEs). However, because input-output analysis is a general equilibrium approach it includes all of the sectors of production of the local economy, some of whom may well be able to enjoy significant economies of large-scale production.

Furthermore, the static approach of input-output analysis may be associated with two areas of concern. The first is part of the issue discussed above in that the snapshot approach fails to include the marginal changes that may result from a change in final demand. However, the second issue relates to the temporal effects in a different way. Tourism and hospitality activities, like agriculture, are noted for their propensity to be seasonal. This seasonality may be the result of the destination's climate or the originating countries' vacation habits, but seasonality is common. Thus, a change in final demand during the peak season period may bring about changes in the establishment's input requirements that may be quite different to those that would have resulted from a change in demand during the off-season periods. This is particularly true with respect to employment. An increase in demand during the peak period may require the hiring of additional units of labour in order to cope. Whereas an increase in demand during an off-peak period may simply utilise some of the slack in the establishment's production function and not lead to any change in employment levels.

Another assumption from the construction of the input-output model is one of no joint production. It is assumed that each good or service is produced by a single industry represented by a single column in the A matrix. However, joint production abounds in economies generally, and with respect to the tourism and hospitality industries in particular. The output of an hotel is not a single good or service, it is a 'package' of goods and services sold to the consumer. Thus, an increase in the output of hotels may be in the form of increased demand for accommodation services, in food and beverage services or in terms of entertainment. Each of these demands may result in a different expenditure pattern in terms of the hotel's input requirements.

The production functions incorporated within the model's framework imply that there is a perfectly elastic supply of intermediate goods and services. That is, if an establishment is subject to an increase in demand for its output it can achieve this by purchasing more inputs, in the same proportions to those purchased on average before. This need not be the case, particularly where the supplying industry is already at full capacity and is unable to respond to an increase in demand. In such cases it is likely that the provision of these goods and services may come from outside the local economy (imports). Thus, the change in final demand will not bring about the same effects per unit of tourist spending as that implied by the average coefficient. So the final income multiplier will be lower than may be expected and the level of imports (leakages) will be correspondingly higher as the inputs are brought in from outside the local economy.

Finally, there is an assumption that there is no substitution between inputs. That is, for example, a sector could not achieve the same level of output by using a different mix of inputs, such as increasing the use of capital at the expense of less labour.

Although the above assumptions may, at first, appear highly restrictive in nature, in effect this is not the case. The assumption relating to the static nature of the model can be overcome by constructing a dynamic model. The technology is easily available to do so, but the cost of constructing such a model is not considered justifiable in terms of the improvement in accuracy achieved. The use of average coefficients rather than the marginal coefficients that should be used results in only minor inaccuracies and these can, to some extent, be alleviated by the adoption of several practices, such as the use of 'best practice' establishment data in order to construct the columns. This would mean that the columns would reflect the future likely impact rather than the past. Alternatively, by greater disaggregation of sectors it should be possible to differentiate between the various types of establishments that may be affected by the particular changes in final demand.

Furthermore, the introduction of a restrictions matrix can be used to counteract the problems associated with the assumption of elastic supply. That is, a matrix can be constructed that reflects the degree of spare capacity evident in each of the sectors. If the change in final demand exceeds that level deemed to be within the boundaries of achievable production then the remaining input requirements of this particular input will be imported from outside the economy in question.

Data requirements

Input-output models are extremely data demanding, far more so than any of the other models that may be considered. As with all models, the final framework chosen will be a compromise between what is ideal and what is affordable, in terms of either time or expense. For most of the weaknesses created by the assumptions that underlie the model there are solutions. The restrictions matrix and the use of marginal coefficients are two such examples. Furthermore, even the contravention of the single product assumption can be overcome by distinguishing between inputs required to produce each product. However, these solutions are expensive in terms of data requirements and judgement needs to be exercised as to whether the returns will justify the costs. In most cases the answer will probably be no, the basic model performs reasonably well and the enhancements do not justify the additional costs in terms of either resources or the additional time that would be needed to collect the data.

The heavy data demands associated with input-output analysis have prompted researchers to explore ways of reducing the data requirements. One way of reducing the data requirements is to increase the level of aggregation in the model. That is, to distinguish between fewer productive sectors, such as opting for a 10-sector model as opposed to a 30-sector model. Clearly, the more aggregated the model the more the single product assumption is violated and hence the greater level of error in the results. Also, a highly aggregated model, even an accurate one, is unlikely to provide those charged with planning with a model suitable as a planning tool. Secondly, because purchases are always easier to trace than sales, the models can be constructed on a column basis rather than on a row and column basis. Nevertheless, the data demands are significant. As an example, the Scottish Tourism Multiplier Study (Fletcher et al, 1992) involved sending out 2500 questionnaires to businesses in Scotland and the follow-up of more than 800 lengthy interviews.

ENVIRONMENTAL IMPACT ANALYSES USING INPUT-OUTPUT ANALYSIS

The environment has become a key consideration in tourism development planning and much has been done to highlight the environmental consequences associated with tourism development. The environmental impacts of tourism can be positive and/or negative, although the literature tends to focus upon its negative impacts. Many of the environmental problems associated with tourism development do not lend themselves to objective measurement; however, there are a number of areas where objective measurement is possible. These latter factors include environmental indicators such as air and water quality, noise, smoke particles, occupational deaths and injuries. There are strong similarities between such objective environmental indicators and their economic counterparts because of the strong correlation between changes in output and changes in each of the indicator levels. Similarly, there are direct, indirect and induced environmental impacts in the same way as there are economic impacts at each of these levels. Thus, because all forms of production will be associated with some environmental impacts, it makes sense to use the general equilibrium approach of input-output analysis to determine the direct, indirect and induced levels of environmental impact. Finally, because this allows the economic and environmental impacts to be assessed within a common framework it provides the policymaker with a more useful information system.

The major difference between the environmental indicators and their economic counterparts is in terms of their common relationship with the level of output. The economic impacts are assumed to be linear whereas the environmental relationships are more likely to be non-linear. Leontief examined the use of input-output analysis in determining environmental impacts at a national level and Cumberland was the first to include environmental indicators within a regional input-output framework. More recently, researchers at Bournemouth University have developed one of the first user-friendly input-output models that combines environmental impacts with those of economic impacts and forecasts these impacts into the future.

USES OF INPUT-OUTPUT ANALYSIS

There are a variety of ways that even the most simple input-output model can be used for the purpose of economic planning. For instance, the *consistency approach* involves the pre-multiplication of a *target* final demand vector by the inverted matrix of interdependence coefficients in order to establish the levels of production required. Input-output analysis is also a useful tool for the determination of supply bottlenecks, methods of import substitution, and manpower planning.

The results of input-output models can be used to structure a destination's marketing strategy in that those tourists with the most beneficial economic impact and the minimum negative environmental impact can be identified and targeted as preferential markets where the supply of such tourists is not seen as being problematic. For instance, a study undertaken in Jamaica in 1985 looked at the economic impact of a wide range of tourists, by country of origin, purpose of visit, season of visit, first and repeat visitors, and so on, in order to determine which visitors offered the greatest benefit to the local economy. Similarly, the study in Scotland allowed for the use of different tourist spending patterns from the special interest visitors who fish for salmon to the overseas visitors to the Edinburgh Festival (Fletcher et al, 1992).

One of the most common uses of input-output analysis, particularly with respect to tourism, is impact assessment. Input-output models generate partial and complete multipliers. Partial multipliers may relate to any of the key economic variables such as income, output, employment, government revenue and imports and apply to each of the different levels of impact (direct, indirect and induced). However, they are related to a single sector only, whereas the complete multipliers, as their name suggests, are derived from aggregating the partial multipliers. The information derived from these models can be used for project appraisals where the development expenditures are used to determine the implementation impact and then the operating expenditures are used to examine the recurrent impact. These multipliers can then be used to assess the economic impacts of various changes in final demand, forecasted or hypothetical, in order to assist future planning. The following chapter examines the multiplier and its uses in more detail.

RECENT AND FUTURE DEVELOPMENTS

The fundamental structure of input-output models has changed little in the past two decades and the most significant developments have taken place with respect to the technique's accessibility. There is little point in developing sophisticated methods of estimating and analysing economic impacts if this information is not accessible to those who may be able to make use of it. To this end, there have been a number of attempts to develop 'user-friendly' computer-based models that can be manipulated by planners and those responsible for decision-making. Early attempts at constructing 'user-friendly' software models achieved limited success and the users of these models required a significant level of input-output knowledge and understanding. However, researchers at the International Centre for Tourism and Hospitality Research at Bournemouth University have constructed integrated economic, environmental and social impact models, based upon the input-output technique, that allow instant and easy access to impact results. It is in this area where future research efforts are likely to be drawn, in an attempt to provide comprehensive planning models, rather than in terms of developing ever increasingly sophisticated economic models that are even more demanding in terms of their data requirements.

SUMMARY

This chapter has examined the various models that can be used to estimate the economic impact of tourist spending on a local economy and found that input-output models are the most powerful and comprehensive tools that can be used. The weaknesses of input-output analysis have been examined and some solutions to these weaknesses discussed. The versatility of the input-output methodology allows for the model to be expanded and used to examine a wide variety of issues from human resource management to environmental impacts. The future of input-output models is assured and new research is focused upon the ease of operation and understanding of the models rather than the development of more sophisticated techniques that might make them less accessible to those who need to be able to use them, the tourism planners.

REFERENCES

Archer, B.H., Owen, C. 1971, Towards a tourist regional multiplier, *Regional Studies*, 5: 289–294

Archer, B.H., Fletcher, J.E., 1988, The tourist multiplier, *Teoros*, 7(3): 6–9

Bagehot, W., 1882, in Wright, A.U., 1956, The genesis of the multiplier theory

Fletcher, John E., 1985, *The economic impact of international tourism on the national economy of Jamaica*, funded by USAID, organised by UNDP/WTO

Fletcher, John E., 1989, Input-output analysis, *Annals of Tourism Research*, 16(4): 541–556

Fletcher, John E., 1993, Employment multipliers and input-output analysis. In Baum, T., ed., *Human resource issues in international tourism management*, Butterworth Heinemann, Oxford, pp. 77–85

Fletcher, John E., Archer B.H., 1991, The development and application of multiplier analysis, *Progress in tourism and recreational research*, Francis Pinter, Vol. Two, July, 32 pp.

Fletcher, John E., Archer, B.H., 1993, Tourism multipliers revisited: models, misunderstandings and multiplier values, *Teoros Revue de Recheche en Tourisme*, 1 (1), October: 83–89

Fletcher, John E., Cooper, C., Wanhill, S., 1992, *Scottish Tourism Multiplier Study*, Vols 1, 2 and 3, ESU Research Paper, No. 31

Johannsen, N., 1908, A neglected point in connection with the crisis; 1925, Business depressions: their causes – both quoted in A.U. Wright, 1956, The genesis of the multiplier theory

Kahn, R.F., 1931, The relation of home investment to employment, *Economic Journal*, 41: 173–198

Keynes, J.M., 1933, The multiplier, *New Statesman and Nation*, April, pp. 405–407

Kottke, M., 1988, Estimating tourism impacts, *Annals of Tourism Research*, 15: 122–133

Leontief, Wassily, 1986, *Input-output economics*, 2nd edn, Oxford University Press, New York

Nathan, R.R. and Associates, 1966, *Recreation as an industry*, a report prepared for the Appalachian Regional Commission, Washington, DC

O'Connor, R., Henry, E.W., 1975, *Input-output analysis and its applications* Charles Griffin, London

Pigou, A.C., 1929, The monetary theory of the trade cycle, *Economic Journal*, **39**: 183–194

Wright, A.U., 1956, The genesis of the multiplier theory, *Oxford Economic Papers*, **8**: 181–193

3 Portfolio Models of Tourism

M. THEA SINCLAIR

INTRODUCTION

Tourism differs from many other economic activities in that it is subject to considerable instability of demand. In periods of rising demand, tourism generates increasing levels of income, employment and government revenue. It is welcomed as a high-growth sector in contexts ranging from developing countries to advanced economies which are undergoing de-industrialisation. The economic contribution that tourism makes has been acknowledged, for instance, by the rapidly expanding countries of South East Asia, which have been concerned to facilitate its ongoing support for the balance of payments as well as for domestic income and employment generation (Wilson, 1994).

Instability of tourism earnings means, however, that in periods of falling demand, the positive economic contribution that tourism makes can swiftly become negative, resulting in rising unemployment, falling income and lower welfare. Public and private investment which are reliant on tourism as a source of finance are deterred and the balance of payments worsens. Such instability may result from 'shocks', for example, political or social unrest (Gunadhi and Boey, 1986), attractions, including the Olympics (Loeb, 1982) and EXPO (Little, 1980), or promotional activity such as the Visit Malaysia Year (Shamsuddin, 1995). It can also result from more frequent changes, such as fluctuations in exchange rates which may be difficult to predict or control.

Instability is not invariably a problem for tourist destinations as some areas have sufficient foreign currency reserves or domestic savings to cover temporary losses in earnings while, in others, instability may encourage rises in the overall savings rate, thereby providing additional resources for investment (Knudsen and Parnes, 1975). None the less, research on the effects of instability of total export earnings indicates that while some economies or economic sectors may be affected positively or remain unaffected, others are affected adversely in terms of income, employment, the budget deficit,

Economic and Management Methods for Tourism and Hospitality Research.
Edited by Thomas Baum and Ram Mudambi © 1999 John Wiley & Sons Ltd.

balance of payments and rate of growth (Love, 1987; Dawe, 1996). Moreover, regions which are highly dependent on unstable activities tend to be affected disproportionately. These findings apply to instability of tourism earnings as well as to instability of total export earnings since, although tourism earnings instability partially offsets instability of earnings from other economic activities in some time periods and countries (Rao, 1986; Buckley and Geyikdagi, 1993), it plays a complementary role in others. Hence, tourism contributes to a net increase in instability in particular time periods and areas (Sinclair and Tsegaye, 1990; Wilson, 1994).

The finding that some tourist destinations are prone to unstable earnings does not imply that such effects are inevitable. In fact, different combinations of earnings and instability are feasible. The reason for this is that different types of tourism activity and nationalities of tourist are associated with different levels of earnings and instability, so that alternative tourism 'mixes' are associated with alternative overall combinations of earnings and instability. For example, destinations specialising in providing tourism activities that are prone to demand fluctuations experience a high level of instability relative to those specialising in activities with more stable demand. Similarly, destinations which receive a high proportion of tourists from countries whose residents are susceptible to exchange rate volatility tend to be subject to a higher level of tourism earnings instability than those receiving a lower proportion, implying that an alternative mix of tourism would decrease overall instability in the former. Thus, a range of instability–earnings combinations apply across destinations at a given point of time, depending upon the specific mix of tourism types that each destination attracts.

The instability–earnings combination resulting from the tourism mix that characterises a given destination may not coincide with the combination that destination policy-makers would select, given an explicit choice. For instance, some may prefer a combination of a high level of earnings accompanied by a high level of instability, while others may prefer reduced instability and lower tourism earnings. The preferred combination is likely to vary between destinations, according to local preferences. Destination policy-makers can attempt to attain their preferred combination by directing their marketing towards attracting the tourism mix which would bring it about. The issue is, therefore, to identify the tourism mix, or portfolio, which would achieve the desired instability–earnings combination.

A technique which can make explicit the range of instability–earnings combinations and associated tourism mixes which are relevant to particular destinations is the portfolio model, drawn from the literature on the economics of finance. By identifying the tourism mixes that are associated with different combinations of tourism earnings and instability, the model can assist policy-makers in identifying the tourism mix that they wish to attract, given their preferred instability–earnings combination. For example, it can identify the tourism mixes that can increase the destination's earnings, for a given level of instability. The following section of this chapter will examine the principles underlying the model and develop the model itself. In order to illustrate the ways in which the model can be applied, a case study of holiday tourism in Spain will then be presented. The final section of the chapter will provide a number of conclusions.

THE PORTFOLIO MODEL

The portfolio model was originally developed by Markowitz (1952a, b, 1959) and has been discussed by, for example, Levy and Sarnat (1984). It has subsequently been applied to the issue of export diversification in developing countries (Alwang and Siegel, 1994). The model is based on the premise that financial assets provide earnings (returns) which vary over time. Those assets which provide high levels of earnings are usually subject to higher instability of earnings, the latter being a measure of the risk associated with holding the asset. The idea underlying portfolio analysis is that the investor wishes to select a portfolio of assets which provide the preferred instability –earnings combination (risk–return trade-off). Assets which provide high earnings but involve a high level of risk can be counterbalanced by assets which provide lower but more stable earnings.

The problem which the investor must resolve is how to choose a portfolio from among the assets which are available. Thus, a risk-averse investor will choose to hold assets with a low instability of earnings, while a risk-taker selects assets whose earnings tend to be higher but subject to a higher level of instability. The choice of assets also depends on the interrelationships (covariance) between the earnings from the different assets over time. For example, earnings on assets from a diverse range of countries are more likely to be inversely related over time (having a negative covariance) and to decrease the overall level of instability (risk) than those from a given country, which are more likely to be positively related over time (having a positive covariance), thereby increasing instability. The portfolio model can be used to determine the investor's optimal portfolio of assets, given knowledge of the anticipated level and instability of the earnings from each asset, the covariance between them and the preferred instability–earnings trade-off. Portfolio theory can show that particular portfolios of assets can decrease the overall level of instability below that which would be associated with the selection of a single asset with the lowest level of instability.

The principles underlying the portfolio model of financial assets can be applied to domestic and foreign tourism mixes. Different types of tourism – holiday, business; cultural, sporting; young, old; domestic, foreign – are associated with different levels of earnings by destination areas (analogous to the earnings from financial assets) and different degrees of earnings instability (analogous to the level of risk). Policy-makers in different destination areas have different preferences concerning their desired combinations of tourism earnings and instability. Some prefer tourism mixes (portfolios) which involve high but variable earnings, while others prefer a lower instability–earnings trade-off. The portfolio model can be used to estimate the level and instability of earnings associated with the current tourism mix, as well as those which would accompany alternative tourism mixes. Given their preferred instability–earnings trade-off, policy-makers can then decide whether to attempt to maintain the prevailing tourism mix or to attempt to promote an alternative tourism mix.

The model is specified as follows. The objective function of the model is used to maximise the predicted level of tourism earnings net of the predicted instability of earnings for a particular instability–earnings trade-off and is written:

$$\max x'h - \phi x'Hx$$

The terms preceding the negative sign give the level of earnings resulting from tourism and the terms following the sign give the level of instability (risk). The term x is a column vector of decision variables of order n, where n is the number of decision variables and the decision variables are chosen according to the requirements of the destination under consideration. For example, policy-makers may aim to alter the prevailing mix of nationalities of tourist, so that x refers to tourist nationalities and n is the number of nationalities. The decision variable is defined as the predicted 'level of operation' of the variable relative to its current level so that if, for instance, the desired number of tourists of the ith nationality were predicted to be 25% higher than the current level, the decision variable x_i would have the value 1.25. The term h is a column vector of order n where h is the predicted earnings associated with the decision variable, for example earnings by tourist nationality. The term H is a symmetric matrix, of order n by n, of the predicted covariances between the elements of the vector h, and ϕ is a parameter providing the trade-off between instability and earnings from tourism.

The objective function is maximised subject to a number of constraints. First, negative values of the decision variables are not permitted so that $x \geqslant 0$. Second, the costs of attaining changes in the decision variables, such as expenditure on publicity or promotion, are equal to the resources available: $c'(x - I) = B$ where c is a column vector of the costs of attaining a change in the predicted level of the decision variable, I is a column vector of values of unity and B is the budget available, to policy-makers, for altering the decision variable. It is assumed that the cost function for changing the level of operation of the decision variable is linear and independent of any other cost function for the destination and that the full effects of policy to change the decision variable occur within the time period under consideration.

The third constraint involves the introduction of upper and lower bounds, beyond which changes in the decision variable are deemed infeasible; for example, increases in tourism demand of extremely large orders of magnitude may be deemed impossible to attain. The constraint may be written as $x_1 \leqslant x \leqslant x_u$ where x_1 and x_u are the lower and upper bounds on x. It is interesting to note that the solutions to bounded portfolio models generally include a proportion of every decision variable, rather than the small numbers of non-zero variables which are more characteristic of the solutions to unbounded models.

The complete portfolio model is:

$$\max x'h - \phi x'Hx \tag{1}$$

subject to $\quad\quad\quad\quad c'(x - I) = B$

$$x_1 \leqslant x \leqslant x_u$$

The solution to equation (1), for a particular set of parameter values, is a vector, x, of the values of the decision variables (for example, the 'level of operation' of each tourist nationality relative to its current level) that correspond to a particular instability–earnings trade-off. The inclusion of alternative values of the trade-off term, ϕ, provides a set of solutions to equation (1) which give rise to an earnings–instability efficient frontier, exemplified in Figure 3.1. It can be seen that a higher level of earnings tends to be accompanied by a higher level of instability, and vice versa. Policy-makers' desired point on the frontier is given by their preferred instability–earnings trade-off.

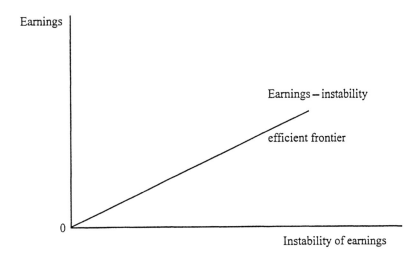

Figure 3.1. Tourism earnings-instability efficient frontier

The portfolio model has been developed, so far, in the context of an individual tourist destination but policy-makers are sometimes concerned with multi-destination contexts such as the different regions or subregions within a country, or with multi-country associations, such as the European Union or the NAFTA. A multi-area portfolio model can be developed to take account of the instability–earnings trade-offs for a set of destinations and the interrelationships between the destinations. The model is specified, analogously to the model for an individual destination, as:

$$\max \bar{x}'\bar{h} - \phi\bar{x}'\bar{H}\bar{x} \tag{2}$$

subject to $\bar{c}'(\bar{x} - \bar{I}) = \bar{B}$

$$\bar{x}_1 \leqslant \bar{x} \leqslant \bar{x}_u$$

where the terms $\bar{x}$, $\bar{h}$, $\bar{c}$ and $\bar{I}$ are stacked column vectors, of order nm, of the corresponding vectors for each of the individual areas, $\bar{H}$ is a symmetric matrix, of order nm by nm, of the predicted covariances of the stacked column vector $\bar{h}$, and $\bar{B}$ is a vector including the budgets available to policy-makers in the different areas. Although the model is specified with an aggregate budget constraint, it could be modified to allow for separate budget constraints for individual areas within the larger group.

PORTFOLIO MODELS OF HOLIDAY TOURISM IN SPAIN

The application of the portfolio model can be illustrated by the case of tourism in a set of Spanish provinces which are popular holiday destinations for a variety of tourist nationalities. The aim is to use the model to make explicit the mix of tourists, by nationality, that would give rise to a specified trade-off between instability and earnings, for example, the minimum level of instability for a given level of earnings. The nationalities considered are the Benelux, France, West Germany, Scandinavia, Spain, the UK, the rest of Europe, North America and the rest of the world. The tourism decision variable is the predicted 'level of operation' of overnight stays, by nationality, in registered hotel and hostel accommodation, where the 'level of operation' is as defined in the previous section. The use of the number of overnight stays is preferable to the number of tourists in that it is a measure of tourism demand which is weighted by the length of stay of the different nationalities. The distinction between different nationalities of tourists is useful as exchange rate elasticities of tourism demand vary by nationality, as shown by the reviews of Archer (1976), Johnson and Ashworth (1990), Sheldon (1990) and Sinclair and Stabler (1997). Moreover, Pearce and Grimmeau (1985), Valenzuela (1988) and Bote Gómez and Sinclair (1996) have shown that the different provinces and regions of Spain experience different patterns of demand by nationality. Time-series data for alternative measures, such as the numbers of tourists by activity or age, are not available.

The level of tourism earnings differed between nationalities but, for any given nationality, was assumed to be unaffected, over time, by policies to change the number of overnight stays. It was also assumed that the gradients of the cost functions for the different nationalities are the same and that the policy budget for the ensuing time period is unchanged, although the latter assumption could easily be modified. Given these assumptions, the original constraint for the individual destination model, $c'(x - I) = B$, (which could not be quantified owing to data limitations), is altered to $x's = I's$ where the column vector s is the predicted number of overnight stays by nationality during the ensuing time period, given the continuation of existing policies. The constraint implies that a rise in overnight stays by some nationalities is offset by a fall in overnight stays by the remainder. The constraint for the multi-area model becomes $x's = I's$. In the case of the multi-area model it was assumed, for simplicity, that the implementation of a policy to increase demand for a given area by tourists of particular nationalities would not affect the other areas in the system. It was also assumed that policies have their full effect within one year – the time period of analysis in the model – and that sufficient spare capacity to cater for additional tourism demand is available. Positive or negative externalities associated with policies to attract additional tourists were not considered but can be taken into account by the types of models considered by Michael Stabler in chapter 15 in this volume.

The application of the models involves estimating the predicted numbers of overnight stays, by nationality, for the Spanish provinces under consideration. Past values of overnight stays can be used to predict the value for the ensuing year, using a variety of methods (for a wider discussion of forecasting methods see, for example, Witt and Martin, 1989). In an initial application of the portfolio model to the Spanish province of Malaga, a two-period autoregressive equation was fitted to the annual numbers of overnight stays, by nationality, for the period prior to the year under consideration and the fitted equation was used to predict the value of overnight stays for the ensuing year (Board et al, 1987). The values of h, predicted earnings from the ith nationality of tourist, were calculated by multiplying the predicted number of overnight stays for the ith nationality by the mean level of expenditure per overnight stay for the ith nationality. A multiplier of unity was, thus, assumed for each nationality. The estimation of the elements of the covariance matrix, H, was carried out by using the residuals from the regression equations estimated for overnight stays by nationality; that is, the differences between the actual numbers of overnight stays and the fitted numbers, given by the regression equation. For the individual area model, the mean expenditure per overnight stay for the ith nationality was multiplied by the residual for the ith nationality, and the resulting values for the range of nationalities were used to calculate the covariance matrix. The multi-area model requires the instability interactions between the different areas to be taken into account and can be achieved using the residuals from the estimated equations for the different areas (see Board and Sutcliffe, 1991).

The lower and upper bounds for the changes in overnight stays can be specified according to the characteristics of the areas under consideration and the likely order of magnitude of the changes which policy-makers can bring about. Thus, in the case of Malaga, Board et al examined lower bounds of $x \geqslant 0$, $x \geqslant 0.5$, $x \geqslant 0.75$ and $x \geqslant 0.9$ so that the number of overnight stays by the ith nationality was constrained to be equal to or exceed, respectively, 0%, 50%, 75% and 90% of the predicted value. Upper bounds of $1.1 \geqslant x$, $1.25 \geqslant x$ and $1.5 \geqslant x$ were considered, as well as an upper bound of infinity. A goal of minimising the level of tourism earnings instability was examined for the period 1966–85. The instability-minimising values of x for the different nationalities in 1986, based on the lowest and highest values of the bounds considered, are shown in Table 3.1.

The results in Table 3.1 indicate the percentage changes in overnight stays by nationality, relative to their values in the preceding year, which are required if policy-makers wish to minimise the instability of tourism earnings. For example, a value of 1.25 would indicate a 25% increase, while a value of 0.75 would indicate a 25% decrease in overnight stays relative to the value for that nationality for the preceding year. The results show that the most important means of decreasing instability in Malaga would be to increase overnight stays by Spanish tourists. The desired increases in overnight stays range between 10% and 80% for a lower bound of zero, and between 10% and 30% for a lower bound of 0.9. The objective of minimising instability indicates decreases in the number of overnight stays by tourists

Table 3.1. Instability-minimising values of x for different tourist nationalities in Malaga

Lower bound	0	0	0	0.9	0.9	0.9
Upper bound	1.1	1.5	∞	1.1	1.5	∞
Benelux	1.1	0.8	0.8	0.9	0.9	0.9
France	1.1	1.2	1.0	1.0	0.9	0.9
West Germany	0.9	0.7	0.6	0.9	0.9	0.9
Scandinavia	1.1	1.1	1.1	0.9	0.9	0.9
Spain	1.1	1.5	1.8	1.1	1.3	1.3
UK	1.1	1.0	1.0	1.0	0.9	0.9
Rest of Europe	1.0	1.1	0.8	0.9	0.9	0.9
North America	0	0	0	0.9	0.9	0.9
Rest of world	1.1	0.5	0	0.9	0.9	0.9
Instability Index	1.1	1.0	1.0	1.2	1.2	1.2

Source: rounded and based on Board et al (1987).

from West Germany and North America and, for almost all combinations of bounds, decreases from the Benelux and the rest of the world. The result for North America would, undoubtedly, change in the context of an alternative policy objective of earnings maximisation, as tourists from this origin tend to incur relatively high expenditure. The instability-minimising changes in overnight stays by tourists from France, Scandinavia, the UK and the rest of Europe are sensitive to the specification of the lower and upper bounds, and the direction and magnitude of change varies in relation to the specific combination of bounds.

The instability index in the final row of Table 3.1 gives the ratio between the level of instability associated with the tourism mix in 1985 and the instability-minimising mix of 1986. It shows that instability could be up to 20% greater in 1985 than in the case of the instability-minimising tourism mix of 1986. The zero change in instability in the case of an upper bound of infinity is unlikely to be relevant to the short run, when policy-makers have limited possibilities of bringing about very large changes in overnight stays by particular nationalities. The main finding from the table is that alternative tourism portfolios could bring about a significant decrease in the instability of tourism earnings, at least in the short run.

The application of the portfolio model in the context of an alternative goal of earnings maximisation for a given level of instability is illustrated by a case study of six Spanish provinces, Alicante, the Balearic Islands, Barcelona, Granada, Malaga and Tenerife, for the same time period (Board and Sutcliffe, 1991). The lower and upper bounds were set equal to the third largest decrease and increase in the proportionate changes in overnight stays to have occurred during the time period. The two largest changes were excluded as they are likely to have resulted from one-off shocks, the magnitude of which would be unlikely to be attained by tourism policy. Unbounded values of x for the ith nationality were also calculated to allow for the effects of tourism policy over the long run. The results are given in Table 3.2.

The results in Table 3.2 show the percentage changes in overnight stays, relative to their values in the preceding year, that are required to achieve the objective of maximising earnings, given the level of instability of the preceding year. For the bounded model, the results indicate increases in overnight stays by tourists from the Benelux, Scandinavia, North America, the rest of Europe and the rest of the world and, for most provinces, from France. Decreases in overnight stays by tourists from Germany, the UK and Spain are required for most provinces. In the case of the unbounded model, the required changes are far greater, with large increases for the rest of Europe and the rest of the world, and large decreases for West Germany, Spain and, for most provinces, the UK. The desired directions of change for the other nationalities vary between the different provinces. The results from a

Table 3.2. Earnings-maximising values of **x** for different tourist nationalities and provinces

	Alicante	Balearic Islands	Barcelona	Granada	Malaga	Tenerife	Sum of provinces
Bounded model							
Benelux	1.5	1.2	1.3	1.3	1.3	1.3	1.3
France	1.2	1.3	1.2	0.8	1.2	1.4	1.3
West Germany	0.8	0.9	0.8	1.1	0.7	0.8	0.9
Scandinavia	1.2	1.1	1.5	1.7	1.3	1.3	1.3
Spain	0.9	1.2	0.9	0.9	1.1	0.9	1.0
UK	0.9	0.9	1.0	1.0	0.8	0.9	0.9
Rest of Europe	1.4	1.2	1.3	1.2	1.3	1.3	1.2
North America	1.3	1.4	1.2	1.2	1.3	1.7	1.3
Rest of world	1.7	1.3	1.2	1.3	1.3	1.2	1.3
Unbounded model							
Benelux	1.8	0	0.8	3.0	0.4	1.8	0.9
France	0	0.8	0	0	1.3	2.3	1.0
West Germany	0	0.6	0	0.9	0.2	0.5	0.5
Scandinavia	0	0	0	4.8	0.9	1.8	0.8
Spain	0.6	0.3	0.6	0.5	0.7	0.3	0.6
UK	0.3	0.2	0.8	1.5	0.5	0.4	0.3
Rest of Europe	16.2	3.9	0.3	2.3	3.2	3.1	3.6
North America	0	0	0.8	0.3	0	2.4	0.4
Rest of world	9.3	38.9	8.2	2.9	8.1	21.8	14.8

Source: rounded and based on Board and Sutcliffe (1991).

multi-area model of the six provinces (not provided here) were very similar to those for the bounded individual areas model, given in Table 3.2. The results for the unbounded case differed from and were more extreme in magnitude than those for the individual areas model.

CONCLUSIONS

Tourism policy-makers are often unaware of the trade-offs which exist between tourism earnings and instability, implicitly accepting the combination which is associated with prevailing tourism demand. A key advantage of the portfolio model is that it can make explicit the range of tourism mixes which are associated with different instability–earnings trade-offs and can quantify the changes, relative to the current tourism mix, which are required to attain them. Policy-makers can then select their desired instability–earnings combination and direct marketing efforts towards the achievement of the tourism mix which will bring it about.

Illustrative applications of the portfolio model to holiday tourism in Spain showed that changes in the tourism mix can lead to gains, relative to the existing tourism mix, of lower instability for a given level of income, or higher income for a given level of instability. The results indicated the implications for tourism policy of differences in the instability–earnings characteristics of different tourist nationalities. North American tourists, for example, were characterised by high instability and high earnings combinations, so that destinations which do not experience significant adverse effects from instability may aim to attract more demand from this origin area. Tourists from Spain appeared to be characterised by lower instability and earnings, implying that risk-averse destinations should attempt to attract increasing demand from the domestic market

The extent to which policy-makers are able to alter tourism demand is likely to vary both between destinations and over time. The portfolio model allows such differences in policy effectiveness to be taken into account via the imposition of alternative lower and upper bounds on changes in the decision variable. In general, a model which is unbounded or which has large lower and upper bounds is more appropriate to the long run, when policy measures have their full effect. The imposition of smaller upper and lower bounds can take account of limitations of policy over the short run. Thus, a further advantage of the model is its flexibility in permitting bounds to be imposed in accordance with the characteristics and requirements of the destination under consideration. In cases where there is some uncertainty concerning the set of bounds which is appropriate and, hence, the precise magnitudes of the desired changes in the decision variable, the model is useful in demonstrating the direction of the desired changes and their broad order of magnitude.

The portfolio model is of wide applicability. It can be applied to a variety of tourism types, such as beach, sporting and cultural tourism, as well as to tourist nationalities, and to alternative types of trade-offs, such as instability and employment, rather than instability and earnings. In this respect, the main limitation is not the theoretical basis of the model but rather the availability of the micro-level data required for its application. Like many economic models, the portfolio model is partial in nature and it would, therefore, be useful to apply it in conjunction with other approaches, such as the target markets analysis proposed by Mudambi and Baum in chapter 11 in this volume. It would also be interesting to apply the model not only to individual countries or areas within them, but also to the multi-country associations which characterise the world economy.

REFERENCES

Alwang, J., Siegel, P.B., 1994, Portfolio models and planning for export diversification: Malawi, Tanzania and Zimbabwe, *Journal of Development Studies*, **30**(2): 405–422
Archer, B.H., 1976, *Demand forecasting in tourism*, Occasional Papers in Economics, No. 9, University of Wales Press, Bangor
Board, J., Sinclair, M.T., Sutcliffe, C.M.S., 1987, A portfolio approach to regional tourism, *Built Environment*, **13**(2): 124–137
Board, J., Sutcliffe, C.M.S., 1991, Risk and income tradeoffs in regional policy: a portfolio theoretic approach, *Journal of Regional Science*, **31**(2): 211–216
Bote Gómez, V., Sinclair, M.T., 1996, Tourism demand and supply in Spain. In Barke, M., Towner, J., Newton, M., eds, *Tourism in Spain: critical perspectives*, C.A.B. International, Wallingford
Buckley, P.J., Geyikdagi, N.V., 1993, Tourism and foreign currency receipts, *Annals of Tourism Research*, **20**(2): 361–367
Dawe, D., 1996, A new look at the effects of export instability on investment and growth, *World Development*, **24**(12): 1905–1914
Gunadhi, H., Boey, C.K., 1986, Demand elasticities of tourism in Singapore, *Tourism Management*, **7**(4): 239–253
Johnson, P., Ashworth, J., 1990, Modelling tourism demand: a summary review, *Leisure Studies*, **9**(2): 145–160
Knudsen, O., Parnes, A., 1975, *Trade instability and economic development*, D.C. Heath, Lexington, MA
Levy, H., Sarnat, M., 1984, *Portfolio and investment selection: theory and practice*, Prentice Hall, Englewood Cliffs, NJ
Little, J.S., 1980, International travel in the UK balance of payments, *New England Economic Review*, May: 42–55
Loeb, P.D., 1982, International travel to the United States: an econometric evaluation, *Annals of Tourism Research*, **9**(1): 7–20
Love, J., 1987, Export instability in less developed countries: consequences and causes, *Journal of Economic Studies*, **14**(2): 3–80
Markowitz, H.M., 1952a, Portfolio selection, *Journal of Finance*, **7**(1): 77–91
Markowitz, H.M., 1952b, The utility of wealth, *Journal of Political Economy*, **60**(2): 151–158

Markowitz, H.M., 1959, *Portfolio Selection*, New York, Wiley

Pearce, D.G., Grimmeau, J-P., 1985, The spatial structure of tourist accommodation and hotel demand in Spain, *Geoforum*, **16**(1): 37–50

Rao, A., 1986, Tourism and export instability in Fiji, Occasional Papers in Economic Development, No. 2, Faculty of Economic Studies, University of New England, Australia

Shamsuddin, S., 1995, Tourism demand in Peninsular Malaysia, MA dissertation in Development Economics, University of Kent at Canterbury

Sheldon, P.J., 1990, A review of tourism expenditure research. In Cooper, C.P., ed, *Progress in tourism, recreation and hospitality management*, Vol. 2, Belhaven, London

Sinclair, M.T., Stabler, M.J., 1997, *The economics of tourism*, Routledge, London

Sinclair, M.T., Tsegaye, A., 1990, International tourism and export instability, *Journal of Development Studies*, **26**(3): 487–504

Valenzuela, M., 1988, Spain: the phenomenon of mass tourism. In Williams, A.M., Shaw, G., eds, *Tourism and economic development. Western European experiences*, Belhaven, London

Wilson, P., 1994, Tourism earnings instability in Singapore, 1972–88, *Journal of Economic Studies*, **21**(1): 41–51

Witt, S.F., Martin, C.A., 1989, Demand forecasting in tourism and recreation. In Cooper, C.P., ed, *Progress in tourism, recreation and hospitality management*, Vol. 1, Belhaven, London

4 Transactions Cost Analysis of Tourism

PETER J. BUCKLEY

INTRODUCTION

This chapter introduces transaction cost economics as a means of unifying and strengthening the analysis of tourism and hospitality. It suggests that a focus on the transaction as the basic unit of analysis can provide a means to unify and clarify the scope of the tourism industry. Further, this method of analysis provides the key to a comprehensive and rational analysis of strategies in the tourism industries. Its results focus on the appropriate scope of the firm, the correct choice of operational means in the industry (ownership versus contractual methods such as franchising versus arm's-length dealing) and it provides insights into marketing strategies.

ECONOMIC TRANSACTIONS ANALYSIS

The transaction is the basic unit of economic activity. The purchase of food, a drink, accommodation, an airline ticket, an aeroplane or a chain of retail travel agents are all single transactions. The buyer and seller come together and a price is fixed (by them or by an outside agency). The ownership of the object of the transaction (goods or service) changes hands. Repeated transactions can be organised either by long-term contracts or by the buyer and seller joining into a single organisation. The joining of buyer and seller is called internalisation and transforms 'normal' external markets into internal markets and arms-length transactions into internal organisational decisions. As long ago as 1937, Ronald Coase made this the basis for a theory of the firm. Internal markets, particularly those for labour services, enable coordination and planning of sets of transactions. Such internal arrangements are often more satisfactory than long-term contracts. This may be because of increased efficiency, largely though the reduction or elimination

Economic and Management Methods for Tourism and Hospitality Research.
Edited by Thomas Baum and Ram Mudambi © 1999 John Wiley & Sons Ltd.

of transactions costs, or it may enable the entrepreneur to appropriate more of the gains from transacting.

Coase's concern was centred on the employment relationship within a firm and in particular with the scope of management's control of the worker. The rationale for the employment contract is that it substitutes a single large and more open-ended contract for many separate smaller transactions. By reducing the number of contracts it economises on the costs of using the price mechanism (Coase, 1937; Buckley and Casson, 1976).

The major motive for internalisation of transactions thus arises from the existence of transaction costs in using the external market. The main sources of these costs of using the price mechanism are:

- Discovering exactly what prices are (and forecasting what they will be)
- The costs involved in negotiating a separate contract for each exchange transaction

The second point is particularly apposite in the hiring of factors of production, especially labour services. The firm represents an alternative institutional arrangement to the market system in that the worker agrees to take orders, within certain limits, in return for continuing remuneration from an entrepreneur. Consequently, a firm is a system of relationships which comes into being when the direction of resources is dependent on an entrepreneur. The firm becomes larger as additional transactions are organised by the entrepreneur, and smaller as the organisation of such transactions is abandoned. The boundary of the firm is set by those transactions undertaken by the market mechanism.

The boundary of the firm is governed by the margin where the costs of organising an extra transaction within the firm are equal to costs involved in carrying out the transaction in the open market. Changes which enable the entrepreneur to carry out direction more effectively (eg the development of systems of communication, the computer, improved management techniques) will increase the size of the firm.

The task of the entrepreneur is thus to carry out the direction of resources at a lower cost than the market. He may be aided in this by exogenous factors such as the tax system. Transfers of intermediate goods and services within the firm are governed by internal transfer prices, largely at the discretion of management, rather than by market prices. Such transfer prices may be manipulated so as to reduce the firm's tax bill. This benefit of internalisation is particularly important in cross-national transactions where transfer prices can be used to move funds and engineer profit increases in low tax regimes (Buckley and Casson, 1976, 1985; see also Williamson, 1975, 1996).

In markets which are information intensive (like tourism) there are additional advantages arising from internalisation. The market for information is subject to uncertainties arising from the possibility that the buyer cannot use or understand the information he is purchasing. Organising insurance for buyer uncertainty is difficult and costly. When buyer and seller are part of the same firm, mutual insurance can be arranged and a satisfactory price can be fixed. Discriminatory pricing of information can also be exercised in an internal market. Where resale is possible, discrimination cannot be practised in external markets. In addition, internalisation avoids difficulties arising from bilateral concentration of market power, for example a hotelier in a favoured location transacting with a tour operator. If the tour operator owns the hotel, uncertainty is avoided.

Consequently, the analysis of transaction costs in particular markets enables a case-by-case analysis of the likelihood of that market being internalised. The benefits to the firm of increased planning control, coordination and opportunities for increased profit must be set against communication and control difficulties. Markets which are most likely to be internalised are those involving a vertical chain of transactions, information intensive markets and those markets where high returns are available from the organisation of teams of individuals with high levels of specialised skills. The relevance of this analysis to tourism is the subject of the following section.

TOURISM – THE TRANSACTIONS CHAIN

A great deal of time and effort is spent on the analysis of the tourism 'product'. Attempts to define the tourism market are also fraught with difficulty. The one element which can easily be defined is the tourist. An analysis of transactions thus proceeds from the main actor – the tourist – and examines all the actor's transactions.

An individual transaction is carried out between two agents. One or both of these agents may then go on to carry out a further transaction until the primary supplier or final consumer is reached. In this way, it is possible to build transactions chains of the types shown in Figure 4.1. Various typical forms of transactions chains may link the tourist with the primary suppliers of goods and services. The tourist product is then defined as all the goods and services for which the tourist transacts and the tourism market as the sum of these transactions.

Figure 4.1 shows four typical transaction chains. Transactions are shown classified by their spatial location – origin (the tourist's home), transit and transport, which may be within the origin country or transnational, and destination, which may be local or international. Tourist transactions are here listed as transport, accommodation, entertainment and amenities, and direct spend on (extra) food and accommodation.

Transaction chain *a* is the unpackaged chain where the tourist purchases all the transactions included in the tourist venture directly from the service

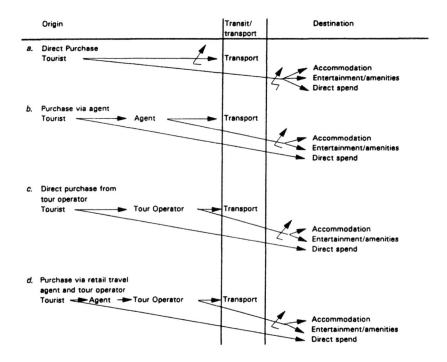

Figure 4.1. Transactional chains in tourism
Notes: The broken arrow indicates opportunity for brokerage
Food may be included with accommodation or be in 'direct spend'

providers. Type *b* shows a tourist purchase via a travel agent, who assembles some or all of the transactional elements, typically transport and accommodation, with some of the attendant entertainment and amenities. Type *c* shows the tourist purchasing a 'package' direct from a tour operator. Such direct selling of an 'inclusive tour' will normally cover transport and accommodation ready assembled and will possibly include certain other services, amenities and entertainment. Type *d* is the purchase of a package tour via a travel agent. Thus a retail sale from agent to tourist is followed by a principal/agent relationship between the travel agent and tour operator, who provides ready assembled services.

There are opportunities for transactional brokers to interpose themselves at various points along the transactions chain. Such brokers will earn a commission by providing services to the transactional partners involving specialist information (including local knowledge), opportunities to reduce costs by consolidating purchases or merely being more efficient transactors. The main such brokerage opportunities are indicated by a broken arrow.

Organisational forces in tourism transactions

The organisation of firms in the tourism transactions chain reflects the forces outlined in the first section. Retail travel agents are able to offer services to tourists superior to those available by direct purchase in many instances. The agents' success depends on their superior access to information and specialist knowledge of markets and conditions. This enables agents to offer a service of advice and guidance to the individual tourist. Agents are also able to act on behalf of the principal, be it hotel, airline, tour operator or shipping company, in a personalised manner. The retail travel agent also offers a one-stop facility allowing choice and enabling the customer to purchase the whole range of tourism products, thereby reducing the tourist's transactional search costs.

The tour operator consolidates the transactions which an independent tourist would make separately and sells a single package to the customer. Tour operators are wholesalers who combine transportation, accommodation and other ground services to make up an inclusive tour, and sell it as a package holiday at an all-inclusive price. This not only gives the customer the convenience of purchasing a single composite product in one transaction, it also enables economies to be obtained on the supply side. The tour operator is able to enter long-term contracts for accommodation and transport (often leading to internalisation of this relationship). Consequently, this permits high load factors for aircraft (ships and trains) and high occupancy rates for hotels. Economies of scale and exercise of monopsony power can also reduce the operator's costs. This packaging enables mass marketing and standardisation to take place. Branding by the tour operators across destinations results in increased consumer loyalty to the operator (and transference of loyalty from destination to operator). The operator can give explicit or implicit quality guarantees to the tourist and thus reduce the perceived risks of default, poor service and other transactional uncertainties. Tour operators can market their products via brochures providing an initial screening of the myriad tourist products potentially available. For the tourist, uncertainty is reduced and quality guarantees are provided. The above analysis leads us to believe that the relationship between travel agents and tour operators is likely to be unstable.

Transactions cost analysis has been applied to the international hotel industry by Dunning and McQueen (1981, 1982). Dunning and McQueen examined the organisational structure of the international hotel industry and found that minority equity ownership and non-equity forms, such as franchising and management contracts, were the dominant forms by which international hotel chains controlled individual hotels. By contrast, the airline business tends to be dominated by wholly owned state or private corporations which have heretofore operated on a national basis because of regulation and restricted landing rights, but now are forming global alliances in order to reap global economies of scale (in booking, reservation systems, world coverage and connections and in shared services).

These forms of doing business (ownership, minority ownership, joint ventures and alliances, licensing, franchising and arm's length arrangements) are often referred to as the governance structure of the industry. They are determined by the interplay of internalisation/transaction costs factors and the locational determinants of where activities are best located. Clearly, in the tourism industry locational factors are substantially fixed (sun, sea, mountains, lakes, cultural attractions and historical sites are generally immovable). Management issues arise from the most profitable means of getting tourists from the destination countries to these fixed locations – but transactions costs substantially interact with these costs to produce the best organisational structure to achieve those objectives. The nature of the contract is particularly important in non-ownership modes of operation as (particularly in the hotel subsector) de facto control can be secured through a contract without equity involvement. Careful micro-analysis here, as elsewhere, is required.

IMPLICATIONS

The marketing implications of transactions analysis can be derived by reversing the transactions flow and looking back over the transactions chain. It is a peculiarity of the tourism market that final service providers must aim their marketing at quite different targets, as illustrated by the different types of transactions chain (Figure 4.1). The direct purchase, self-assembly package implied by chain *a* requires final service providers to reach the individual tourist directly. In the other types of transactions chain, intermediaries occur and marketing needs to be directed at them. These intermediaries may be tour operators and/or travel agencies. (A parallel analysis can be conducted for the strategies of National Tourism Promotional Agencies.) Similarly, tour operators must target marketing efforts at individual tourists and travel agencies.

The analysis of linkages and the flow of intermediate products has implications not only for the packaging of tourism services but also for the nature of tourism enterprises in general. The above analysis shows that the nature of the transport function is crucial. The transport function is an important point in the exchange of rights in the tourism transaction chain. If this function is subcontracted to an independent operator this delicate and central function can go out of control. Hence the close integration of transport with other facilities in the integrated multinational. There are important cost implications also. Efficient utilisation of capacity is crucial in keeping costs down in transport as well as accommodation. Complete control of a fleet of aircraft or ships (one ship or aircraft for smaller companies) will impose severe cost penalties if these facilities are not fully utilised. Consequently there is considerable instability arising from the necessity to balance control of transport with cost-efficient utilisation.

The transport function is also important because it, uniquely, involves the transnational transfer of rights (and tourists). Its management therefore requires great skill and sensitivity. Further, it affords opportunities for international arbitrage and utilisation of transfer-pricing techniques which may have a significant impact on profitability.

Finally, the theory has important implications for quality management in tourism. Control of the transactions flow enables the integrated multinational to monitor and control the quality of services. This is often difficult to achieve through external contracts because of the intangible nature of services and the difficulties of exercising day-to-day control other than by direct line management.

The application of transaction cost analysis to tourism is not yet extensive. Examples include the work of Dunning and McQueen (1981, 1982), referred to above, McQueen (1989), Davé (1984) on US multinationals in hotels, Buckley and Papadopoulos (1988) on foreign investment in Greek tourism, Tremblay (n.d) on the impact of transactions costs and information on the corporate structure of tourism multinationals, Dwyer and Forsyth (1994) on the motivation and impact of foreign tourism investment in Australia and Buckley and Geyikdaki (1996a, b) on Turkey. Other studies of foreign investment and multinationals in tourism include Ajami (1988) on Belize and Zammit (1981) on developing countries. The internationalisation of the hotel industry is examined by Dunning and Kundu (1995).

CONCLUSION

The analysis of transactions and transaction costs provides a framework for the unification of concepts and analysis in tourism research. It provides a core theory which allows the analysis of tourism demand through the transactions chain and the organisation of supply by its distinctive view of the forces driving organisational developments. The changing pattern of industry analysis and the scope of firms can be explained and predicted by internalisation pressures. The approach has implications for marketing and for the future organisation of the tourism industry.

REFERENCES

Ajami, R.A., 1988, Tourism multinationals in Belize, *Annals of Tourism Research*, **15**,(4): 517–530

Buckley, Peter J., 1987, Tourism – an economic transactions analysis, *Tourism Management*, 8(3), September: 190–194

Buckley, Peter J., Casson, Mark, 1976, *The future of the multinational enterprise*, Macmillan, London

Buckley, Peter J., Casson, Mark, 1985, *The economic theory of the multinational enterprise*, Macmillan, London

Buckley, Peter J., Geyikdaki, Necla V., 1996a, A theoretical explanation of international tourism investments, *Annals of Tourism Research*, 23(4): 941–943

Buckley, Peter J., Geyikdaki, Necla V., 1996b, Explaining foreign direct investment in Turkey's tourism industry, *Transnational Corporations*, 5(3) December: 99–110

Buckley, Peter J., Papadopoulos, S.I., 1988, Foreign direct investment in the tourism sector of the Greek economy, *Services Industries Journal*, 8(3) July: 110–120

Coase, Ronald, 1937, The nature of the firm, *Economica* (New Series), 4: 386–405

Davé, V., 1984, US multinational involvement in the international hotel sector, *Services Industries Journal*, 4(1), March: 48–63

Dunning, John H., Kundu, S.K., 1995, The internationalisation of the hotel industry, *Management International Review*, 35(2): 101–133

Dunning, John H., McQueen, Matthew, 1981, The eclectic theory of international production: a case study of the international hotel industry, *Managerial and Decision Economics*, 2(4): 199–210

Dunning, John H., McQueen, Matthew, 1982, *Transnational corporations in international tourism*, United Nations Centre on Transnational Corporations, New York

Dwyer, Larry, Forsyth, Peter, 1994, Foreign tourism investment: motivation and impact, *Annals of Tourism Research*, 21(3): 512–537

McQueen, Matthew, 1989, Multinationals in tourism. In Witt, S.F., Moutinho, L. eds, *Tourism marketing and management handbook* (1st edn) [NB: not in 2nd edn], Prentice-Hall, Hemel Hempstead, 285–289.

Tremblay, Pascal, n.d., The corporate structure of multinational enterprises in tourism: transaction costs and information. International Sociological Association – XII World Congress of Sociology

Williamson, Oliver E., 1975, *Markets and hierarchies*, The Free Press, New York

Williamson, Oliver E., 1996, *The mechanisms of governance*. Oxford University Press, Oxford

Zammit, A., 1981, Transnationals in developing countries, *International Tourism Quarterly*, 1: 37–56

5 Behavioral Models Related to Tourism

STEPHEN J. HIEMSTRA AND JOSEPH A. ISMAIL

OBJECTIVES AND CONCEPTS

Behavioral or demand models are designed primarily to identify the causal factors associated with a dependent variable of interest. For example, such a model may be developed to 'explain' the number of tourist arrivals at a given destination such as a country. It may focus on only those tourists originating from a given location, such as another country, or it may include tourists from all other countries, depending on the objectives of the study.

This chapter will focus on (A) the usefulness of behavioral models in contrast to time-series models, (B) the structural form of typical models and variables commonly found to be significant in behavioral models, (C) interpretation of the results and the usual basis for determining significance for some simple demand models related to tourism demand, and (D) the assumptions, diagnostics and solutions to some problems commonly encountered when estimating behavioral models. Some examples will be presented as illustrations.

TIME-SERIES VS BEHAVIORAL MODELS

The objective of using behavioral models to explain past events is in contrast with that of time-series models whose objective is primarily to project past trends into the future based on observed patterns in past data. Behavioral models are concerned with estimating the impacts of one or more independent variables on a particular variable of interest such as tourist arrivals or the demand for tourism services. The term 'behavioral' stems from the notion that the independent variables explain the behavior of the dependent variable over time or cross-section. Time-series models on the other hand are univariate in nature and do not provide any information on events or conditions that may have impacted the variable of interest. This dichotomy

Economic and Management Methods for Tourism and Hospitality Research.
Edited by Thomas Baum and Ram Mudambi © 1999 John Wiley & Sons Ltd.

is not entirely pure because some aspects of time are sometimes used in behavioral models when time itself is found to be an explanatory variable, or when dynamic models are used to measure long-term relationships.

For example, seasonality itself may be considered an important behavioral variable, or sometimes longer term trends are entered as explicit variables in behavioral models as an indicator of changes in habits or changes in technology. However, trend variables should be used sparingly because they usually are not truly explanatory, but themselves are a proxy for more basic motivating factors that should be included if possible. In concept, seasonality is not a root variable either, and it does change slowly over time, but in this case the calendar may be a more substantive variable. Ultimately, of course, seasonality may be a reflection of vacation, business, and school schedules but these factors can be lumped together in terms of seasonal impacts.

Dynamic or long-run models incorporate time by lagging the effects of key variables, such as price, from previous time periods. For example, a model explaining the level of price by changes in quantities sold (plus other variables) could include a variable for price in previous time periods (P_{t-1}). These long-run effects can be interpreted as measuring the effects of 'habit,' that is, the proclivity to continue purchasing similar items over long periods of time (Hiemstra and Ismail, 1994). Discussion of distributed lag models of this sort is an advanced topic which is beyond the scope of this chapter (see Phlips, 1990; Intriligator, 1978). It is mentioned here only because it is an important time-related component of many models.

Behavioral or causal models are often considered to 'explain' or 'cause' past events, but theoretically this statement is true only when the data being analyzed have been derived from controlled experiments. More typically, when analyzing survey data the independent variables should be thought of as being 'associated with' rather than truly explaining or causing changes in the dependent variable. To regard a regression model as explanatory, one must assume that (A) the variables included in the model are actually independent, (B) the errors in the data are normally distributed, and (C) that all other possible impacts on the dependent variable are held constant or controlled. These are stringent assumptions, and the first two assumptions can be tested empirically for multicollinearity and heteroscedasticity or equal variance. The third assumption, often referred to as the ceteris parabus assumption (all things remain constant), is more difficult to examine. Some degrees of such problems are hidden below the surface in analyzing most socioeconomic data whereas in a controlled experiment, all other things, besides the independent variables, are held constant.

There are times when behavioral models are used for projection purposes even though that is often not their primary objective. One can argue that any model that truly explains the past should be useful for projection purposes, and should be better for that purpose than more 'mechanical' projections of unknown trends. In order to use a behavioral model for forecasting purposes, forecasted levels of the independent variables need to be known because the dependent variable in the future is a function of the independent variables. But behavioral models are usually based on independent variables such as prices and income which themselves may not be known with any more certainty for the projected periods than is the dependent variable which is being forecast. Consequently, the forecasting errors will pyramid by combining the errors of first projecting the independent variables and then using those results to project the dependent variable.

For this reason, it is not surprising that time-series models often have been shown to do a better job of projection than behavioral models. The advantage of time-series models is particularly important for relatively short projections (Martin and Witt, 1989; Witt and Witt, 1990). Behavioral models usually do relatively better for projections made over longer time periods when the underlying factors have more time to be expressed.

One of the most useful aspects of behavioral models is their use in playing 'what if' in order to understand or test relationships among a set of projected variables or alternative scenarios at some future time period. The simplest approach is to use a 'dummy' or 'indicator' variable (a variable which usually takes on a value of 1 during the period of interest and 0 elsewhere), to indicate the occurrence of specific incidents over time that may have an impact on the dependent variable. For example, one can use dummy variables to indicate periods of terrorist activity in a given destination, periods of high energy cost or even recessionary periods. If the level of the dependent variable shows significant changes from its average behavior during or after the occurrence of some event, the forecaster can use this information to estimate the likely impacts if these events occur in the future.

The relationship of continuous variables such as income, prices, exchange rates, or Gross Domestic Product can also be used to examine different scenarios. For example, if it were found that the price of lodging in a specific destination had a significant negative impact on the number of visitors to a destination, then a forecaster could estimate the impacts of changes in lodging prices. It must be remembered that several independent variables are being projected so the relationships among them are an important objective.

FORMS OF THE MODEL AND VARIABLES

Behavioral or demand models owe their basic constructs to classical consumer utility theory based on analysis of indifference curves from the days of Alfred Marshall and his followers (Marshall, 1890/1920), and later refinements related to income and substitution effects by John Hicks (1946). These basic models hypothesize that the quantity of a product demanded is a function of the price of that product, the price of competing products, and the income of consumers. The theory has been expanded further to include non-economic characteristics of demand. These include such variables as population, when the underlying structure is hypothesized to be in per capita terms, and other socioeconomic and demographic variables such as household size or type. They also include various segmentation and situational variables that may have a one-time impact in shifting the level or rate of demand. Sometimes marketing costs are included in the model to allow for demand shifts due to advertising and promotion. More complex models include price lags to make the model dynamic.

A common demand model can be characterized as:

$$Q_i = f(P_i, P_j, I, \text{CPI}, D_k, S_1), \text{ to be fit by ordinary least-squares regression,} \quad (1)$$

where Q_i is the quantity of good 'i' that is purchased, P_i is the price of that good, P_j is the price of competing goods, I is the income level of consumers buying the good, CPI, the Consumer Price Index, is the general level of prices (inflation), D is a vector 'k' of population and other demographic characteristics, and S_1 is a vector of various segmentation and situational variables. This model includes a variable to measure the effects of inflation on prices and incomes. An alternative formulation could be to 'deflate' the economic variables by dividing each observation by the CPI or some other price index such as the deflator for Gross Domestic Product for the same period of time. A separate inflation variable is preferable because it avoids a forced one-to-one relationship between inflation and current prices imposed by dividing by an inflation index, however this is not always possible due to the multicollinearity (high correlations among two or more independent variables) usually found among prices, income and Gross Domestic Product.

The model can be based either on annual or quarterly data depending on the period of concern and data available. Monthly data should usually be avoided to reduce problems of multicollinearity. If quarterly data are used, three additional dummy variables would be included to measure the differential effects of seasonality on three quarters. The fourth quarter, which must be excluded, is the base or reference to which the three quarterly variables relate; it is measured by the intercept variable.

As an alternative, models can be fitted to each of the four quarters of the year independently and the coefficients compared. However, this procedure requires a much larger sample size, since the sample used for each model will now only be one-fourth as large. For the same level of confidence, running separate quarterly models is not as efficient in the use of degrees of freedom as putting all the data into a single model.

By using a single dummy variable for each quarter, the implicit assumption is that only the intercepts of the models differ by quarter. If one hypothesizes that the coefficients associated with other predictor variables also differ by quarter, then interaction terms for each quarter must also be added to the model. Interaction variables are defined by multiplying 1 times each observation for a given quarter plus 0s for each other quarter. It is often useful to test this hypothesis by entering the interaction terms into the model to see if their impact on the dependent variable is significant. If a quarterly dummy variable and the interaction term are both significant in the model, it would indicate that not only are the absolute levels of the dependent variable different on average from quarter to quarter but also the rate of change in the dependent variable associated with a one unit change of the dependent variable is different from quarter to quarter. This procedure will efficiently yield full information with no advantage to fitting separate models to each quarter.

Sometimes 'quantity' as the dependent variable is redefined to relate to expenditures rather than simply number of items purchased. Often, in measuring the demand for tourism products or services, the dependent variable is measured in terms of expenditures. Many such models continue to use the same independent variables as in the case of true quantities, even though expenditures are technically equal to price times quantity. This formulation may cause specification errors in the model because price is also an independent variable. A better formulation of expenditures is to deflate the expenditures so the results are in real terms (Pyo and Warner, 1996).

The basic model (1) as specified above is linear in form, but some other model specifications may still be handled by ordinary least squares by modifying the variables themselves. For example, one common specification allows multiplicity (curvilinearity) in the model by transforming some or all of the variables into logarithms (logs). Log-linear or double-log models – being in percentage terms already – offer the convenience of the coefficients of the variables being identical to the elasticities. For example, the model:

$$\ln Y_t = \alpha + \beta_1 \ln X_1 + \beta_2 \ln X_2 + \varepsilon \text{ is equivalent to } Y = \gamma_0 X_1^{\gamma_1} X_2^{\gamma_2} \varepsilon$$

where ln represents the natural log of the variable indicating that X_1 and X_2 have a mulitiplicative impact on Y rather than a weighted additive impact implied by

$$Y_t = \alpha + \beta_1 X_1 + \beta_2 X_2 + \varepsilon$$

But one gets the impression that this ease of calculating elasticities guides too many analysts into using this model without considering the appropriateness of the underlying functional form. The ease of interpretation of log-linear models may not be worth the small effort necessary in calculating elasticities. Coefficients in natural numbers are translated into elasticities by multiplying them by the ratio of the mean of the associated variable (for example, prices or income) divided by the mean of the dependent variable.

Often food-demand models are found to fit better in semi-log form, that is quantities in nominal units are hypothesized to be explained by prices and incomes in log form. Another common variation is the polynomial form in which squared or higher order terms of an independent variable are included in the equation. In this case, the higher order terms would likely be in addition to the linear term, which would allow changes in income or time to have either an increasing or decreasing impact on quantities purchased.

The log-linear model has the disadvantage of requiring consumer responses to be constant over income levels of consumers and the prices they face. To gain flexibility in consumer responses and avoid some of the other specification problems caused by using expenditure data as the dependent variable, Deaton and Muellbauer (1980) developed the Almost Ideal Demand System (AIDS) which specifies budget shares of expenditures on a particular commodity as the dependent variable. Budget shares are specified as a function of (A) the log of expenditures deflated by a complex form of prices of own products (which is usually replaced by a geometric price index) and (B) prices of substitute products as independent variables. As in the case of linear regression, other demographic and situational variables can be added to the model as appropriate.

The AIDS model is flexible by allowing varying responses to a wide range in prices and consumer incomes. But this flexibility leads to complexity in calculating price elasticities of demand. This model has not often been used in tourism demand analysis, to the knowledge of these authors, but it offers the opportunity to avoid the fixed restrictions of the commonly used log-linear model.

Ordinary multivariate, least-squares regression is by far the most commonly used form of behavioral models used to explain tourism demand. But some other useful forms of such models include discriminant analysis and logistic models. Discriminant analysis derives the factors responsible for distinguishing between two or more predetermined outcomes. For example, it could be used for determining why travelers prefer destination A as opposed to destination B.

Tobit and probit are the two most commonly used logistic models, with tobit the predominant choice in recent years. Logistic models predict the probability of each of two or more choices being made. They could be used to measure probabilities associated with travelers vs non-travelers. They in essence allow the use of indicator dummy variables as dependent variables, whereas in ordinary least squares regression dummy variables are usable only as independent variables.

EXAMPLE OF A TOURISM MODEL

Model specification

Regardless of the format of the model, a model explaining the number of tourist arrivals in a given country would be expected to include some form of prices or relative prices between originating and destination countries, changes in exchange rates among these countries, disposable income or gross domestic product in the country of origin, and population in the inbound compared with the outbound region of concern.

As an example, Martin and Witt (1989) used the basic model shown in Table 5.1 to explain the number of tourist visits outbound to six selected countries from the United Kingdom in their study comparing alternative forecasting models. The same basic model was used for outbound tourism to each of the six countries, even though the same model may not have been the best possible model explaining travel to each of the six countries individually. But this model suits our purpose because it demonstrates the most

Table 5.1. Tourism model used by Martin and Witt to explain number of tourism visits from the United Kingdom to six selected destination countries

Model: $\ln \dfrac{V_{ijt}}{P_{it}} = a_1 + a_2 \ln \dfrac{Y_{it}}{P_{it}} + a_3 \ln C_{jt} + a_4 \ln CS_{it} + a_5 \ln EX_{ijt} + a_6 \ln TA_{ijt}$
$+ a_7 \ln TAS_{it} + a_8 \ln TS_{ijt} + a_9 \ln TSS_{it} + a_{10}DV1_t + a_{11}DV2_t + a_{12}DV3_t + a_{13}\text{Trend}_t + U_{ijt}$

i = country of origin, United Kingdom
j = 1...6 countries of destination
t = 1,2...,16(1 = 1965,...,16 = 1980)

where
V_{ijt} is the number of tourist visits from origin i to destination j in year t
P_{it} is the origin i population in year t
Y_{it} is personal disposable income in origin i in year t (1980 prices)
C_{jt} is the cost of living for tourists in destination j in year t (1980 prices)
CS_{it} is a weighted average of the cost of tourism in substitute destinations for residents of origin i in year t (1980 prices)
EX_{ijt} is the rate of exchange between currencies of origin i and destination j in year t
TA_{ijt} is the cost of travel by air from origin i to destination j in year t (1980 prices)
TAS_{ijk} is a weighted average of the cost of travel by air to substitute destinations from origin i in year t (1980 prices)
TS_{ijt} is the cost of travel by surface from origin i to destination j in year t (1980 prices)
TSS_{it} is a weighted average of the cost of travel by air to substitute destinations from origin i in year t
$DV1$ is a dummy variable which measures effects of the 1974 oil crisis, $DV1_t = 1$ if $t = 10$ (1974) or 11 (1975) and $= 0$ otherwise
$DV2$ is a dummy variable which measures effects of the 1979 oil crisis, $DV2_t = 1$ if $t = 15$ (1979) and $= 0$ otherwise
$DV3$ is a dummy variable which measures effects of the 1967–69 UK currency restrictions, $DV3_{it} = 1$ if i refers to the UK and $= 0$ otherwise
$TREND_t$ is a time trend over t

U_{ijt} is a random disturbance term, and
$a_1, a_2,..., a_{13}$ are unknown parameters

common variables usually expected to 'explain' international travel. The model is fit by ordinary least squares in log form.

Note that the United Kingdom is termed 'i' as one of a family of such countries of origin that is being analyzed as a set. The variables in this model differ somewhat from those in equation (1). In this case, population and other demographic variables are not included as separate variables in the model but rather population is used to deflate the dependent variable; that is, the number of travelers is defined on a per capita basis. The Martin and Witt model includes a set of cost variables which take the place of the price and substitute prices specified in (1). It omits any segmentation variables but includes some dummy variables related to abnormal situations, which are not specified in (1). When behavioral models use data that occur across time as opposed to cross-section, models usually do not include many demographic and segmentation variables because of a lack of such detailed information available over time, plus the necessity of conserving degrees of freedom.

Cost variables are often used in place of price variables because of the lack of detailed information. Cost, which is price times quantity purchased, is more readily available than the two components that it replaces, but it is not as conceptually preferred. Sometimes distance traveled is used in place of costs but average distance traveled is not generally available. Further, costs of travel are not as closely correlated with distance traveled as before the advent of yield management programs, which are more attuned to reflecting differences in demand for travel than in reflecting cost differences. The cost of travel to alternative locations attempts to allow for the purchase of substitute products by p_j in equation (1). The cost data are refined in the Martin and Witt model by separating costs of air as opposed to costs of surface transportation, as well as costs of travel to designated locations as opposed to substitute locations.

Crouch (1994), in his excellent syntheses of various studies related to international tourism demand, indicated that 'economic determinants alone account for much of the variation in tourist numbers and expenditures.' He found that 'a reading of the past research leads one to conclude that income alone is the single most important determinant of demand for international tourism.' He found that most income elasticities are in the range of 1.0–2.0. But he continues by pointing out that 'non-economic factors are also important.'

Crouch goes on to point to the problem of measuring prices as related to international tourism demand. Various studies have measured prices differently, so measured price elasticities are quite varied. Many studies have had difficulty in incorporating prices of competing products. Loeb (1982) used a rather unique and elaborate process of incorporating relative prices in competing countries by defining a set of price variables in which various weights were assigned to alternative countries of destination, in relation to the country of origin. Tourism itself is a composite of anomalous products (services) so it is not surprising that its price is difficult to capture in the context of an explanatory model. It is more straightforward to think of prices in relation to quantity of services provided by hotels (room rates) or restaurants (menu prices).

Interpretation of the model

The results of the Martin and Witt models for two of the destination countries referred to in Table 5.1 are given in Table 5.2. These findings contain

Table 5.2. Results of Martin and Witt model to explain number of tourism visits from the United Kingdom to Austria and Germany

Explanatory variable	Destination	
	Austria	Germany
Constant	−47.819	−20.482
	(−38.51)*	(−7.81)*
$\ln Y/P$	4.550	2.387
	(24.00)*	(6.16)
$\ln C$	−0.235	−0.361
	(1.60)	(−1.75)
$\ln CS$	0.130	
	(0.23)	
$\ln EX$	1.869	
	(6.62)*	
$\ln TA$		
$\ln TAS$		0.540
		(3.03)*
$\ln TS$		−1.765
		(−3.73)*
$\ln TSS$		
$DV1$	−0.258	−0.265
	(−10.64)*	(−4.27)*
$DV2$	−0.619	
	(−10.23)*	
$DV3$	−0.061	−0.052
	(−2.82)*	(−1.60)
TREND		0.056
		(2.82)*
F	252.16	19.46
Adj R^2	0.983	0.803
R^2	0.991	0.895
DW	2.34	1.95

The figures in parentheses are t values.
* Indicates statistical significance level of 0.5.

income coefficients of 4.55 for tourists traveling to Austria and 2.387 for travelers to Germany from the UK. The 't' values for these income coefficients are higher than for any other independent variable, 24.0 in the case of Austria and 6.16 for travelers to Germany. These values are noted as being significant at the 5% level or more, and in these cases their significance level is much greater than 5% that is, the significance level is likely at the 1% level or better. Normally, a t value of around 2.0 is significant at the 5% level.

The t value for a regression coefficient is calculated as the estimate of that coefficient divided by the standard error of that estimate. The hypothesis being tested by the t statistic is that the coefficient in question is equal to zero, that is (H_o: $\beta_i = 0$). When the t value is approximately 2.0, or larger, it indicates that the estimate of the coefficient falls two or more standard errors from the mean of zero, indicating that there is a 0.05, or less, probability that the regression coefficient is zero, provided the distribution of the estimate of the regression coefficient is normally distributed.

The income coefficients in the model indicate that for every 1% increase in income in the UK, there is expected to be a 4.5% increase in rate of tourists going to Austria and nearly a 2.4% increase in rate of tourists going to Germany. Note that these increases are measured from their respective bases of travelers to these countries. It provides an indication of percentage changes but gives no indication as to which destination country has the larger number of tourists from the UK. The rates are measured in terms of tourist visits relative to size of the population in the UK, or in number of travelers per capita.

Other significant variables (other than the intercept term) in the case of travelers to Austria include exchanges rates and the three dummy variables for the two oil crises and the 1967–69 UK currency restrictions. The exchange rate variable indicates that during the period of this study, there was an increase in outbound travel to Austria as the UK's currency increased in value relative to Austria's currency. Specifically, there were 1.859% more (less) travelers per capita from the UK to Austria for each percentage increase (decrease) in the value of the British pound relative to Austrian currency.

During the period of the 1967–69 UK currency restrictions, the increase associated with the relative value of the pound was less than usual (to the extent of 0.061 to 1.0). Dummy variables are usually entered into a model in terms of zeros and 1s. That is, during the period of 1967–69, the value of $DV3$ would be 1 and during all other periods, the value of $DV3$ would be zero.

The other two dummy variables show that the two oil crises both had significant negative impacts on travel to Austria, to the extent of the rate of travel per capita being less by 0.258 during the 1974 crisis and less by 0.619 during the 1979 crisis. The significance levels on both of these variables was very high, with t values exceeding 10.

The remaining variables in the model for Austria were found to be not significantly different from zero. For this reason, the model could have been rerun and these variables omitted from the model, likely without much impact, provided the non-significant variables were not highly correlated with each other. In this case, the two cost variables (C and CS) likely could have been omitted without harming the remaining model. The coefficients for the remaining variables would likely have been altered because all variables are interrelated to some degree in their impacts. However, sometimes when insignificant variables are omitted, there are strong impacts on the remaining variables. When that is the case, there likely is a problem of multicollinearity or relatively high correlation among the independent variables because variables that are closely related are partly substituting for each other. For example, it may be found that the elimination of either C or CS would result in the remaining variable being found significant in the equation. This situation violates one of the important assumptions underlying the model, that of independence among the independent variables.

In the case of the model for Germany, there are some significant variables that are different from those in the model for Austria. The dummy variables for the 1967–69 currency restrictions are not significant in the case of UK travel to Germany. But in this model, TAS (travel by air to substitute countries) and TS (travel by surface to Germany) are significant variables. In addition, the trend variable is significant. One expects substitute purchases to be positively related to demand for a given product, and this result is demonstrated by this model. As the weighted average of the cost of travel to substitute countries (for example to the US) increases, it becomes more desirable to travel to Germany from the UK. In the case of surface travel costs to Germany for travelers to Germany (TS), increased costs will reduce the number of travelers from the UK, which suggests that travelers are economically rational.

The trend variable indicates that time itself is a factor in explaining increases in travel from the UK to Germany, after allowing for all other significant variables in the model. The trend coefficient of 0.056 indicates that each year the travel per capita ratio has increased 0.056 per year over the period of the study. The significance of trend variables in a model usually indicates that the behavioral factors in a model are not doing a very good job of explaining changes in the dependent variable.

The model for travel to Austria accounted for most of the variation in per capita visitors from the UK based on the values of R^2 (0.991) and adjusted R^2 (0.983) given. The R^2 of 0.991 indicates that 99.1% of the total variance is expanded by the combination of variables in the model. The adjusted R^2 adjusts for changes in the degrees of freedom due to the inclusion of additional variables in the model. It can be shown that R^2 will increase with the addition of new variables into an equation regardless of the significance of the additional variable. As the degrees of freedom available to estimate the error term approach zero, the difference between the calculated R^2 and the adjusted R^2 will increase. When the degrees of freedom to estimate the error term reach zero the model cannot be estimated. This would occur if there were one less explanatory variable in the model than observations available to estimate the model since regression coefficients and the intercept each need one degree of freedom.

In the case of travel to Germany, the model explains only 89.5% of the total variation in the system, and 80.3% after adjustment for degrees of freedom. Thus, the model for Germany is not nearly as strong as in the case of travel to Austria, and the degrees of freedom were more of a limiting factor. This conclusion is also supported by the F statistic that is much higher for the Austrian model than for the German model, and also by the significance of a trend variable in the model.

It is likely that both of these equations originally suffered from serial correlation since the authors indicate that both equations were estimated with the use of a Cochran–Orcutt transformation which is used to correct for serial correlation. The Durbin–Watson (DW) test provides a measure of serial correlation in the system. A DW value of 2.0 is optimum, so the level of 2.34 for the Austria model is probably in the 'indeterminate' range of serial correlation being a problem, but one would need to consult the DW tables of distribution to be sure. The DW level of 1.95 for the Germany model is much better. Numbers that depart significantly on either side of 2.0 indicate significant serial correlation. Problems of serial correlation and multicollinearity can often be corrected, or at least reduced, by introducing lagged terms or autoregressive terms in the model (see later discussion).

Implications of the model

The striking conclusion from the models explaining outbound tourism to Austria, and to a lesser degree to Germany, is the overriding importance of income. This finding supports the generalization by Crouch. However, relative exchange rates between the two countries are also quite important. It is disappointing but not surprising that the cost variables are not significant in the Austrian model, but two of them are quite important in the German model.

One of the reasons that income is such a strong variable in explaining tourism behavior is the lack of being able to introduce prices directly in these models. In this sense, there may be a specification error in the available models which is likely, as will be discussed below. Prices have an impact through exchange rates and also through various cost of travel variables, but in demand systems for most other products prices of own products as well as prices for substitute products play a more dominant role in affecting purchase behavior.

ASSUMPTIONS AND DIAGNOSTICS RELATED TO MULTIPLE REGRESSION MODELS

When estimating a multiple regression model of the form described earlier, it is important to understand not only the interpretation of the model but also the assumptions related to the model. A generic multiple regression model can be written as:

$$Y_i = \alpha + \beta_1 X_{1i} + \beta_2 X_{2i} + \ldots + \beta_j X_{ji} + \varepsilon_i \tag{2}$$

The interpretation of the model is as follows: Y_i is the dependent variable, for example travelers per capita per year from the UK to Austria during year i (Table 5.1); α is the intercept or constant term which is the predicted value of Y when all Xs are zero; each β_j represents the average change in Y for each unit change in X_j across all i (observations) from 1 to n with all other $X_{s_{*j}}$ held constant. Finally, ε_i is the error associated with the ith estimate of Y_i.

Specifications of the model

The assumptions related to the model directly affect how confident we can be in the results of the model. There are a number of assumptions that must be made in order to insure that the results of the model are not biased or misleading. The most basic assumptions relate to the specification of the model. As can be seen from equation (2), Y is a linear combination of the Xs. This specification is too limiting since models remain linear if the variables can be transformed so that the model is linear with respect to the coefficients β_j. Examples cited earlier are the log-linear, semilog and polynomial models which allow nonlinear relationships to be estimated through appropriate transformations of the variables. Not all models can be transformed in this manner, in which case they would be considered inherently nonlinear (Pindyck and Rubenfeld, 1991). Therefore, an initial assumption when using multiple regression is that the underlying model is inherently linear and the appropriate transformations are made for nonlinear relationships.

A further assumption related to the specification of the model is that no relevant variables are omitted from the equation and no irrelevant variables are included in the equation. Either of these cases would lead to a misspecified model. In the case of an omitted variable that is correlated with variables that are in the model, the impacts of the omitted variable on Y will be partly accounted for by the coefficients of the remaining variable, thereby biasing the estimates of the coefficients. The degree and direction of bias on the remaining variables' coefficients will be dependent on the degree and sign of the correlation between the omitted relevant variable and the remaining variables. To the degree that the omitted variable is uncorrelated with the remaining variables, the loss of the omitted Xs explanatory power of Y will appear in the error term as serial correlation, which will be discussed later.

The inclusion of an irrelevant variable, meaning the coefficient on the variable is close to zero, does not bias the other coefficients nor does it affect the consistency of the estimates. It can, however, make it more difficult to reject the hypothesis that a relevant variables' coefficient is zero if the relevant and irrelevant variables are correlated.

Assumptions related to variables

Two important assumptions related to the variables themselves are (A) that they are measured without error, and (B) that no two independent variables or combinations of independent variables are perfectly correlated. If the independent variables are measured with error the estimates of the regression coefficients will be biased and inconsistent. For example, if for larger values of X, the error associated with its measurement increases, then as X increases the error associated with the model ε increases so X and ε will be correlated. A similar problem will arise if Y is measured with error. There are no clear solutions to measurement errors since often there is no knowledge about these errors, especially in the social sciences. The technique of instrumental-variable estimation can help solve a measurement error problem but that problem is beyond the scope of this book.

The second assumption related to the independent variables is that there are no combinations of independent variables that are perfectly correlated. When two or more variables are perfectly correlated it is not possible to calculate the parameter estimates and no solution to equation (2) can be estimated, so one of the variables must be dropped from the equation. It is for this reason that one of four quarterly dummy variables discussed earlier must be dropped from the equation since any particular dummy variable is equal to 1 minus the other three variables. The problem is not as straightforward when variables are not perfectly correlated but are highly correlated. It is assumed that the independent variables in the equation are in fact independent of each other. When this is not the case and the variables are correlated, the problem identified earlier as multicollinearity exists. In non-experimental data, there is almost always some degree of correlation among the independent variables. When the correlations are very high, serious problems arise with the estimation and interpretation of the regression coefficients. Some symptoms of the existence of multicollinearity include: (A) a high R^2 for the equation but no highly significant coefficients; (B) dropping or adding a variable in the equation causes large changes in the size or significance of the coefficients; (C) the sign on a coefficient is not as expected, for example a negative sign on an own price coefficient; (D) adding additional observations to the analysis causes large changes in some coefficients.

High multicollinearity creates the problems described above because (A) it inflates the variances of the coefficient estimates, and (B) two or more variables are sharing their explanatory power. As explained earlier, the calculation of the t statistic for any particular coefficient is the coefficient divided by its standard error. If the standard error is inflated, it becomes more difficult to reject the hypothesis that the coefficient is zero, leading to a possible incorrect conclusion that the coefficient is zero and therefore insignificant in the regression. The reason two variables that are highly correlated share explanatory power can be shown by the interpretation of the model. The interpretation of a specific coefficient is that it reflects the change in Y for each unit change in that X variable with all other X variables held constant. It cannot be assumed that all other variables are staying constant if two or more variables are highly correlated since one will tend to move with the other or others. In this case, it becomes difficult to determine which of the highly correlated variables movements is truly associated with the changes in the Y variable.

The symptoms of multicollinearity described above are not conclusive evidence of multicollinearity, merely the common results. To determine the extent of multicollinearity in a regression equation one can inspect the pairwise correlation coefficients of the independent variables to see if they exceed some value, typically around 0.80. If the correlations between two variables are 0.80 or higher one should consider dropping one of the variables from the equation to analyze the effect, or alternately combining the variables into one composite variable. Even though it may be found that none of the pairwise correlations are very high, it does not mean multicollinearity does not exist. The easiest way to determine if there is some combination of two or more variables that are highly correlated with another variable, is to regress each of the independent variables on the remaining independent variables to see if they are highly predictive (R^2 approaching 1.0 for that variable).

Statistical analysis packages such as SAS allow researchers to easily test for multicollinearity by requesting that the Variance Inflation Factor (VIF) be calculated for each parameter estimate. For any particular coefficient β_j, the $(VIF)_i = 1/1 - R_i^2$ where R_i^2 is the multiple coefficient of determination for the model which regresses the independent variable X_i, associated with β_j on the remaining independent variables as described above. It is easy to see that as R_i^2 increases say to 0.90, the (VIF) will increase to 10. Another statistic that can be requested is the 'Tolerance'(TOL) which is simply the reciprocal of the VIF_i or $(1 - R_i^2)$. Many statistical packages allow the user to set (TOL) limits so that an independent variable with an $R_i^2 > 0.90$, or (TOL) < 0.10, for example, will be excluded from the equation.

When multicollinearity is a problem in a regression model, the solutions are limited. Before committing to a solution, however, the purpose of the model must be considered. If the model is being used solely for prediction or forecasting purposes, the problem is not as serious as if the model is being used to measure behavioral relationships. In small sample sizes, the best solution is to increase the sample size. If this is not possible, or still does not help solve the problem, one should consider combining variables or dropping one or more of the offending variables from the equation. If these solutions lead to misspecification or do not solve the problem, it is possible to modify the least squares estimation method with a technique known as Ridge Regression. Ridge Regression improves the stability of the coefficients but the usual inferences regarding the coefficients and their distribution are not applicable.

Assumptions related to error terms

The final topic related to assumptions and diagnostics of a regression model relates to the error term. The error term can be thought of as consisting of two components; the effects on Y due to misspecification of the model, and secondly a residual random element in the dependent variable. The basic assumptions are that the errors: (A) have an expected value of zero; (B) have constant variance for all observations; (C) are independent and uncorrelated for different observations; and (D) are normally distributed.

The assumptions related to the error term (ε) are sometimes categorized as diagnostic techniques related to the residuals. This is somewhat misleading since the residual is composed of the true error (ε) in addition to errors associated with estimation of the model such as: (A) specification errors which are due to the true regression model being misspecified by failing to include all appropriate variables in their proper form, (B) sampling errors which relate to the expected random variation in the data set, and (C) non-specification and non-sampling errors due to problems such as data entry or problems associated with poor survey design which can result in observations that are well outside of normal expectations (outliers). The error that is measured by subtracting the estimated value of Y for each observation from the actual value of Y for each observation is a combination of all three types of error. Therefore, residual analysis must be approached with the realization that the analysis contains the true error associated with Y as well as additional errors associated with misspecification and other problems.

With these limitations in mind, an analysis of the errors, or residuals, can proceed by first observing any unusual patterns in the distribution of the residuals. A plot of the residuals across time or over observations of some X variable will reveal if estimation of one particular observation is distinctly different from others. An observation probably would be considered an outlier if the residual falls more than three standard deviations from the expected mean of zero.

Analysis of outliers can be performed in a number of ways other than inspection of the residual plot. In SAS© regression programs (SAS Institute, 1993), influence diagnostics provide a number of statistics to help detect extremely influential observations. Options such as 'R' and 'Influence' can be requested in the model statement of a 'Proc REG' SAS program which will provide a number of statistics to help detect outliers. The primary statistics provided are the Studentized Residuals and Dfbetas, which are similar to another statistic related to influential observations called Cook's D. If any of these statistics exceed the absolute value of two for any predicted value, the associated observation should be analyzed to determine if there is some abnormality associated with it. Cook's D shows the change to the estimates of Y that would occur if each individual observation were removed from the data set.

Further analysis of the patterns of the residuals can reveal further problems with the assumptions related to the ε. The first assumption that the error has an expected mean of zero is not of great concern since properties associated with the least squares estimation insure that the sum of the residuals must equal zero. The assumption that there is constant variance implies that the residuals are homoschedastic (equal) across observations. If the variance has some specific pattern such as getting larger or smaller with increased values of X or Y, it is relatively easy to observe. A common approach used to diagnose this problem is to plot the residuals against each X value. The plot will show visually if the residuals are systematically expanding or contracting as the value of X increases or decreases. When heteroscedasticity appears to be a problem, there are a number of potential solutions primarily related to transformation of the data in order to correct the problem. Specific transformations are appropriate for different forms of heteroscedasticity; a more complete discussion can be found in Mendenhall and Sincich (1989).

The final point on diagnostics related to the error term is that of serial correlation, which is often present in time-series data. Violation of the assumption that the error terms are uncorrelated is referred to as serial or auto correlation. If errors are negatively serially correlated, they will tend to cycle negative, then positive, and then negative again when arranged across observations or time. Positive serial correlation is present when the errors have long negative and then positive cycles. Serial correlation is most often a problem in data that are analyzed across time and, in fact, was a problem in the example provided earlier in this chapter. The primary effect of serial correlation is that the estimated standard error of the regression seriously underestimates the true standard error. This may lead to the belief that the regression coefficients are much more precise than is actually the case, so

that absolute size of the coefficients in the regression may change significantly if the serial correlation is removed. In presence of serial correlation,
the t and F tests used to test the significance of the model are no longer
strictly applicable.

The most common test for the presence of serial correlation is the
Durbin–Watson (DW) test which was mentioned earlier. The DW statistic
ranges from 0 to 4 with the midpoint 2.0 indicating that there is no serial correlation present. Positive serial correlation is associated with DW values
below 2.0, and negative serial correlation with values above 2.0. Positive
serial correlation is by far the most common problem. Most statistical packages will print out the DW statistic on request. To determine if the value of
DW indicates a problem with serial correlation it is necessary to use a table
which will provide an upper and lower limit for the statistic given the
number of observations and the number of independent variables. If the statistic falls between the upper and lower tabled figures the results of the test
are inconclusive. If the value of DW is above the upper limit of the tabled
value then serial correlation is not present. If the DW value is below the
lower limit then serial correlation is present and the results of the regression
are highly suspect.

The most common cause of serial correlation is that a significant explanatory variable has been left out of the equation, meaning the equation is misspecified. The missing variable is thought to be highly correlated with the
error term, in essence the variable should explain the correlation in the
errors. The first choice in correcting for serial correlation is to determine
which significant variable is missing from the equation and to introduce that
variable into the equation. Often, analysis of the residuals will indicate some
significant shift at some point in time which may be associated with the
occurrence of a specific event. However, it may not always be possible to
determine which variable is missing if that variable is unknown or if appropriate data are not available. In this case, it is necessary to correct the
problem, using some estimate of the correlation in the error terms. Two
common methods of correcting or transforming data to remove the effects of
serial correlation are the Cochrane–Orcutt procedure, and the Hildreth–Lu
procedure. Both of these procedures focus on ρ, the correlation coefficient
associated with the error term. Specific calculations of these remedial
measures are discussed in Pindyck and Rubenfeld (1991).

SUMMARY AND CONCLUSIONS

This chapter has focused on the usefulness and derivation of behavioral
models in contrast to time-series models in understanding and explaining
tourism behavior. Behavioral models are best used when the objective is to
'explain' trends in a dependent variable, or to identify associated variables,

whereas time-series models often give the best forecasting procedures by mechanically projecting the trend. A typical origin–destination model was used in demonstrating the concepts, variables, and results that can usually be expected from use of a behavioral model. The coefficients were explained as the basis for understanding their interpretation. A discussion of functional forms of the model encourages users to choose them on the basis of their statistical implications rather than ease of computation and use.

Behavioral models can be especially useful to managers of tourism facilities because they allow the manager to explore various scenarios, or play 'what-if,' regarding the impacts of various independent variables on the dependent variable. For example, if the impact of exchange rates, advertising expenditures, price or even specific events is included in the model, the manager can assess the likely impact of changes in the levels of these variables.

Finally, model diagnostics were discussed to show how some of the major assumptions that underlie least-squares regression can be tested, and if problems are found, how appropriate adjustments may be made in the model. Important assumptions relate to specifications of the model, the individual variables, and perhaps most important, the errors or residuals between the observations and their predicted values. Only after the assumptions are tested can one be reasonably certain that the chosen model is performing according to expectations and the results can be relied upon for decision-making.

REFERENCES

Crouch, G.I., 1994, The study of international tourism demand: a review of findings, *Journal of Travel Research*, **32**(4): 41–57

Deaton, A., Muellbauer, J., 1980, *Economics and consumer behavior*, Cambridge University Press, Cambridge

Hicks, J.R., 1946, *Value and capital*, Oxford University Press, Oxford

Hiemstra, S.J., 1991, Projection of world tourism arrivals to the year 2000, *World Travel and Tourism Review*, **1**: 59–65

Hiemstra, S.J., Ismail, J.A., 1994, Analysis of room rates in the lodging industry, paper presented at annual meetings of the Council on Hotel, Restaurant, and Institutional Educators, Palms Springs, CA

Intriligator, M.D., 1978, *Econometric models, techniques and applications*, Prentice-Hall, Englewood Cliffs, NJ

Loeb, P.D., 1982, International travel to the United States: an econometric evaluation, *Journal of Travel Research*, **9**(1): 7–20

Marshall, A., 1920, *Principles of economics*, 8th edn, London

Martin, C.A., Witt, S.F., 1989, Accuracy of econometric forecasts of tourism, *Annals of Tourism Research*, **16**: 407–428

Mendenhall, W., Sincich, T., 1989, *A second course in business statistics: regression analysis*, Dellen, San Francisco

Phlips, L., 1990, *Applied consumption analysis*, revised and enlarged edn, Elsevier Science, New York

Pindyck, R.S., Rubenfeld, D.L., 1991, *Econometric models and economic forecasts*, 3rd edn, McGraw-Hill, New York

Pyo, S.S., Uysal, M., Warner, J.T., 1996 SURE estimation of tourism demand system model: US case, *Journal of Travel and Tourism Marketing*, 5:(1/2): 145–160, (Haworth Press)

SAS Institute, 1993, *SAS/STAT© user's guide*. Version 6, 4th edn, Vol. 2, Cary, NC

Witt, C.A, Witt, S.F., 1990, Appraising an econometric forecasting model, *Journal of Travel Research*, 28(3): 30–34.

6 An Empirical Analysis of Oligopolistic Hotel Pricing: The Case of Bermuda Resort Hotels

TOM BAUM AND RAM MUDAMBI

INTRODUCTION

Products of the resort hotel industry have characteristics which make their supply relatively inflexible. The number of hotel rooms or other units of accommodation cannot be changed overnight. Yet the industry faces demand which tends to be highly volatile. These two factors make the industry conform closely to the theoretical Ricardian model of rent generation. Ricardian analysis offers several insights into the process of price-setting and demand forecasting in the resort hotel industry. In this chapter, we use the Bermuda resort hotel industry as a case study to illustrate such analysis.

In a competitive market, Ricardian analysis predicts that the price of the marginal unused unit (the empty hotel room whose neighbour is occupied) will be competed down to zero. Competitive hotels will be willing to let unrented rooms for virtually nothing, provided that the marginal revenue from other hotel services justifies this strategy. In an oligopolistic situation, this need not occur. Oligopolistic hotels recognise their interdependence and know that by adjusting availability, they can influence price. Hence it is likely that in periods when demand is expected to be slack, rooms may be renovated (and hence unavailable for rental) or wings may be closed down. This has the added benefit of savings in terms of material and labour costs.

Such strategies involving the withdrawal of hotel rooms from the market may be termed 'withholding' strategies. They are unavailable in the competitive case because of the complete absence of market power. A competitive player is a small operator and does not control enough units to influence price. Hence withholding offers no or, at best, limited strategic advantage.

However, an oligopolistic player controls a large proportion of units and can influence price through varying availability. Thus withholding strategies

Economic and Management Methods for Tourism and Hospitality Research.
Edited by Thomas Baum and Ram Mudambi © 1999 John Wiley & Sons Ltd.

become crucially important. Not surprisingly, it may be shown that withholding strategies introduce considerable instability into the market.

It may be shown that this instability appears only in the case of excess supply. In the case of excess demand, both competitive and oligopolistic operators are able to extract maximal revenue from their units.

We have two objectives in this chapter. The first is to test the predictions of the Ricardian model within the context of the resort hotel industry. The second is to address the impact of changing demand through fluctuating tourist arrivals on hotel occupancy within the specific context of island tourism. In undertaking this task, we wish to complement the technique of yield management, which has gained wide acceptance and is extensively used all over the world, particularly within larger hotel organisations. The technique, which originated in the airline industry and gained ground in the hospitality sector from the mid-1980s onwards, is designed to assist hotels to go beyond traditional occupancy objectives and achieve maximum revenue from each room available for sale. The literature on yield management is relatively extensive and good illustrations include Orkin (1988); Relihan (1989); Lockwood and Jones (1990); Russo (1991); Jones and Hamilton (1992); Shaw (1992); and Lieberman (1993). What we attempt to do here is to go beyond the environment of the individual hotel property or discrete hotel corporation and apply Ricardian techniques as an alternative mechanism by which destinations can attain maximum yield from their accommodation stock.

Island tourism represents an ideal source for the testing of this approach to supply and demand analysis. Islands do have characteristics which set them apart from other tourism destinations. Baum (1993) identifies a number of characteristics of island tourism which accentuate these differentials. These include:

- A high economic dependence on a small range of industries and products, including tourism
- A focused and, frequently, limited range of tourism products
- Targeting of high spend tourism, often long-haul, markets, requiring 5 star or equivalent product standards
- A high level of foreign investment in resort facilities, imposing multi-national standards without much scope for local interpretation
- A restricted pool of skilled personnel with the aptitude, training and language requirements for employment in the international tourism industry, reflecting limited service industry culture and traditions
- Limited or non-existent education and training facilities for tourism

While not all these characteristics are directly applicable to our case-study destination, Bermuda, the island does, in fact, represent an ideal location for the purposes of this study. In particular, Bermuda, as a vacation destination, has a number of features which make it particularly suited to a discussion of this nature. These include Bermuda's remote location in the west Atlantic which means that it is very unlikely to act as a 'shared' destination with any other location, in that it is not a likely participant in dual or multiple destination packaging. Secondly, its size means that data collection, relating to Bermuda, is likely to be far more complete than is the case with other destinations, where inaccuracies through sampling may affect analysis. Additional factors include Bermuda's high dependence on one relatively homogeneous market, with respect to arrivals and the characteristics of visitor stays, namely the United States (accounting for approximately 82% of air arrivals and 92% of cruise ship visitors mainly from the mid-Atlantic and north-eastern states [Department of Tourism, 1993a]); and the small number of major hotels on the island (the seven which are utilised in this study accounted for almost 60% of the total accommodation units on the island in 1991 [Archer, 1992]).

In the next section of the chapter, we discuss the nature of the tourism and hotel industries in Bermuda. Subsequently, we present the application of the theoretical Ricardian model to the resort hotel industry. Then we describe our data, discuss the estimation procedure and present our results. A conclusion follows.

THE TOURISM AND HOTEL INDUSTRIES IN BERMUDA

Before embarking on our analysis, it is valuable to provide a brief introduction to the tourism and hotel environment within which this discussion has been based. Bermuda, as a destination, has certain characteristics which appear to set it apart from many competitor islands, for example those further south in the Caribbean. Brown and Riley (1993) describe Bermuda in the following terms.

> Bermuda has always marketed itself as an upscale tourist location, a place for fun and frolic and relaxation for the wealthy and well-known. Assiduously avoiding any characterisation as a mass market tourist destination, Bermuda has eschewed introducing any new approaches aimed primarily at increasing the number of tourists with deeply discounted packages or mass appeal entertainment – such as gambling or amusement

This approach to marketing of the island was one which appears to have been relatively successful during the years of growth, up to the late 1970s, but the experience of the 1980s demonstrated the island's vulnerability to fluctuations with respect to economic and political factors within its main originating market, the United States. The influence of currency changes and international tensions and terrorism has had a marked effect on the number

of tourists visiting the island. At the same time, the underlying trend within
land-based tourism (those visitors using hotel stock within their visit) is
downwards, with 1992 marking a 15 year low. Arrivals data for the period in
question are shown in Table 6.1. The underlying decline in tourist arrivals
has been reflected in both annual average hotel occupancy performance and
average length of stay of visitors since 1980. Table 6.2 summarises these data
for the period 1980–1992.

Brown and Riley (1993) acknowledge international factors behind this
trend of decline but also note that 'part of the reason why Bermuda has lost

Table 6.1. Annual tourist arrivals in Bermuda 1980–92

Year	Air arrivals	Cruise arrivals	Total arrivals	% USA
1980	491 640	117 916	609 556	88
1981	429 801	105 445	535 246	89
1982	420 288	124 178	544 466	88
1983	446 864	120 846	567 710	88
1984	417 461	111 410	528 871	88
1985	406 687	142 903	549 590	89
1986	459 711	132 202	591 913	89
1987	477 877	153 437	631 314	89
1988	426 850	158 368	585 218	88
1989	418 273	131 322	549 595	86
1990	434 909	112 551	547 460	86
1991	386 178	128 151	514 329	86
1992	375 231	131 006	506 237	85

Source: Department of Tourism, Bermuda, 1991 and 1993a.

Table 6.2. Annual occupancy and average length in hotels, 1980–92

Year	Average occupancy (%)	Average length of stay (days)
1980	73.9	5.1
1981	60.1	5.0
1982	58.8	5.2
1983	63.9	5.0
1984	60.7	4.9
1985	65.0	4.9
1986	68.5	4.9
1987	67.1	5.0
1988	60.5	4.9
1989	65.2	4.9
1990	66.4	4.9
1991	59.9	4.8
1992	54.9	4.6

Source: Bermuda Hotel Association, 1993.

some of its lustre in that exclusive domain is that its value has been threatened in a number of areas, externally and internally'. They acknowledge factors such as recession but also point to a number of internal product- and environment-related deficiencies as factors in accelerating the decline. Archer (1992) also points to the weather-induced seasonal nature of Bermuda tourism and, thus, it has been difficult for the island to counter low occupancies during the off season in the way that other island destinations, such as Hawaii, have been able to (Cook, 1993).

In this paper, we use accommodation indicators, primarily derived with respect to large resort hotels, as the main gauge of the relationship between supply and demand within Bermuda tourism. The Bermuda accommodation stock consists of a diversity of prestige large resort hotels, smaller establishments, cottage colonies (a unique Bermudian type of establishment) and guest houses. The accent is, very much, on quality accommodation and some of the smaller hotels are also of exceptional standard, falling into what might be called the boutique category. The hotels, that form the basis for the discussion here, are the larger properties on the island but, even within that categorisation, show considerable variation in their range of facilities and the services on offer. This caveat is of some importance to the theoretical discussion in this paper.

Recognition of the overall decline in arrivals is reflected in the embargo on new hotel construction which has been in place since 1980, and when combined with the loss of a number of small hotels, has contributed to an overall reduction in hotel stock. This reduction in hotel rooms has been something in the order of 8% between 1980 and 1992 (Department of Tourism, 1993b).

Dodswell (1993) notes the steady erosion of profits within the hotel sector in Bermuda since 1980, commenting that 'the hotel industry as a whole has seen red ink for the past four years'. While Dodswell speaks from the position of someone with a clear vested interest in the issues under discussion, it is worth noting that he continues by arguing that the problems faced by hotels are the result of very high and inflexible operating costs, especially with respect to labour.

> Labour is at a minimum of approximately US $10 per hour. Utility rates are triple those in the United States. All of our supplies must be imported from abroad with high shipping, government duty and delivery costs. As a result we cannot lower our hotel rates and yet we have been criticised that prices are too high here in Bermuda. Recognizing that we cannot reduce our rates without seriously affecting future viability, we can regain our former levels of occupancy by giving more for less and we have to acknowledge that it is our responsibility to provide our guests with what they want rather than what we think they want.

Dodswell notes that 'numerous studies' have been carried out in order to identify remedies for the underlying decline in Bermudan tourism, sponsored by government, the private sector of the tourism industry and academics acting in an independent capacity. The study reported here may provide an alternative analytical methodology in support of this process.

THE MODEL

We use Ricardian analysis to study the Bermuda hotel market. This economic analysis is appropriate for the study of markets where sunk costs have a large impact. For a detailed discussion of sunk costs and their impact on market structure, see Sutton (1991). Other relevant literature includes Gabszewicz et al (1981) and Shaked and Sutton (1982). The Ricardian analysis is based on some assumptions:

(a) The quality of hotels varies and this places restrictions on prices which may be charged.
(b) Hotel quality can be measured and ranked in terms of revenue-generating capacity.
(c) Hotel room rentals are completely unstorable. An empty hotel room represents revenue lost forever.
(d) The Bermuda resort hotels market is dominated by a relatively small number of firms which have market power and a considerable degree of oligopolistic interdependence.

It may be pointed out that many of these assumptions are really just fundamental characteristics of the hotel industry. Thus, our choice of the Ricardian methodology is particularly appropriate in this context.

We illustrate the Ricardian analysis with a simple model, drawn from Baum and Mudambi (1994). A full game theoretic presentation of the results is available in Masson et al (1994).

Suppose that there is a total of six hotel units, ranked by quality from 1 to 6. Consider the following outcome:

Revenue Generating Capacity	100	90	80	70	60	50
QUALITY RANKING	1	2	3	4	5	6

It is important to bear in mind that the units are quality-differentiated and cannot be aggregated together. Hence a simple demand-supply model (with a homogeneous output) is inappropriate in this context.

We wish to concentrate on the strategic aspects of oligopolistic price-setting, and hence restrict our attention to the case where price affects market share, but not market size. This is not an unreasonable simplification, particularly in the Bermudian context, where travel prices would tend to outweigh hotel prices in determining the pool of potential customers.

First, consider the 'underestimated demand' scenario. Suppose that the demand is for six or more units. Now all the available units can be sold at their maximum revenue-generating potential. The equilibrium price vector is [100, 90, 80, 70, 60, 50]. This 'high-price' equilibrium is insensitive to market structure, that is, regardless of whether the ownership of units is dispersed or concentrated, these equilibrium prices prevail.

Now consider the more common 'overestimated demand' scenario. Suppose that the demand is for only four units. Here the equilibrium is sensitive to the pattern of unit ownership.

The competitive case

Suppose that the ownership of the units is completely dispersed, that is, there are six hotels each with control over one unit. Then, although its revenue-generating capacity is 60, the price of the fifth unit is competed to zero (since only four are demanded). This unit then determines the Ricardian equilibrium price vector to be [40, 30, 20, 10, 0, 0], since $100 - 60 = 40$ and so on.

This is the essence of Ricardian analysis. In Ricardo's classic analysis, when the firms (or rentiers) are competitive, the best unused unit determines the equilibrium prices generated by the superior quality of the units which are used.

The oligopoly case

Concentrated unit ownership, as in the Bermuda resort industry, is now considered. For notational simplicity, let there be two hotels, A and B. Let hotel A own units 1, 3 and 5, while hotel B has the remainder, that is, units 2, 4 and 6.

If hotel A charges the Ricardian prices 40 and 20 for its two best units (and obtains a total payoff of 60), it can sell these in the face of any non-negative prices chosen by hotel B. Hence any strategy involving lower prices for these units cannot be an equilibrium. Similarly, hotel B can always obtain 30 and 10 for its best two units (with a payoff of 40).

If either hotel charges prices higher than the Ricardian prices and offers all its units for sale, the best response of its rival will be to undercut these prices by a small amount and divert sales to itself. Thus, any price vector higher than the Ricardian price vector cannot be an equilibrium if all units are offered for sale.

If hotel A withholds unit 5, it can charge 50 and 30 for its best two units and sell these in the face of any non-negative prices offered by hotel B. Clearly this option is made possible by the ownership of multiple units. This strategy yields a certain payoff of 80.

Hotel B's best response to this is to withhold the last unit and charge 90 and 70 for its best two units. Hotel A counters by charging 100 and 80 for its best two units. Hotel B now responds with price undercutting – charging $90 - \varepsilon$, $70 - \varepsilon$, and $50 - \varepsilon$, for its three units, where ε, is arbitrarily small. As hotel A responds with further price shading, this leads inexorably back toward the Ricardian prices and the cycle begins again.

Hotel B knows that hotel A will not accept a payoff of less than 80. Thus, hotel B can add $2/3(10) = 6.667$ to the price of its best two units. This strategy yields a payoff of $36.667 + 16.667 = 52.334$. Hotel A has no incentive to undercut these prices, since by doing so, and selling all its units, it gets a payoff marginally smaller than 80, that is, $(46.667 - \varepsilon,) + (26.667 - \varepsilon) + (6.667 - \varepsilon)$ $= 80 - 3\varepsilon$.

Thus, in the oligopoly case, prices fail to fall to the Ricardian (or competitive) level even in the face of excess supply. Hotel A's payoff is at least 80 and hotel B's payoff is at least 52.334. These compare with the Ricardian payoffs of 60 and 40 respectively.

More importantly, there is no single price configuration which can be sustained as an equilibrium. Any prices chosen by one hotel are subject to opportunistic undercutting (with an appropriate pattern of withholding) by its rival. In the language of game theory, there does not exist an equilibrium in pure strategies. The actual prices chosen cannot be predicted analytically; they are likely to vary widely in a manner unconnected with the actual level of excess supply. (It is possible to prove, however, that there always exists an equilibrium in mixed strategies for any number of players. See Masson et al [1987].)

THE DATA

Monthly data are analysed for the period 1980–1992. The market segment we study is the large resort hotel sector. Peak (Spring and Summer) rates and off-peak (Fall and Winter) rates are compiled from various issues of the *Bermuda Hotel and Guest House Rates* published by the Department of Tourism. The deficiencies inherent in the use of published rate sources are recognised but these provide the only consistent and comparable data for the purposes of this study. Reliable data on actual, achieved rates are not available in published form. There were a total of ten resort hotels operating in Bermuda during the period studied. Seven of these reported rates throughout the period of study. The rate used is the double occupancy rate per person with the modified American plan (MAP), the most common rate charged in Bermuda. The rate includes room, breakfast and dinner. Rates are quoted in terms of the Bermuda $ which is tied 1 : 1 to the US $.

In 1992, these seven hotels controlled 2527 rooms, capable of accommodating 6464 guests. This compares with the total of 81 hotels of all types registered under the Hotels (Licensing and Control) Act of 1969, and the total of 8539 rooms on the island.

Monthly tourist arrivals and the monthly consumer price deflator are taken from the *Bermuda Digest of Statistics 1992* published by the Ministry of Finance. In addition, an alternative deflator is constructed using the wages of hotel staff reported in the *Digest*. The most recent figures are obtained directly from the Department of Tourism. Monthly hotel occupancy figures are obtained from the Bermuda Hotel Association.

Hotel rates must be deflated since they pertain to a period of over a decade. Deflating with the overall Bermuda consumer price index, we obtain what we term the 'A' hotel rate series.

To guard against the chance that resort hotel prices may move asynchronously with overall inflation, we construct a deflator from the wages of hotel workers (tipped and untipped). This deflator increases by more than the overall consumer price index, lending support to the belief that Bermuda hotels have been under input cost pressure through the 1980s. Using this latter index generates what we call the 'B' series. We analyse both the 'A' and 'B' series.

ESTIMATION AND RESULTS

Methodology

The fundamental prediction of the model is that hotel rates should behave asymmetrically relative to demand forecasts. If demand is underestimated (excess demand), then the rates should remain relatively high. However, if demand is overestimated (excess supply), the absence of a genuine market equilibrium should ensure that rates do not behave systematically.

Testing the model involves two steps. First we generate demand forecasts and combine these with the actual level of demand to determine whether a period is characterised by excess demand or excess supply. If forecasted demand in a period is less than the actual level of demand for that period, there is excess demand. Similarly if forecasted demand for a period is greater than actual demand, the period is characterised by excess supply. (Since the rates used are published rates which are put out in advance, there is reason to believe that they would be based on forecasts.)

Second, after the periods have been categorised into excess demand and excess supply periods, the rates in these periods are examined. Periods with excess demand should show rates which vary systematically, that is, the greater the excess demand, the higher should be the rates. Periods with excess supply should not exhibit this characteristic, that is, higher excess supply *need not* be associated with lower rates.

We use four measures of excess demand (and supply). The first two measures are generated by forecasting occupancy. We forecast occupancy first using total arrivals and then using air arrivals only. The latter forecast is expected to be the finer one, as total arrivals include cruise arrivals who are not generally hotel customers; statistically this proves to be the case.

The second two measures are generated by forecasting total arrivals and air arrivals. It may be argued that arrivals give hotels an idea of the potential clientele. We expect these measures to be cruder than the measures based on occupancy and expect the results to provide supporting, rather than primary evidence. Of these two measures, total arrivals is the cruder one, for the reason mentioned above.

Demand forecasting

In the demand forecasting stage, arrivals and occupancy are estimated. No quantitative or qualitative forecasts of hotel demand for Bermuda are available. Hence we are obliged to construct forecasts from available data. We attempt to be as parsimonious and as simple as possible in our specification of the forecasting equations. We then subject the specification to diagnostic testing. The tests appear to support the specification adopted.

The following equations, which form a recursive system, are estimated, using monthly data. The appropriate estimation technique is OLS:

$$ARR = \alpha_0 + \alpha_1 {}^*YEAR + \alpha_2 {}^*DUM + u_{1t} \tag{1a}$$

$$AARR = \beta_0 + \beta_1 {}^*YEAR + \beta_2 {}^*DUM + u_{2t} \tag{1b}$$

$$OCC = \nu_0 + \nu_1 {}^*ARR + w_{1t} \tag{2a}$$

$$OCC = \delta_0 + \delta_1 {}^*AARR + w_{2t} \tag{2b}$$

Here ARR denotes total tourists arrivals, AARR denotes air arrivals, OCC denotes the monthly average hotel occupancy, YEAR is a linear trend term and DUM is a bi-variate peak period dummy. In (2a) and (2b), both YEAR and DUM affect OCC through arrivals, that is, recursively through (1a) and (1b).

Not surprisingly, tourist arrivals in Bermuda show a strong seasonal pattern, with the peak season roughly covering the second two quarters of the year. Estimating (1a) and (1b) brings out the strong seasonal pattern, as well as demonstrating that the trend term (YEAR) has limited impact. This is true for all arrivals (1a), as well as for air arrivals (1b). We may conclude that, by and large, the hotels are competing against each other in a zero-sum game and no time deflator is necessary.

The results of the estimation of (1a) and (1b) are presented in Table 6.3. The fit of (1a) and (1b) is fairly good. The values of R^2 (adjusted for degrees of freedom) are in excess of 60% and the F-statistic is extremely significant. The Durbin–Watson statistic indicates that autocorrelation is not a problem. The hypothesis of a linear functional form is accepted using Ramsey's RESET test.

In order to assess forecasting ability, we test for parameter stability (the

Table 6.3. Demand forecasting: tourism arrivals – equations (1a) and (1b)

Dependent variable	ARR (all arrivals)		AARR (air arrivals only)	
Regressor	Coefficient*		Coefficient*	
Constant	29 264.8	(11.58)	26 979.7	(15.64)
YEAR	−14.30	(0.53)	−22.94	(1.25)
DUM	36 612.1	(16.00)	20 660.6	(13.23)
Regression diagnostics				
R^2 (Adj.)	0.635		0.543	
F (2, 144); (*p* value)	127.92;	(0.000)	87.822;	(0.000)
Durbin–Watson statistic	1.6691		1.6472	
Functional form: @				
F(1, 143); (*p* value)	0.08378; (0.773)		0.001515; (0.969)	
Forecast diagnostics:				
Forecast periods	*Parameter stability:# F(3, 141); (p* value)			
24	1.03140; (0.381)		1.27880; (0.284)	
12	0.96951; (0.413)		1.05610; (0.370)	
6	0.93806; (0.424)		0.98670; (0.401)	
	*Predictive failure:**			
24 F(24, 120); (*p* value)	0.85362; (0.662)		0.83686; (0.684)	
12 F(12, 132); (*p* value)	0.75024; (0.700)		0.73382; (0.716)	
6 F(6, 138); (*p* value)	0.69896; (0.651)		0.62820; (0.707)	

* '*t*' statistics in brackets.
@ Ramsey's Reset Test (F Version).
# Chow Test.
** Chow's 2nd Test, as generalised by Pesaran et al (1985).

Chow test) and predictive failure (the generalised form of Chow's 2nd test, as presented in Pesaran et al, 1985), with 6, 12 and 24 forecast periods. In all cases, the null hypotheses of stable parameters and predictive accuracy cannot be rejected.

The results of the estimation of (2a) and (2b) are presented in Table 6.4. It is found, equally unsurprisingly, that arrivals have a strong significant effect on occupancy. The fits of these equations are extremely good. The values of adjusted R^2 are over 90% and the F-statistic is extremely significant. Again, the Durbin–Watson and Ramsey RESET tests are easily passed; the forecast diagnostics indicate excellent forecasting ability.

The predicted values from (2a) are denoted by FOROCC1. Now consider

$$ERROCC1 = OCC - FOROCC1$$

that is, the difference between the actual and forecasted resort hotel occupancy rate. This represents the demand-supply status of the resort hotel market. If this value is positive, the actual occupancy rate is higher than forecasted and there is excess demand. Conversely, if it is negative, the actual

TOM BAUM AND RAM MUDAMBI

Table 6.4. Demand forecasting: hotel occupancy – equations (2a) and (2b)

Dependent variable: OCC	All arrivals	Air arrivals only
Regressor	Coefficient*	Coefficient*
Constant	18.887 (13.42)	5.859 (5.15)
ARR	0.0009421 (34.46)	–
AARR	–	0.001596 (53.41)
Regression Diagnostics		
R^2 (Adj.)	0.8904	0.9513
F (1, 145); (*p* value)	1187.80; (0.000)	2852.60; (0.000)
Durbin–Watson statistic	1.7403	1.7607
Functional form:@		
F(1, 144); (*p* value)	0.99798; (0.432)	0.12312; (0.674)
Forecast Diagnostics:		
Forecast periods	*Parameter stability:#* F(2, 143); (*p* value)	
24	1.57040; (0.212)	0.19983; (0.819)
12	1.65360; (0.195)	0.34318; (0.710)
6	1.34210; (0.265)	0.34194; (0.711)
	*Predictive failure:***	
24 F(24, 121); (*p* value)	0.62236; (0.911)	0.36687; (0.997)
12 F(12, 133); (*p* value)	0.71563; (0.734)	0.40637; (0.959)
6 F(6, 139); (*p* value)	1.09060; (0.371)	0.65698; (0.684)

* '*t*' statistics in brackets.
@ Ramsey's Reset Test (F Version).
\# Chow Test.
** Chow's 2nd Test, as generalised by Pesaran et al (1985)

rate is lower than forecasted and there is excess supply. The variable FOROCC2 is generated using (2b), and

$$ERROCC2 = OCC – FOROCC2$$

The secondary proxy for the demand-supply situation is generated from (1a) and (1b). The predicted values from (1a) are denoted by FORARR1 and the difference ERRARR1 = ARR – FORARR1, is constructed. As above, if this value is positive, the actual tourist arrivals are higher than forecasted and there is excess demand; if it is negative, actual arrivals are lower than forecasted and there is excess supply. Similarly, the variable FORARR2 is generated using (1b) and ERRARR2 = ARR – FORARR2.

Forecast analysis

The resulting values of ERROCC1 and ERROCC2 are divided into five classes, creating proxy variables which are denoted by OCEXALL and OCEXAIR respectively. Similar construction using ERRARR1 and ERRARR2 creates a second pair of proxies which are denoted by AREXALL and AREXAIR respectively. The quantitative definitions of OCEXALL and OCEXAIR and AREXALL and AREXAIR are as follows:

ERROCC1 and ERROCC2(%)	OCEXALL and OCEXAIR
> + 20	1
+5.0 to +19.9	2
−4.9 to −4.9	3
−5.0 to −19.9	4
< −20	5

ERRARR1 and ERRARR2(%)	AREXALL and AREXAIR
> +10	1
+2.5 to +9.9	2
+2.49 to −2.49	3
−2.5 to −9.9	4
< −10	5

Periods when the proxies take the value of 1 or 2 are characterised by excess demand, while those when they take the value 4 or 5 are characterised by excess supply. Periods when they take the value 3 represent times of rough market clearing. The Ricardian model predicts that such periods should witness price behaviour that dovetails with the systematic price pattern of excess demand periods. Note that the construction of all the excess demand proxies takes into account the seasonal effect, as the seasonal dummy enters into the creation of the estimates FORARRi and (through recursion) FOROCCi, $(i = 1, 2)$. Hence, further introduction of the seasonal component into the Ricardian analysis is unnecessary; indeed, it would be methodologically incorrect.

We present our analysis of hotel rates in Tables 6.5–6.8. Only overall results for 'A' rates are presented, since the results for 'B' rates are not qualitatively different.

Analysing the hotel rate data along the dimension of OCEXALL (see Table 6.5) using analysis of variance (ANOVA), it is found that for excess demand and equilibrium periods (1, 2 and 3), rates behave systematically. The 'A' rates decline from 141.10 in periods of high excess demand (OCEXALL = 1) to 110.17 in equilibrium periods (OCEXALL = 3). A Least Significant Difference (LSD) test for paired means indicates that these means are significantly different.

However, during periods of excess supply, rates behave quite erratically. The average rate for periods of low to medium excess supply

Table 6.5. Hotel rate@ analysis: OCCUPANCY proxy for excess demand based on all arrivals

OCEXALL	Mean rate (A)*	No. of obs.
1	141.10	28
2	134.76	35
3	110.17	35
4	132.39	35
5	146.45	42
Pooled mean	132.79	175
Pooled S.D.	43.56	

Analysis of variance: (A)*

Source	D.F.	Sum of squares	Mean square	F statistic; (p value)
OCEXALL	4	34 375	8594	4.53; (0.002)
Error	170	322 524	1897	
Total	174	356 899		

@ Hotel rates used are the modified American plan, per person, double occupancy.
* Rates deflated by the Bermuda Consumer Price Index.

(OCEXALL = 4) is 132.39. It *increases* to 146.25 for periods of high excess supply (OCEXALL = 5). Again, the LSD test indicates that these means differ significantly from those in excess demand periods, and from each other. The pattern is mirrored by the 'B' rates, but not as strongly. However, the LSD test still indicates that the 'B' rates for different excess demand levels are significantly different, from each other and from the excess supply periods.

The OCEXALL proxy is constructed using all tourist arrivals and is thus contaminated by the large cruise arrivals component, which should not affect hotel rates. The OCEXAIR proxy is constructed using only air arrivals, and is a cleaner representation of the excess demand scenario. Indeed, as expected, the predictions of the Ricardian model are supported much more strongly by analysis using OCEXAIR. Both 'A' and 'B' rates decline smoothly as excess demand declines, but behave erratically during the excess supply periods. The analysis of variance suggests much more significant rate differences for both 'A' and 'B' rates. The F-statistic rises from 4.53 to 10.02 for 'A' rates and from 3.11 to 4.04 for 'B' rates. These results are presented in Table 6.6.

Similar results using the cruder AREXALL and AREXAIR proxies are presented in Tables 6.7 and 6.8. The results mirror those discussed above, and can be considered as further evidence supporting the main thesis.

We consider three final issues. The Ricardian model specifies that the quality of the good supplied be non-uniform. Analysing rates along the dimension of hotel identity, it is found that there is significant rate variation. The F-statistic for the 'A' rates is 3.01 with (6173) degrees of freedom

Table 6.6. Hotel rate@ analysis: OCCUPANCY proxy for excess demand based on air arrivals

OCEXAIR	Mean rate (A)*	No. of obs.
1	149.64.	42
2	105.79	28
3	71.57	14
4	142.00	42
5	117.02	49
Pooled mean	132.79	175
Pooled S.D.	41.22	

Analysis of variance: (A)*

Source	D.F.	Sum of squares	Mean square	F statistic; (*p* value)
OCEXALL	4	68 102	17 026	10.02; (0.00)
Error	170	288 796	1 699	
Total	174	356 899		

@ Hotel rates used are the modified American plan, per person, double occupancy.
* Rates deflated by the Bermuda Consumer Price Index.

Table 6.7. Hotel rate@ analysis: ARRIVALS proxy for excess demand based on all arrivals

AREXALL	Mean rate (A)*	No. of obs.
1	156.44	35
2	127.45	28
3	120.18	42
4	119.45	28
5	138.17	42
Pooled mean	132.79	175
Pooled S.D.	43.63	

Analysis of variance: (A)*

Source	D.F.	Sum of squares	Mean square	F statistic; (*p* value)
OCEXALL	4	33 260	8315	4.37; (0.002)
Error	170	323 638	1904	
Total	174	356 899		

@ Hotel rates used are the modified American plan, per person, double occupancy.
* Rates deflated by the Bermuda Consumer Price Index.

compared with a critical value of 2.15 at the 5% level and 2.91 at the 1% level. Further, qualitative observations support this conclusion. There is considerable variation in the facilities available at the major resort hotels. For example, the Hamilton Princess, one of the largest properties in our sample, has virtually no sporting or major leisure facilities, while its sister hotel, the Southampton Princess, offers golf, tennis and swimming among other

Table 6.8. Hotel rate@ analysis: ARRIVALS proxy for excess demand based on air arrivals

AREXAIR	Mean rate (A)*	No. of obs.
1	155.05	42
2	142.50	35
3	98.04	14
4	102.86	35
5	138.10	49
Pooled mean	132.79	175
Pooled S.D.	40.81	

Analysis of variance: (A)*

Source	D.F.	Sum of squares	Mean square	F statistic; (p value)
OCEXALL	4	73 759	18 440	11.07; (0.00)
Error	170	283 140	1 666	
Total	174	356 899		

@ Hotel rates used are the modified American plan, per person, double occupancy.
* Rates deflated by the Bermuda Consumer Price Index.

facilities. This is evidence supporting the claim that the 'quality' among the resort hotels is not uniform.

Secondly, we address the question of heterogeneous market perceptions by the different hotels. If the hotels arrived at differing forecasts, it could lead to asymmetric rate variation of the type we have discovered. If this were true, then calculated excess demands should vary systematically across the hotels, that is, each forecasting equation should give rise to an identifiably different pattern of forecasting errors.

In order to test this hypothesis, we randomly select from the excess-demand-proxy/hotel-identity matrix to obtain balanced blocks. We then carry out two-way ANOVA to examine the interaction term. We find that in all cases the interaction term is insignificant. We are led to reject the hypothesis that the hotels react to excess demand proxies differently. This supports the contention that the hotels' market perceptions are uniform and that the results we have obtained do, in fact, support the predictions of the Ricardian model.

Lastly, we consider whether excess demand periods occur mostly in the 'peak' season and excess supply periods occur mostly in the 'off-peak' season. If this were the case, it would suggest that perhaps it is the nature of the season rather than the nature of the forecast error that is driving the results. We find, however, that the correlation between our four excess demand proxies and a peak–off-peak dummy to vary between a low of −5.3% and a high of 5.5%. Ordinal measures using Spearman's rank correlation coefficient yield similar results. Forecast errors seem to be unrelated to the nature of the season.

CONCLUSIONS

Conclusions from this paper must necessarily be somewhat tentative but they can be drawn to reflect both the practical and theoretical. We can see that the Ricardian model has a contribution to make within the context of hotel occupancy forecasting. The predictions of the model are shown to be valid in the context of Bermuda's resort hotels. Thus, drastic price cutting and potentially suicidal price wars have not been a feature of this sector of the Bermuda hotel industry over the period under analysis. While the oligopolistic nature in the large resort hotel sector is not the only contributing factor to this situation, its significance should not be underestimated.

Bermuda, in many respects, represents the ideal destination for the application and testing of the Ricardian model because of its size, location, wealth and comprehensiveness of data sources and the nature of the tourist markets with which it deals. However, the model does have application and implications in the context of other island tourism destinations. It is the authors' intention to undertake further studies in this area. In general, the approach which we pilot here can be used as a vehicle to support supply and pricing policies within resort hotels elsewhere, complementing the more short-term benefits of yield management techniques already utilised within the industry.

ACKNOWLEDGEMENTS

The authors would like to acknowledge the assistance of the Department of Tourism, Bermuda, and in particular, Deanna Wade, Statistical and Research Officer, for providing data utilised in this study.

REFERENCES

Archer, B., 1992, *The economic impact of tourism in Bermuda, 1991*, Department of Tourism, Hamilton, Bermuda

Baum, T., 1993, Human resources: the unsung price-value issue. In Hawkins, D.E, Ritchie, J.R.B., eds, *World travel and tourism review*, Vol. 3, CAB International, Wallingford, Oxon

Baum, T., Mudambi, R., 1994, A Ricardian analysis of the fully inclusive tour industry, *Service Industries Journal*, **14**(1): 85–93

Bermuda Hotel Association, 1993, *Monthly room occupancies, 1980–1992*, Bermuda Hotel Association, Hamilton, Bermuda

Brown, W.C., Riley, C.W., 1993, The determinants of value in a Bermuda vacation: the good, the bad and the possibilities. In Hawkins, D.E., Ritchie, J.R.B., eds, *World travel and tourism review*, Vol. 3, CAB International, Wallingford, Oxon

Cook, L., 1993, Tourism awareness programs. *Proceedings of the Second Island Tourism International Forum*, Bermuda

Department of Tourism, Bermuda, 1991, *A statistical review of the years 1980–1989*, Department of Tourism, Hamilton, Bermuda

Department of Tourism, Bermuda, 1993a, *Ten year tourism arrivals history, 1983–92*, Department of Tourism, Hamilton, Bermuda

Department of Tourism, Bermuda, 1993b, *The Hotels (Licensing and Control) Act, 1969: The normal bed count and the number of properties licensed under the above Act*, Department of Tourism, Hamilton, Bermuda

Dodswell, D., 1993, Price-value considerations for hotels and resorts. In Hawkins, D.E., Ritchie, J.R.B., eds, *World travel and tourism review*, Vol. 3, CAB International, Wallingford, Oxon

Gabszewicz, J.J., Shaked, A., Sutton, J., Thisse, J.-F., 1981, Price competition among differentiated products: a detailed study of Nash Equilibrium, *ICERD Working Paper 37*, London School of Economics, UK

Jones, P., Hamilton, D., 1992, Yield management: putting people in the big picture. *Cornell Hotel and Restaurant Administration Quarterly*, 33(1): 89–95

Lieberman, W.H., 1993, Debunking the myths of yield management, *Cornell Hotel and Restaurant Administration Quarterly*, 34(1): 34–41

Lockwood, A., Jones, P., 1990, Applying value engineering to rooms management, *International Journal of Contemporary Hospitality Management*, 2(1): 27–32

Masson, R.T., Mudambi, R., Reynolds, R.J., 1987, Equilibrium in non-cooperative 'Ricardian' games. *Martindale Center Discussion Paper 4/87*, Lehigh University

Masson, R.T., Mudambi, R., Reynolds, R.J., 1994, Oligopolistic product withholding in Ricardian markets. *Bulletin of Economic Research*, 46(1): 71–79

Orkin, E.B., 1988, Boosting your bottom line with yield management, *Cornell Hotel and Restaurant Administration Quarterly*, 28(1): 52–56

Pesaran, M.H., Smith, R.P., Yeo, S., 1985, Testing for structural stability and predictive failure: a review, *The Manchester School*, 53, 280–295

Relihan, W.J., 1989, The yield-management approach to hotel-room pricing, *Cornell Hotel and Restaurant Administration Quarterly*, 29(2): 40–45

Russo, J.A., 1991, Variance analysis: evaluating hotel room sales, *Cornell Hotel and Restaurant Administration Quarterly*, 32(1): 60–65

Shaked, A., Sutton, J., 1982, Relaxing price competition through product differentiation, *Review of Economic Studies*, 49, 3–13

Shaw, M., 1992, Positioning and price: merging theory, strategy and tactics, *Hospitality Research Journal*, 15(2): 31–40

Sutton, J., 1991, *Sunk costs and market structure*, MIT Press, Cambridge, MA.

7 A Positioning Analysis of Hotel Brands

CHEKITAN S. DEV, MICHAEL S. MORGAN AND
STOWE SHOEMAKER

Hotels attempt to establish a unique market position in an effort to boost market share. In the end, however, position is in the eye of the customer. Identifying that position is an essential element in determining the effectiveness of a hotel's marketing strategy.

A hotel brand's unique selling proposition – the argument it makes to convince travellers to book its hotels instead of someone else's properties – is known as its market position. The position comprises the bundle of attributes that the hotel offers in an effort to meet guests' wants and needs.

A hotel brand's position can be viewed from two perspectives, that of the brand's management and that of the guests. The brand's management must have a firm concept of the hotel's intended position and its promotional efforts must articulate not only what the brand offers but how its offerings are distinct from those of other brands.

In the final analysis, however, a brand's position is determined by its customers. A hotel company might offer a luxury-level package of services and amenities in an effort to attract business travellers, for instance if the resulting room rates are higher than corporate travel managers are willing to pay, that brand is in reality not positioned for the bulk of business travellers. Instead it may attract only those who are price insensitive, or it may attract luxury-oriented leisure guests. In another example, if a hotel has positioned itself as the most effective and efficient conference hotel in the market, customers will expect their meetings to occur flawlessly. Should that not occur, the hotel's position from the customer's point of view will in reality be 'an o.k conference hotel' or worse.

Customers' perceptions of a hotel brand's position can be subdivided into specific attributes that can, in turn, be depicted graphically on coordinate axes known as perceptual maps. Likewise, the position of an individual hotel or brand can be graphed, to allow a comparison of the brand's position in relation to those of competitors and to demonstrate any changes in the brand's position over time. In this article, we demonstrate how such a perceptual map can show the way a hotel brand's customers view the chain and, further, how that map can assist in determining a hotel's competitive set. The maps we discuss were constructed using data drawn from surveys of travel managers and travel agents published in 1990, 1991 and 1992.

POSITIONING

Each hotel booking represents a purchase decision that is based on the customer's perception of the attributes represented by that brand. In the case of corporate travel offices, the customer is the person who makes the booking regardless of who actually stays at the hotel. Those attributes are both tangible (the physical property) and intangible (services offered).[1] Typical attributes might include a low price, convenient location, a frequent-traveller programme, or a helpful and courteous staff. The package of attributes offered by the brand constitutes its market position, which is usually viewed in relation to other brands. Brands that have similar bundles of attributes are considered to be in the same competitive set.[2]

The part of the position that derives directly from the product's physical attributes is its objective position.[3] The fact is that the Four Seasons offers the most services of any hotel brand, AmeriSuites offers a suite at a price often charged by conventional mid-price competitors,[4] and Motel 6 offers consistent, low-cost rooms.

The other portion of the position is subjective, involving people's perceptions of a brand or an individual property's intangible attributes. These can only be experienced during the hotel stay. As Robert Lewis succinctly put it, you cannot take a hotel stay home to use.[5] Hyatt Hotels, for example, positioned itself in the 1980s as operating hotels whose dramatic architecture created an exciting hotel stay.

Most of a hotel's attributes are intangible, making it difficult for a customer to distinguish among competitive offerings.[6] To enable customers to make that distinction, marketers attempt to establish a position using brand names and specific images or slogans that signify some of the intangible attributes. Lewis suggested that a successful position comprises three elements: it differentiates the brand, it 'locates' the brand on specific benefit dimensions, and it creates an image.[7] Lewis continued: 'To combine these elements, the positioning statement should be designed to create an image reflecting the perception of the hotel that management wishes its target market to hold and reflecting promises on which the brand can deliver and make good.' The subtext of this definition is that the key to a hotel's position is in how it is viewed by the customer.

Through market research hoteliers can determine which attributes travellers (or travel managers) consider in choosing a brand and how travellers view a hotel brand in light of those attributes.[8] From that information, the researcher can apply discriminant analysis to develop a 'map' of the brand's position as seen by its customers.[9] In assessing those attributes, researchers must be careful to distinguish the determinant attributes (those that actually cause a purchase) from the salient attributes which might not be so keenly noticed, because both contribute to the view that a customer has of a given brand's position. It is possible, however, to establish positioning maps based solely on determinant attributes.[10]

BUSINESS TRAVELLERS

Different classes of travellers use different attributes to determine their view of a hotel brand's position. Moreover, even when they use the same attributes, various classes of travellers assign different weights to those attributes. A principal point of differentiation among travellers is whether they are travelling on business or for pleasure.[11] This study concerns itself with hotel brands' positions among business travellers. As a proxy for the travellers themselves, we used data from corporate travel managers and travel agents whose clients are chiefly business travellers. These travel planners are growing in importance as a distribution channel.[12] At the time of our study some observers estimated that these channels delivered 25% of all hotel room reservations. That percentage is higher for up-scale hotels than for mid-market and economy properties.

Data for the study described in this article were drawn from summary statistics published in the yearly US Hotel Systems Survey for 1989, 1990 and 1991 by *Business Travel News*.[13] The survey compiles the views of corporate travel managers and business travel agents' opinions of the nation's hotel brands on a variety of attributes.

UNUSUAL SITUATION

At the time our data were compiled the hotel industry was at the bottom of its worst shakeout in at least two decades. In 1991 the US hotel industry's average occupancy dropped to 60.8%, a 20-year low.[14] Moreover, many hotels were in the red. An Arthur Andersen study revealed that US hotels in 1990 lost some $5.5 billion and another $2.7 billion in 1991.[15] Coopers and Lybrand estimated that 60% of hotels were operating at a loss in mid-1992. Data from Smith Travel Research suggested that increases in hotels' ADR lagged the consumer price index from 1987 to 1991.[16] It was well known that the supply of new hotel rooms was vastly outstripping demand. Because this period represented a dynamic environment for the industry, we chose it for our study.

The hotel brands were divided a priori by *Business Travel News* into five market segments: luxury, up-scale, mid-price, economy, and all-suite. Because of the number of hotel brands under consideration, each respondent rated hotel chains in only one or two segments. The attributes used included ease of arranging individual travel, timely commission payment, quality of food and price-value. See Figure 7.1 for the complete list of attributes used to create perceptual maps for the up-scale segment. The attributes respondents used to rate the brands varied for each segment simply because different attributes apply to each segment. The graph in Figure 7.1 shows the relative importance of each of the attributes for this sample.

The Survey's sampling method remained consistent over the three-year period. The magazine's researchers mailed a questionnaire to approximately 7500 randomly selected subscribers who were business travel managers and travel agents focusing on business accounts. One month after the first mailing, the questionnaire was sent again to non-respondents. There was no further follow-up. This methodology obtained the following response per-centages: 23% in 1990, 21.4% in 1991 and 19.2% in 1992. The *Business Travel News* researchers made no effort to control for non-response bias, and the findings represent only the opinions of those who answered the question-naire. Moreover, summary characteristics of those who responded are unavailable. Consequently any projections to the industry at large should be made with caution. Nevertheless, the data provide a positioning map of several chains based on the perceptions of these travel managers and agents.[17]

Respondents rating each hotel brand were qualified in the following way. They were asked whether they had booked their clients into a property affil-iated with a given hotel brand in the previous 12 months. A respondent's attribute ratings for that brand were tabulated only if the respondent answered this question in the affirmative. The consequence of this method-ology is that the sample size from brand to brand in the same year's survey shows considerable variation.

As a final note on the data, the ratings used were means for each hotel brand. We attempted to obtain the entire data set but it was not available. We had no way to determine the level of homogeneity for the sample because variance estimates were not given.

ANALYSIS

Our goal was to create perceptual maps showing the relative positions of the various brands against each other and to examine any movement in a brand's position during the three years, as viewed by the business travel managers and agents. We analysed the relative positions of the ten most used brands in each tier in the data published in 1990 and then compared those brands' positions

89

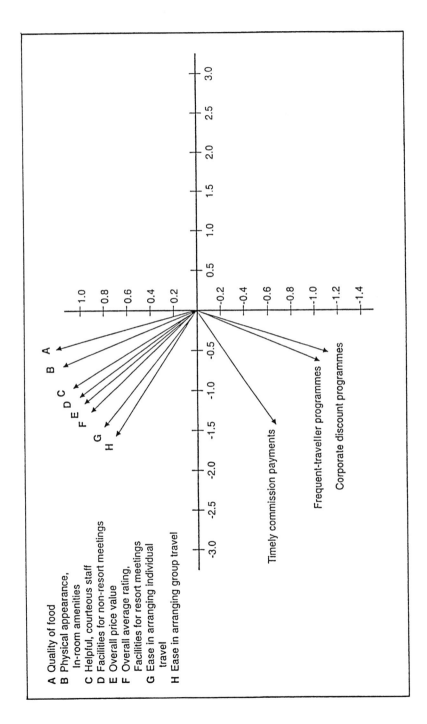

Figure 7.1. Relative importance of hotel attributes (this study): up-scale tier, 1990–1992

in 1991 and 1992. Each analysis was conducted for 30 hotel brands (10 chains for each of three years in each market segment). We also analysed the positions of the top two brands in each of the five tiers over the three years (another 30-brand analysis). In making the perceptual maps, however, we excluded the luxury tier due to an insufficient number of respondents.

The outcome of our analysis was perceptual maps that revealed how each brand was positioned relative to its competitors and how each brand's position changed over the three years we studied. Our goal was more than simple description, however. We wanted to test statistically the changes in market position over time to determine the extent to which brands occupy the same perceptual space.

We applied probabilistic multidimensional scaling (MDS) algorithms to derive the coordinates for the perceptual map.[18] Multidimensional scaling is a method of calculating similarities between objects on a set of attributes. The calculations result in coordinates that can be plotted on coordinate axes to form a map. The distances thus calculated give an indication of the extent to which the respondents view brands as similar.

We obtained the MDS algorithms from the computer programme 'Multiscale', described in the Appendix. The algorithms found in Multiscale require that some sort of distance matrix be applied. We used a dissimilarities matrix, created using the following Euclidean distance metric:

$$(d_{ij})^2 = \Sigma_k \, (x_{ik} - x_{jk})^2$$

for chains i and j, and attributes, $k = 1, 2, \ldots, p$. The distances d_{ij} were then represented to the best extent possible on a two-dimensional map.

Positions of the firms or brands on the perceptual map can assist managers in identifying potential competitive threats and opportunities. The coordinates of a brand's location on X and Y axes reflect underlying composites of attitudes toward the brand among the survey respondents. It is important to bear in mind that the 'distances' are in psychological space, measured in terms of customer perceptions and preferences rather than on differences derived from more objective measures.[19]

It is also important to note that the position maps are essentially value-neutral. That is, one spot on the map does not inherently have to be better or worse than another, except if a chain intends to be one place (with one particular competitive set) and finds itself at some other place. Perceptual maps can indicate how 'close' one's brand is to competing brands. Brands that are positioned relatively far away from each other on the map are interpreted to be less directly competitive, while hotel chains that have nearby coordinates are considered to be strongly competitive with each other. The map also can identify open space, which is interpreted to be an available market niche either for repositioning existing operations or for a new entrant.

A frequent complaint about MDS is that the plotted points and distances are derived purely algorithmically, without respect to the probability distribution of errors in the space. We have applied an algorithm that conducts statistical tests of significance to ensure the points are, in fact, different. Such a test alleviates the concerns raised by the following questions. If the distance between two points cannot be perfectly reflected in a reduced two-dimensional MDS map, how is the error distributed? Moreover, how can one tell whether two points are really different from one another in a statistically significant way? Even points that look different may contain random error that makes them, in reality, not different.

Because we have the ability to test for the significance of differences between points on the perceptual map, we can determine which chains have positions that are at significant distances from each other. We can also tell whether a movement by a brand from year to year is significant. The benefit of using probabilistic scaling is that it allows one to focus only on position differences that are statistically significant. Such an approach clears much of the clutter surrounding position differences.

The outcome of the calculations is a set of points on a map. The location of each hotel brand is depicted according to how customers perceive them on the attribute dimensions in the graph in Figure 7.1. Although the brands are arrayed on coordinate axes, their positions in relation to the axes (and attributes) themselves are less important than their positions in relation to one another or the change in a brand's own position from one year to another. Changes in perceptual distances experienced by a brand over time that are statistically significant we term 'direction', while changes that involve motion that is not statistically significant we term 'drift'.

CARTOGRAPHY

Statistical tests allow us to examine whether the points on the coordinate axes shown in Figure 7.2 are at a significant distance from each other. (Note that Figures 7.2, 7.3 and 7.4 can be overlaid on Figure 7.1.) The differences shown in two dimensions may actually be larger in three dimensions. The circles drawn around the points on this map depict clusters of points that are not at statistically significant distances from each other. So, for example, the map of the 1990 data (collected in 1989) makes it appear that Stouffer's position was considerably different from that of Meridien. The statistical tests showed otherwise, as indicated by the circle around those two chains. Likewise, there was no significant difference in the perceived positions of Wyndham and Meridien. However, the distance between Wyndham and Stouffer is significant.

Viewed another way, the business-travel managers and travel agents in the 1990 survey viewed Hilton, Radisson, and Sheraton as competitive

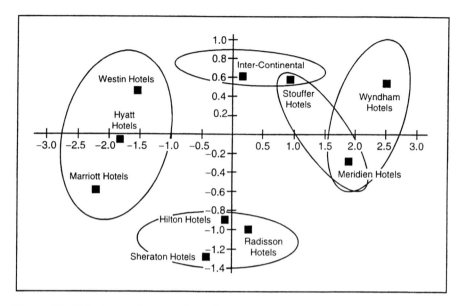

Figure 7.2. Relative market positions (this study): up-scale tier, 1990

brands whose essential positions were not particularly distinct from one another. Hyatt, Marriott, and Westin formed another competitive group, with a position significantly different from that of Hilton, Radisson, and Sheraton, but not from each other. This map provides a baseline against which to compare the other two.

Changes coming

The 1991 data (collected in 1990) may reflect the results of the severe recession that began in 1990. This map (Figure 7.3) allows two levels of analysis. First, we can once again compare the chains' relative positions against each other. We can also compare the positions of each chain in 1991 with its 1990 position. Indeed, there was considerable movement in managers' and agents' perceptions of the chains' positions. For instance, Marriott has 'moved' out of its former competitive group with Hyatt and Westin to be more competitive with Hilton and Sheraton. It is interesting that none of those other four chains moved substantially from 1990 to 1991. The movement of Meridien and Wyndham was substantial.

1992

The data published in 1992 record the positions hotel brands held in the nightmare year of 1991, when it appeared that the industry would never

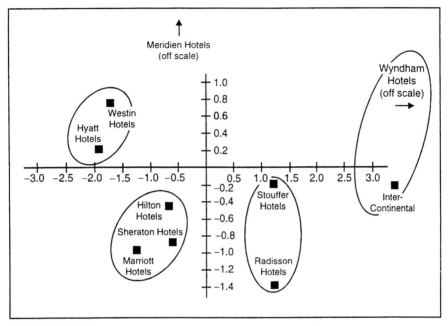

Figure 7.3. Relative market positions (this study): up-scale tier, 1991

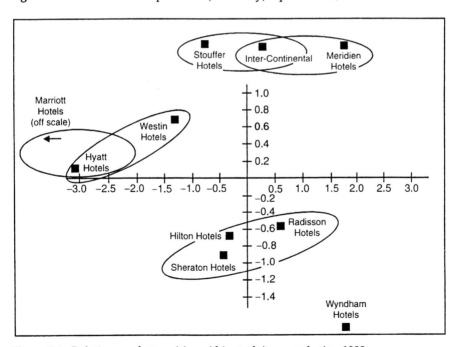

Figure 7.4. Relative market positions (this study): up-scale tier, 1992

recover from the effects of war, overbuilding, and recession (Figure 7.4). Ironically, the competitive clusters found in the 1992 data are similar to those in the baseline 1990 chart (Figure 7.2). Hilton, Westin, Sheraton, and Hyatt remain fairly consistent. Marriott has moved substantially but is again viewed as competitive with Hyatt, albeit not with Westin. Likewise, Radisson is once again viewed as competitive with Sheraton and Hilton.

CHAIN MOVEMENT

The perceptual maps give us an idea of how individual brands did or did not attempt to change customers' perceptions of their positions. The maps capture the movement of individual brands from year to year based on customers' perceptions of differences among the chains, which the attribute arrows help to illustrate. The decisions the companies make to emphasise one or another discriminating dimension shifts their position in the minds of their customers.

In the 1990 map, Stouffer is on a par with Inter-Continental on price and product quality, but in 1991, customers' price-value perception of Stouffer moved it away from Inter-Continental's competitive set, a movement that reversed in 1992 following considerable advertising, acquisitions and product upgrades. Marriott moved downward on the cost scale between 1990 and 1991. The chain responded to the hotel industry's recession (and its own real-estate-driven difficulties) by emphasising the economic dimension, particularly its incentive programmes. As examples, Marriott beefed up its frequent-guest and corporate-discount programmes and courted travel agents and managers by guaranteeing commission payments in 30 days. By 1992 that focus was softened and the chain moved to compete more with Hyatt and less with Hilton and Sheraton. For its part, Hyatt maintained a fairly consistent position during the entire period.

MANAGERIAL IMPLICATIONS

Managers should monitor the implications of their marketing strategies. They need to examine the attributes that customers use to differentiate one hotel brand from another, checking the dimensions on which that position is based both for their own brand and for their competitors.

Ratings such as those by *Business Travel News* can give marketing managers an indication of the effectiveness over time of the brand's marketing strategies in positioning against the competition.

Such an approach will prevent hoteliers from making the mistake of presuming a competitive set based only on physical attributes. Two similar appearing hotels may or may not actually compete directly against each other, and all up-scale hotels are not necessarily part of a given competitive set. By developing a perceptual map, marketing managers can determine which brands are actually in the competitive set.

More important, by maintaining the perceptual map over time, managers can assess whether changes in the brand's marketing strategies are causing the hotel's position to change. Changes in position should be intentional and not accidental, lest a brand find itself competing in a set that puts it at a disadvantage. On the other hand, intentional changes in the competitive set can make sense. Marriott's $49-room programme, for instance, substantially changed its position on the 1991 map, compared to 1990 and 1992. For that time, the brand moved out of one competitive group and into another one. Our data set does not give an indication of intention, but we may infer that Marriott's move was a deliberate strategy.

While the technique in this example is based on historical data, the lessons of how a hotel's position moves as a result of operating or marketing changes – intentional or unintentional – can be used for future strategic planning. In 1992 Ramada launched an advertising campaign with the following positioning statement: 'Ramada's in, Holiday's out'. Ramada's president Stephen Belmonte explained the strategy as one of positioning Ramada close to Holiday Inn in the customer's mind, or, in other words, to position Ramada with Holiday in the customer's consideration set.[20] The strategy was chosen, Belmonte said, because Ramada was a 'sleepy and stagnant company' with an 'identity crisis', and was falling out of favour as a mid-market brand.[21] According to Scott Deaver, Ramada's vice president of marketing, the objective of the campaign was for 'Ramada to be part of a "competitive pair" with Holiday in the same way that Reebok and Nike, Burger King and McDonald's, or MCI and AT&T are competitive pairs'. In commenting on the results of the campaign, Deaver noted that there was no way of knowing whether the campaign achieved its objective of having Ramada considered with Holiday.[22] Using the technique presented in this article, however, would help determine whether that objective was achieved.

NOTES AND REFERENCES

1. See G. Lynn Shostack, Breaking free from product marketing, *Journal of Marketing*, **41**, April 1977: 73–80
2. Positioning by attribute is the most common but not the only strategy. See David A. Aaker, Positioning your product, *Business Horizons*, May–June 1982: 56–62
3. Robert C. Lewis, Advertising your hotel's position, *Cornell Hotel and Restaurant Administration Quarterly*, **31**(2), August 1990: 85
4. Mark Harris, Economical positioning *Cornell Hotel and Restaurant Administration Quarterly*, **29**(2), August 1988: 97
5. Lewis, Advertising your hotel's position, p. 87

6. See John M. Rathmell, *Marketing in the service sector*, Winthorp, 1974, Cambridge, MA
7. Robert C. Lewis, The positioning statement for hotels, *Cornell Hotel and Restaurant Administration Quarterly*, 22(1), May 1981: 53
8. For example, see Paul E. Green and Yoram Wind, New ways to measure consumers' judgements, *Harvard Business Review*, July–August 1975: 107–115
9. For an explanation of discriminant analysis, see Robert C. Lewis, The market position: mapping guests' perceptions of hotel operations, *Cornell Hotel and Restaurant Administration Quarterly*, 26(2), August 1985: 88–89
10. Ibid., p. 93
11. For a specific analysis of the differences in attributes applied by business and pleasure travellers, see Robert C. Lewis, Predicting hotel choice: the factors underlying perception, *Cornell Hotel and Restaurant Administration Quarterly*, 25(4), February 1985: 91
12. See Russell A. Bell, Corporate travel-management trends, *Cornell Hotel and Restaurant Administration Quarterly*, 34(2), April 1993: 30–39
13. *Business Travel News*, 29 January 1990: pp. 36–41; 28 January 1991: pp. 13–19; 27 January 1992: pp. 15–18
14. Pauline Yoshihashi, Hotel recovery will be a late arrival, *Wall Street Journal*, 27 July 1992: p. B1
15. Ibid
16. Ibid
17. The data used for this study were selected to illustrate the perceptual-mapping method and should not be used for strategic interpretation of the up-scale lodging market
18. See J.O. Ramsay, Some statistical approaches to multidimensional scaling, *Journal of the Royal Statistical Society*, Series A, **145**, 1982: 285–312; and M.L. Davison, *Multidimensional scaling*, John Wiley, 1983, New York
19. The significance of psychological positioning is explored in George Overstreet, Creating value in oversupplied markets: the case of Charlottesville, Virginia, hotels, *Cornell Hotel and Restaurant Administration Quarterly*, 34(5), October 1993: 84–91
20. Aaker, Positioning your product, pp. 56–62; also see Michael S. Morgan, Travellers' choice: the effects of advertising and prior stay, *Cornell Hotel and Restaurant Administration Quarterly*, 32(4), December 1991: 40–49
21. Phillip Swann, Raging Belmonte, *Lodging*, **70**(10), June 1992: 28–29
22. Jim Galb, Taking off the gloves, *ASTA Agency Management*, August 1993: p. 95

APPENDIX

Basic points of probabilistic multidimensional scaling (Multiscale)

1. Points are located in Euclidean space based on variable ratings (in this case based on perceptions of product attributes), and fitted to a two-dimensional perceptual map. Inter-point distances are calculated.
2. The differences between true and fitted inter-point distances (errors) are compared using statistical tests of whether those distances are due to random chance or whether they are statistically significant.
3. All distances are considered positive (absolute value). Statistical tests are based on the assumption that variables have a log-normal distribution.

4. Any extreme values (outliers) must be transformed. Before applying a Multiscale fitting to these distances, the outliers must be smoothed out so that the final graph shows a more log-normal distribution.
5. Finally, z-tests are applied to the inter-point distances, testing whether those distances are significant at the $p < 0.05$ level.

8 A Utility Analysis of Cross-Time Tourism Consumption

ZHENG GU

INTRODUCTION

This chapter will use utility theory, the foundation of modern investment and other finance theories, to analyze individuals' cross-time tourism consumption decision-making and the factors that affect tourism utility and tourism consumption. An individual's tourism utility is the satisfaction that he derives from cross-time consumption of tourism goods, services, and leisure. In the chapter, the analysis will concentrate on how optimal allocation of tourism consumption across time through saving or investing can lead to the maximization of an individual's tourism utility. Furthermore, the impact of age, the interest rate and inflation on cross-time tourism consumption will be analyzed. Their implication to tourism forecasting and marketing will be discussed. Empirical cases of tourism consumption and non-tourism consumption based on real data from the US will be provided and assessed to support the theoretical analysis.

TOURISM CONSUMPTIONS AND INVESTMENT

Utility theory is a theory of consumer behavior in choosing different bundles of consumer goods and services. Utility can be defined as an individual's perception of his satisfaction from consumption of goods and services (Maurice et al, 1982). The essence of utility theory is that a rational individual makes his consumption decision in a way that maximizes his utility or satisfaction. Utility theory is the core component of modern economic and finance theories. While economic utility theory emphasizes individual utility maximization through optimal allocation of different consumption goods, financial utility theory concentrates on optimal allocation of consumption in two periods – current consumption and future consumption. In the financial utility analysis, an individual's current consumption decision cannot be

Economic and Management Methods for Tourism and Hospitality Research.
Edited by Thomas Baum and Ram Mudambi © 1999 John Wiley & Sons Ltd.

separated from his saving or investing decision which is ultimately for future consumption.

According to the utility analysis of modern investment theory, an individual is a consumer as well as a saver or investor (Levy and Sarnat, 1984). The individual's utility is derived from his consumption of goods and services at present and in the future. An optimal allocation of cross-time consumption through investing will lead to the maximization of the individual's utility (Copeland and Weston, 1988; Levy and Sarnat, 1984). Any individual has his subjective time preference of consumption between present and future. The existence of the capital market makes investing for the future possible, and hence the exchange of today's consumption for tomorrow's possible. The interest rate of the capital market, or the reward for delaying consumption, interacts with an individual's subjective time preference and affects the allocation of cross-time consumption.

A tourist is also an investor. He can save on today's tourism consumption for more tourism consumption tomorrow. Therefore, the interest rate should play a role in his tourism consumption decision-making. An individual's tourism consumption decision should not be isolated from his investment decision. Previous research studies have examined tourism demand in isolation of people's investing activities and have identified discretionary income and leisure time as two determinants of tourism consumption (McIntosh and Goeldner, 1986; Sessa, 1983). An examination of the interrelationship between an individual's tourism consumption decision and investment decision will add a new dimension to tourism research. This chapter analyzes a tourist's utility maximization in cross-time tourism consumption and empirically investigates the impact of the interest rate on such consumption.

INDIFFERENCE CURVE AND UTILITY MAXIMIZATION

Modern utility theory was finalized when the indifference curve was first introduced by Vilfred Pareto in 1906 (Maurice and Smithson, 1985). In modern utility theory, economists use the concept of utility to explain consumer behavior without the assumption of cardinal measurability. Different levels of indifference curves represent different levels or ranks of utility. An indifference curve is located in a two-commodity space. It is a locus of points which represent different combinations of goods or services yielding the same level of satisfaction or utility for an individual. Figure 8.1 shows three indifference curves consisting of two goods, X and Y. The characteristics of an indifference curve are: (A) negative slope which implies the trade-off between goods X and Y for the same level of satisfaction; (B) no intersection of two indifference curves of the same individual because of their representation of two different levels of utility; (C) convexity to the origin

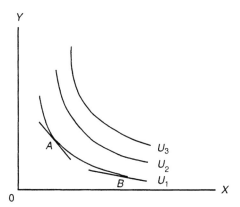

Figure 8.1. Utility derived from two commodities

because of diminishing marginal utility of consumption; and (D) no common indifference curve for different individuals.

In Figure 8.1, the indifference curve $U3$, which is the farthest from the origin, represents a higher level of utility than the indifference curves $U1$ and $U2$. Each point on $U1$ represents a consumer's consumption of goods X and Y generating the same utility, $U1$. A tangent line can be drawn at any point along the indifference curve, representing the consumer's subjective marginal rate of substitution (MRS) of X for Y at the given utility level. At point B where more Xs are being consumed than at A, the MRS of X for Y is low. One unit of X can be exchanged for less Y than at A, implying diminishing marginal utility from the consumption of X.

In the financial utility analysis, an indifference curve is located in a two-period space, instead of a two-commodity space, where the Y axis represents future consumption and the X axis, current consumption. The curve is a locus of points representing different allocations of two periods' consumption that generate the same level of utility. The contents of the consumption are ignored. Figure 8.2 shows three indifference curves, $U1$, $U2$, and $U3$, consisting of current consumption, C_0 and future consumption, C_1. The slope or the tangent line of an indifference curve at any point is the MRS, or the ratio at which the individual is willing to exchange C_0 for C_1. The MRS measures the subjective time preference of consumption at a given level of utility. The indifference curve in a two-period space has the same characteristics of the indifference curve in a two-commodity space.

In Figure 8.2, a capital market line, W_1 W_0, is drawn. The capital market line represents the marginal rate of exchange (MRE) between current wealth, W_0 and future wealth, W_1. It is also the exchange rate between current consumption and future consumption because consumption is backed up by wealth.

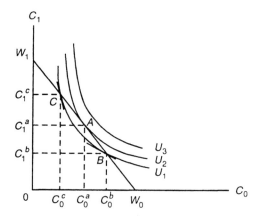

Figure 8.2. Utility maximization from two-period tourism consumption

The slope of the MRE is $-(1 + i)$, in which i is the implied interest rate determined by the capital market. The negative sign of the MRE implies the trade-off between current and future wealth.

According to financial utility theory, a consumer with current wealth endowment of W_0 would choose the consumption combination represented by Point A. At Point A, the MRE line is tangent to the indifference curve $U2$ and the individual's utility is maximized. At B and C, the MRE line intersects the indifference curve $U1$ which represents a lower level of utility. B and C or any other points along the MRE line $W_1 W_0$ are inferior to A, because they would intersect inferior indifference curves. Given current wealth W_0, a rational individual would not choose any points along $W_1 W_0$ other than Point A. Points on $U3$, which represents higher utility, are not attainable. They would require wealth endowment greater than W_0. Point A is the maximum achievable utility for the individual with wealth W_0. At A, the individual would choose to consume OC_0^a at present and invest $C_0^a W_0$ in exchange for future consumption of OC_1^a.

UTILITY ANALYSIS OF TOURISM CONSUMPTION IN TWO PERIODS

A tourist is not only a consumer but also an investor. By spending less on tourism today and investing more, he can spend more on tourism tomorrow. A tourist can maximize his tourism utility through optimal allocation of tourism spending between today and tomorrow. With slight modification, Figure 8.2 can be used to explain the two-period tourism consumption behavior. In Figure 8.2, W_0 and W_1 now represent the discretionary income available for tourism consumption today and tomorrow. C_0 and C_1 represent each period's consumption of tourism goods and services.

With the modification, the indifference curves in Figure 8.2 now represent a tourist's combinations of current and future consumption of tourism goods and services at different levels of utility. The slope of a tangent line along a particular curve is the tourist's subjective MRS between today's and tomorrow's tourism consumption for a given level of utility or:

$$\text{MRS} = \frac{\delta C_1}{\delta C_0}\bigg|_{U=\text{constant}} = -(1+r) \tag{1}$$

The negative sign of MRS implies that to keep the tourism utility unchanged, a tourist would need $(1+r)$ units of future consumption to compensate for one unit of consumption given up today. The additional term r is the 'interest' required by the tourist. If the required interest is zero, then the tourist would need exactly one unit of tomorrow's tourism consumption to exchange for one unit of today's. At Point C of Figure 8.2 where the individual is having little current tourism consumption, the slope or the tangent line of the MRS is steep, implying that current tourism consumption is valuable and he is willing to exchange one unit of current tourism consumption for a lot of future tourism consumption. At Point B where the individual is enjoying plenty of current tourism consumption, the MRS is almost flat, implying that current consumption is less valuable and he is willing to exchange one unit of current tourism consumption for little future tourism consumption.

The declining MRS from C to B implies the diminishing marginal utility of current tourism consumption or the decreasing satiation as current tourism consumption increases. The convexed indifference curve shows that when current tourism consumption increases, the satisfaction or utility derived from the last unit of consumption diminishes and the individual is willing to exchange current consumption for less future consumption. Moving from C to B, the individual's increasing current tourism consumption is associated with decreasing marginal satisfaction, while his decreasing future tourism consumption is associated with increasing marginal satisfaction, leaving the total tourism utility unchanged.

In Figure 8.2, with the modification, W_0 is a tourist's current discretionary income available for tourism consumption and W_1 is the future discretionary income for tourism consumption if the entire W_0 is invested. The slope of the capital market line W_0W_1, $-(1+i)$, is the MRE of the tourism money between the two periods. Any point along the $W_0 W_1$ line represents the tourist's feasible combination of current tourism consumption and savings, or his feasible combination of current and future tourism consumption given a current discretionary income W_0. At Point B, he could consume OC_0^b and invest $C_0^b W_0$ to obtain future tourism consumption OC_1^b. The tourist, however, would not choose B because at B, the MRE is greater than his subjective MRS. In other words, the market offers a higher rate of return than what he requires. Moving upward, or consuming less and saving more, the tourist can achieve higher utility represented by $U2$. On the other hand, at point C, the tourist can consume OC_0^c and invest $C_0^c W_0$ to exchange for OC_1^c of tomorrow. However, he would not choose C where his subjective MRS is greater than the MRE. The market is offering a reward rate lower than what he requires. Moving downward or consuming more and saving less, he can arrive at a higher utility level, $U2$. For this tourist with discretionary income W_0, the highest attainable tourism utility is at A where the MRE line is tangent to the indifference curve $U2$. The tourist would stay at A, consuming OC_0^a and saving $C_0^a W_0$ in exchange for tomorrow's consumption OC_1^a. At A, the tourist's required interest rate r, or his required reward for delaying tourism consumption, is equal to the market determined interest rate i, and the MRS is equal to the MRE:

$$MRS = -(1 + r) = -(1 + i) = MRE \qquad (2)$$

Tourism consumption is backed up by discretionary income. A tourist can spend his discretionary income today or save it for tomorrow's tourism consumption. The analysis above shows that the tourist's utility is maximized when the market interest rate equates his required compensation for delaying tourism consumption. When a tourist plans for his current and future tourism consumption, the market determined interest rate must play a role.

CROSS-PERIOD ALLOCATION OF LEISURE TIME

Different from non-tourism consumption, tourism consumption typically involves a significant amount of traveling time. Tourism consumption is backed up by not only discretionary income but also leisure time and is, by essence, twofold consumption: consumption of money and time. Leisure time is a critical factor in tourism consumption decision-making.

Leisure time generates pleasure or utility. A tourist is not only a money investor but also a time investor. He also can maximize his utility by optimally allocating his leisure time between today and tomorrow. The utility analysis of cross-time tourism spending can be easily extended to cross-time allocation of leisure time. Leisure time has its price or opportunity cost. The opportunity cost is the additional discretionary income that can be earned. Less leisure time enjoyed today implies more leisure time saved for tomorrow. A tourist can give up some leisure time today and work more days to earn additional discretionary income. The additional discretionary income can be invested and enable him to work less and enjoy more leisure in the future. The capital market makes it possible for a tourist to choose between consuming leisure time for current pleasure or saving it for future pleasure.

Because of the existence of non-regular working opportunities, such as overtime work, second jobs, summer teaching, and so on, a tourist has the flexibility of allocating his leisure time between today and tomorrow. The tourist's utility maximization in his allocation of leisure time can be analyzed in the same manner as the analysis of the consumption of tourism goods and services.

With leisure time treated as a special type of tourism consumption, Figure 8.2 can be utilized to illustrate how an individual may maximize his utility from an optimal allocation of leisure time in two periods. The MRE line used for the leisure time analysis, however, needs some adjustment because the wage rate may change over time. The MRE for the leisure time analysis should be:

$$L_1 \times w_1 = L_0 \times w_0 \times -(1 + i)$$
$$MRE = L_1/L_0 = -(1 + i) \times w_0/w_1 \tag{3}$$

where: L_0 and L_1 = leisure time of today and tomorrow
w_0 and w_1 = wage rates of today and tomorrow
i = the market determined interest rate

If the wage rate remains constant across the periods ($w_0 = w_1$), then the MRE for the leisure time analysis is the same as the MRE for the analysis of the consumption of tourism goods and services. If the future wage rate is expected to be higher than the current wage rate ($w_1 > w_0$), then the MRE for the leisure time analysis should be smaller. W_1, which now represents available future leisure time measured in terms of money, in Figure 8.2 would be adjusted downward and the MRE line would be less steep. In a macro analysis of cross-time tourism demand, the expected average current/future wage ratio of a nation, w_0/w_1, should be used to adjust the MRE line. In a micro analysis of the tourism demand of a particular individual or a group, each individual or group would have a different MRE for leisure time, depending on expected future wages. Higher expected future wages or lower w_0/w_1 ratios will result in a more flat MRE line and more current consumption of leisure time.

To maximize the utility from consuming leisure time in two periods, a tourist would choose the point where his MRS of leisure time equates the MRE. The detailed analysis is omitted here because it is identical to the utility maximization analysis for the consumption of tourism goods and services.

THE IMPACT OF THE INTEREST RATE ON TOURISM CONSUMPTION

The MREs for the consumption of tourism goods and services and the consumption of leisure time have a common interest rate term, i, which is determined by the capital market. A change in the interest rate will change the slopes of the MREs and the allocation of tourism consumption. The interest rate change should have a greater impact on cross-time tourism consumption than on non-tourism consumption because of the twofold consumption nature of tourism activities.

Figure 8.3 illustrates how a change in the interest rate would affect a tourist's cross-time tourism consumption. The individual's indifference curve was originally tangent to the middle MRE line, $W_1 W_0$. A decrease in the interest rate would rotate the MRE line downward to $W_1' W_0$ and the line would be tangent to a lower indifference curve. Repositioned at a lower utility level, a tourist would consume more today and save less for tomorrow. The present value or the current price (CP) of future consumption is the future consumption (FC) discounted back by the MRE, or $CP = FC/(1 + i)$. The price of future consumption becomes greater when the interest rate i decreases. Declining i implies more expensive future consumption and the tourist would choose to consume more today and save less for tomorrow. On the other hand, an increase in the interest rate would turn the MRE line upwards to $W_1'' W_0$ and the line would be tangent to a higher indifference curve. Repositioned at a higher utility level, the tourist would consume less today and save more for tomorrow. The higher interest rate makes current consumption more expensive and shifts the tourist toward more future consumption.

The impact of an interest rate change on leisure time allocation is similar to its impact on the consumption of tourism goods and services. The price of future leisure time (FL) measured in terms of present leisure time (PL), is:

$$PL = FL/(1 + i) \times w_1/w_0 \qquad (4)$$

A decrease in the interest rate i would result in a greater PL and make the future leisure more expensive. As a result, a tourist may choose to have more leisure time now and reduce future leisure time. On the other hand, an increase in interest rate would make the future leisure time cheaper and the

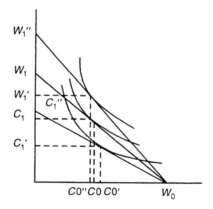

Figure 8.3. Interest rate change and two-period tourism consumption

tourist may choose to work more and enjoy less leisure at present. Involving leisure time is a unique feature of tourism consumption. It makes tourism consumption more affected by a change in the interest rate than other consumption.

THE EFFECT OF INFLATION

The interest rate discussed in the previous section is the real interest rate exclusive of the influence of inflation. In reality, an observed interest rate is a nominal rate that contains an inflation term. With inflation present, the MRE used for the analysis of consumption of tourism goods and services should be:

$$MRE = -(1 + R) = -(1 + i) \times (1 + h) \tag{5}$$

where R is the nominal interest rate, i the real rate, and h the inflation rate. From the equation above the following can be derived:

$$(1 + R) = (1 + i) \times (1 + h) \tag{6}$$

$$R = i + h + ih$$

The interaction term ih is trivial and can be omitted. Therefore, the real rate is the nominal rate minus the inflation rate, $i = R - h$, and the real MRE for consumption of tourism goods and services is the observed MRE minus inflation rate h, or $MRE = -(1 + R - h)$. The real MRE for the leisure time analysis would be $-(1 + R - h) \times w_0/w_1$. Graphically, the real MRE lines would be less steep than the nominal MRE lines. In Figure 8.3, if $W_1''W_0$ and $W_1'W_0$ are observed nominal MRE lines, then the real MRE lines would be below the nominal MRE lines. Inflation will affect the positions of W_1'' and W_1' on the Y axis, but not the position of W_0 on the X axis.

When the observed nominal interest rate increases, current consumption of tourism goods and services and leisure time may not decrease as much as previously discussed for the real interest rate change. Inflation rate h may partially or totally offset the increase in nominal rate R and the real MRE may increase little or remain the same. If the inflation rate exceeds the increase in the nominal interest rate, the real rate will actually decrease and current consumption of tourism goods, services, and leisure time will increase. The decreased real MRE can stimulate current tourism consumption and discourage future tourism consumption.

On the other hand, inflation should always enlarge the impact of a decrease in the nominal rate on tourism consumption. When a decrease in the nominal rate is accompanied by an inflation h, the real rate drops more than the nominal rate by h. This would further stimulate current tourism consumption. Inflation implies a smaller increase or a greater decrease in the real rate than the observed increase or decrease in the nominal rate. Therefore, it is always a plus factor or a stimulant for current tourism consumption. In a highly inflationary economic environment, saving becomes less attractive or not attractive at all.

AGE AND TOURISM CONSUMPTION

Utility theory suggests that the indifference curve differs across individuals. However, indifference curves of people with same age may have some commonalities. Old people have limited future time. For them, current tourism consumption of goods, services, and leisure time is precious. They prefer to enjoy more and work less. To exchange for even little current tourism consumption, they would require a large premium from future tourism consumption. Their MRS should contain a large r term and their indifference curves should be steeper than those of a younger generation. On the contrary, young people have ample future time. Current tourism consumption may not be as precious as for the old generation. They tend to enjoy less tourism but work more and save more for future tourism. Their indifference curves should be relatively flat.

Age also has an impact on the location of indifference curves. Old people are generally wealthier and have more leisure time available (longer paid vacation, for example) than young people. They have more current 'endowments' to support their tourism consumption. Their indifference curves should be positioned far away from the Y axis but near the X axis. By contrast, being less wealthy and having fewer current 'endowments,' the young generation should have their indifference curves positioned near the Y axis and far away from the X axis. Based on the data of US Bureau of the Census, McIntosh and Goeldner (1986) find that age groups under 25 are less active in travel than age groups between 25 and 64.

Figure 8.4 presents the indifference curves of two individuals, an old individual and a young one. The curves represent either consumption of tourism goods and services or leisure time. To make it simple, the MRE for leisure time consumption is assumed to be the same as that for the consumption of tourism goods and services ($w_0/w_1 = 1$) and the inflation is ignored. The two individuals' curves intersect at A. A MRE line is drawn through A and has an intercept of W_0L_0 on the X axis, implying same current discretionary income and leisure time endowments for both individuals. The two individuals would behave differently. To maximize his cross-time tourism utility, the young individual would move to B by giving up some of his current tourism consumption in exchange for more tourism consumption in the future. The old individual would move to C to maximize his cross-time tourism utility by increasing current tourism consumption and reducing future tourism consumption.

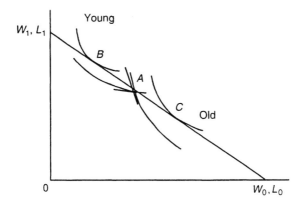

Figure 8.4. Age and two-period tourism consumption

Age is an important factor in tourism consumption. When the average age of a nation increases, we may observe an increase in tourism consumption. Of course, we also need to consider the physical constraints imposed on people who are extremely old and whose tourism consumption is restricted by their mobility.

EMPIRICAL CASES OF THE IMPACT OF THE INTEREST RATE

The utility analysis of cross-time tourism consumption suggests that if the interest rate rises, current tourism consumption will become more expansive and people will postpone current tourism consumption and save more money and time for future tourism consumption. On the other hand, lower interest rates encourage current tourism consumption.

An empirical investigation was conducted to examine the impact of interest rates on air travel, national park stay and restaurant sales in the United States. In particular, it examined whether there were significant correlations between interest rates and the tourism activities and whether interest rates could provide additional explanation to the variation in the tourism activities. The impact of interest rates on the consumption of two non-tourism categories, drug and furniture/appliance, was also examined for comparison purposes.

Variables and data sources

Monthly average yields of US government short-term (2–4 years) bond were used as the interest rate variable. Air passenger miles and national park visitors' days of stay per month were used as measures for air travel and national park patronage. Monthly restaurant sales were used to measure the nation's restaurant consumption. In the two comparison categories, monthly drug sales and furniture/appliance sales were used as non-tourism consumption variables. National park days of stay were obtained from *US Travel Data Center Microfiche (1993)*. All the other data were obtained from *Security Price Index Record* and *Current Statistics* by Standard & Poor's Statistical Service (1992). The period covers January 1985 through December 1990, a total of 72 monthly observations. All the consumption activity data were seasonally adjusted. The monthly interest rate and sales were adjusted for monthly inflation rates derived from the monthly Consumer Price Index. Because air travel and national park stays normally need planning and reservation in advance, the impact of the interest rate should have a time lag. Therefore, air travel passenger miles and park stays were lagged for two months in the empirical study.

Methodology of the empirical study

To test the relationship between the interest rate and consumption activities, Pearson product moment coefficient of correlation, r, was calculated. Statistical significance level, represented by P value, or the probability of making a Type I error, was computed. Pearson coefficient of correlation ranges from -1 to $+1$. It is a measure of the strength of the linear relationship between two variables. Great absolute value of the coefficient and low P value suggest strong and significant linear correlation. High P value indicates that the coefficient of correlation between two variables is not significantly from zero and the no-relationship null hypothesis cannot be rejected.

Furthermore, to examine if the interest rate contributes to the explanation of the variation in tested activities, time-series regressions, with and without the interest rate, were run and compared. Regression was first run with a trend variable alone. Then the interest rate variable was added as the second explanatory variable. R^2 of the two-variable model was compared with that of the one-variable model. A significant increase in R^2 would suggest additional explanatory power provided by the interest rate variable. To test the significance of the additional explanation contributed by the interest rate, the partial F test as discussed by Kleinbaum et al. (1988), was performed. The partial F test is a test for the significance of the variable added last, given other variables already in the model. SAS statistical program was used for the statistical analyses.

Empirical findings

Table 8.1 presents the Pearson coefficients of correlation between the interest rate and the tested consumption activities.

Table 8.1. Pearson product moment coefficients of correlation between interest rate and other variable

	Int	Trnd	Park	Air	Rstr	Frap	Drug
r	1.0000	−0.1766	−0.3569	−0.4356	−0.1706	−0.1892	−0.1496
P	0.0000	0.1437	0.0024	0.0002	0.1580	0.1168	0.2164

Notes:
r = Pearson coefficient P = probability of Type I error
Int = interest rate   Trnd = trend variable
Park = natl. park days of stay   Air = air passenger miles
Rstr = restaurant sales   Frap = furniture/appliance sales
Drug = drug sales

The coefficient of correlation (r) of the interest rate variable (Int) with itself is 1 and the associated P value is zero. The interest rate is, of course, perfectly correlated with itself. For the rest, Air passenger miles (Air) has the greatest absolute r value, 0.4356 and lowest P value, 0.0002, followed by National park stays' (Park) 0.3569 (r) and 0.0024 (P). Both Air and Park are significantly and negatively correlated with Int at the 0.0025 significance level. The coefficients of correlation of the other three consumption categories, restaurant sales (Rstr), furniture and appliance sales (Frap), and drug sales (Drug) with Int are all not significant at the 0.05 level. Also, the trend variable (Trnd), with a P value of 0.1437, is not correlated with the interest rate variable, Int.

Table 8.2 shows the regression results. Since the purpose of the regression was to find out if the added interest rate variable contributes to the

Table 8.2. Results of regression

	t(Trnd)	t(Int)	Partial F(Int)	R^2	F(Model)
Park:					
One-var model:	3.1447	NA	NA	0.1270	9.2393
Two-var model:	2.7550	−2.7615	7.6260	0.2162	9.8892
Air:					
One-var model:	20.055	NA	NA	0.8553	402.28
Two-var model:	27.029	−8.6822	75.38	0.9319	458.73
Rstr:					
One-var model:	52.041	NA	NA	0.9748	2708.2
Two-var model:	51.150	0.2526	0.0638	0.9748	1336.1
Frap:					
One-var model:	31.815	NA	NA	0.9353	1012.2
Two-var model:	30.959	−0.4291	0.1842	0.9354	500.28
Drug:					
One-var model:	55.442	NA	NA	0.9774	3073.7
Two-var model:	54.697	1.1653	1.3579	0.9778	1545.3

Note: Underlined statistics are not significant at the 0.05 level. All the other t, F, and partial F values indicate significance at least at the 0.01 level.

explanation of the variation in the dependent variables, only the test statistics, t of each explanatory variable, partial F of Int, F of the model, and R^2 are presented in the table. The constants and coefficients of independent variables are omitted.

Table 8.2 shows that adding interest rate to the one-variable model has raised the R^2 from 0.127 to 0.2162 for national park stay and from 0.8553 to 0.9319 for air passenger miles. The partial F values of Int in both Park and Air models are highly significant, at the 0.0025 level. R^2 indicates the percentage of variation in the dependent variable that has been explained by the model. The significant increase in R^2 of the two models and the associated high partial F values show that with the trend variable already in the model, the interest rate provides significant additional explanation for the variation in air passenger miles and national park stays. The significant contribution of the interest rate variable to the two models is also confirmed by the significant t values of Int and the increased model F values. The negative sign of the t values of Int suggests that the interest rate affects the two tourism activities negatively.

For the other three consumption activities, Rstr, Drug and Frap, the increases in R^2 due to the additional interest rate variable are trivial and the partial F tests are all not significant at the 0.05 level. Thus, the null hypothesis of zero contribution of Int to the models cannot be rejected. The insignificant contribution of the interest rate variable in the three models is confirmed by their insignificant t values associated with Int and the decreased model F values. The signs of Int are even distorted to become positive in the models of Rstr and Drug. Adding interest rate to the three models will not improve their explanatory or predictive power.

Explanation of the empirical results

Air travel and national park vacation are tourism activities involving a significant amount of money and time. The interest rate, as discussed in the previous utility analysis, should have a greater impact on the two activities because of its dual impact on money and leisure time. The significant contribution of the interest rate to the explanatory power of the Air and Park models is consistent with the utility theory. Higher interest rates encourage people to delay tourism consumption whereas lower interest rates encourage current tourism consumption. There is a significant negative relationship between the interest rate and current tourism consumption.

Restaurant consumption was not significantly affected by the interest rate, probably due to the fact that its main patronage is local residents. For local residents, restaurant patronage involves small amounts of money and no traveling time. Although some parts of restaurant sales are contributed by tourists, the insignificant relationship between the interest rate and restaurant consumption does not necessarily conflict with the utility analysis of cross-time tourism consumption.

Unlike tourism consumption, the drug is a necessity that requires no leisure time and is not purchased with discretionary income. People cannot delay the consumption of a necessity. There should be no cross-time consumption exchange for the drug. The insignificant relationship between the interest rate and drug consumption is expected. Furniture and appliance involve a large amount of money but no leisure time. They can be considered as quasi-necessities. The insignificant relationship between Frap and Int is also expected.

The empirical results suggest that the interest rate does affect people's cross-time tourism consumption, particularly in activities that require a substantial amount of money and time, such as air travel and vacation in national parks. On the other hand, partial-tourism activities that involve little money and leisure time, such as restaurant patronage, may be less affected by the interest rate. The interest rate has no impact on the cross-time consumption of necessities or quasi-necessities involving no leisure time. The empirical cases are consistent with the utility analysis of cross-time tourism consumption.

SUMMARY

A tourist is a consumer and an investor as well. A rational tourist budgets not only his short-run tourism spending but also his long-run tourism consumption. By saving on today's tourism consumption, in terms of either money or leisure time, a tourist can have more future tourism consumption. The tourist can maximize his tourism utility by optimizing the allocation of his cross-time tourism consumption. The optimal allocation is realized when the tourist's required reward for delaying tourism consumption is equal to the capital market determined interest rate. Therefore, the interest rate should play a critical role in a tourist's cross-time tourism consumption decision.

The interest rate determines the slope of the MRE line. A change in the interest rate will change the optimal allocation of an individual's tourism money and leisure time. Because of the dual impact of the interest rate on tourism activities, tourism consumption should be more sensitive to changes in the interest rate than non-tourism consumption. An increase in the interest rate is likely to cause a decrease in current tourism consumption. A decrease in the interest rate should encourage current tourism consumption. With inflation present, however, an increase in the nominal interest rate may not necessarily reduce current tourism consumption. Different age groups have indifference curves of different shapes and locations, resulting in different patterns of cross-time tourism consumption. While current tourism consumption is more precious for old people, young people are likely to delay their tourism consumption.

The empirical cases presented in the chapter are consistent with the utility analysis of the impact of the interest rate on tourism consumption. The findings of this study suggest that in the future, the tourism industry and academia should pay more attention to the impact of the interest rate on tourism demand, particularly during periods of unstable interest rates. Tourists, after all, are investors and their tourism consumption decisions should be tied to their investing decisions. The utility analysis of tourism consumption could be incorporated into tourism demand forecasting. Besides discretionary income and leisure time, a forecasting model may include interest rate, inflation, average age, and expected future wage rate as additional explanatory variables. Adding those variables to a tourism demand model may help increase its predictive power and improve forecasting accuracy. The utility approach of tourism consumption may also be incorporated into tourism marketing strategies. If the economy of a target market is experiencing low interest rates and/or high inflation, it may be a good time to remind people of the relative inexpensiveness of current tourism consumption. For tourism researchers, based on the theoretical analysis of the chapter, more hypotheses can be tested to provide further empirical evidence. Listed below are some testable hypotheses:

1. Tourism revenue is more sensitive to the interest rate than local recreational and entertainment revenues.
2. High inflation is associated with high inflation-adjusted tourism revenue.
3. The lodging industry revenue is negatively correlated with the interest rate.
4. An aging population has larger per capita tourism spending than a relatively young population.

By providing a link between an individual's tourism consumption decision and his investment decision, the utility analysis opens a new dimension in tourism research. This chapter is only an initial attempt to apply financial utility theory to an individual's cross-time tourism consumption. The analysis is neither thorough nor comprehensive enough. Many issues remain undiscussed and should be further explored. For example, the subjective MRS may differ across not only age groups but also sex, race, and profession groups. To establish a sound utility theory of tourism consumption useful for tourism demand forecasting and tourism marketing, more in-depth research studies are needed.

ACKNOWLEDGMENTS

The discussion of the Empirical Cases of the Impact of the Interest Rate, including Tables 8.1 and 8.2, is reprinted from *International Journal of Hospitality Management*, **14**, No. 3/4, Zheng Gu, The relationship between interest rate and tourism activities, pp. 239–243, © 1995, with permission from Elsevier Science.

REFERENCES

Anderson, D.R., Sweeney, D.J., Williams, T.A., 1995, *Quantitative method for business*, 6th edn, West Publishing Company, Minneapolis

Copeland, T.E., Weston, J.F., 1988, *Financial theory and corporate policy*, 3rd edn, Addison-Wesley, Reading, MA

Kleinbaum, D.G., Lawrence, L.K., Muller, K.E., 1988, *Applied regression and other multivariable methods*, 2nd edn, PWS-KENT Publishing Company, Boston

Levy, H., Sarnat, M., 1984, *Portfolio and investment selection: theory and practice*, 1st edn, Prentice-Hall, Englewood Cliffs, NJ

Maurice, S.C., Phillips, O.R., Ferguson, C.E., 1982, *Economic analysis: theory and application*, 4th edn, Richard D. Irwin, Homewood, IL

Maurice, S.C., Smithson, C.W., 1985, *Managerial Economics*, 2nd edn, Richard D. Irwin, Homewood. IL.

McIntosh, R.B., Goeldner, C.R., 1986, *Tourism principles, practices, philosophies*, 4th edn, John Wiley, New York.

Sessa, A., 1983, *Elements of tourism economics*, CATAL s.r.l., Roma

PART II

9 Multidisciplinary Methods: Introductory Note

TOM BAUM

Part I of this book addressed a diversity of theoretical tools in quantitative research as applied to the travel, tourism and hospitality (TTH) industry group. These approaches represent largely unidisciplinary analytical tools which, in methodological terms, draw from one specific area in seeking to provide an explanatory framework for aspects of TTH.

TTH phenomena, however, are not always amenable to unidisciplinarity and the analysis which derives from this approach. TTH, indeed, is an ill-defined activity which impinges across a range of other established sectors of the economy, and, from an academic perspective, derives its conceptual, methodological and practical impulse from across the disciplines in the academy (Baum, 1997).

These are contexts, therefore, where the analytical tools employed by those researching and interpreting TTH phenomena cannot assume the environment of a single discipline. Particularly in relation to the formulation and implementation of practical tourism policy, multidisciplinary research tools provide a natural complement and extension to the more restricted interpretation afforded by the methodologies discussed in Part I. Multi-disciplinarity, of course, is not without problems, as it can result in imprecision and complexity in terms of data analysis.

Policy formulation and the identification of strategic direction within TTH, whether in the public sector or in tourism enterprises, cannot take place in isolation. Rather, it must factor into consideration a diversity of external and internal variables, which may or may not be predictable or controllable.

These variables reflect economic, political, social, cultural and technological influences on the TTH area and are, in themselves, an acknowledgement that decision-making in tourism is rarely undertaken on the basis of entirely rational economics operating on the basis of a single paradigm.

Part II of this book represents discussion of a series of tools and approaches

Economic and Management Methods for Tourism and Hospitality Research.
Edited by Thomas Baum and Ram Mudambi © 1999 John Wiley & Sons Ltd.

which recognise multidisciplinarity as an important dimension within decision-making in the TTH industry group. The six chapters which follow in Part II are diverse in their focus, but have a common strand in that they focus on supporting the decision-making process at a policy or strategic level. There is a strong but not exclusive market research and marketing theme in these chapters, indicating the extent to which consumer research is built upon multidisciplinary assumptions.

Marja Paajaren's chapter represents a multidisciplinary approach at its simplest. The Nordic Model of Tourism, devised and agreed at the governmental level, is in fact a composite of two methods – income and expense analysis which utilises data collected from both the demand side (tourists) and the supply side (tourism enterprises and their local suppliers). The model is designed to assess the income and employment impact of tourism at a local level and this has clear links to the contributions by John Fletcher in Part I. Data collection is by way of local sample fieldwork with the consequent likelihood of imprecision but the model permits penetration into the direct, indirect and induced impacts of tourism at a local level. It is thus an important tool for local policy-makers involved in decisions about public sector support and incentives, allocation of resources to tourism or to other competing sectors and in support of political case-making.

Ram Mudambi and Tom Baum's chapter also considers tourist expenditure, but it is assessed as a policy aid to marketing planning at a national level. The chapter presents a methodology which is designed to assist countries (but also regions) to target those national tourist groups which deliver maximum benefits in terms of tourist expenditure. Using a comprehensive tourism panel data set, the first objective of the method is to isolate characteristics which explain the overall level of tourist expenditure, based on different tourist originating countries. The second stage is the application of a quantitative method which permits optimal targeting of a finite tourism promotional budget through the use of panel data estimates.

This strongly demand-side-focused chapter is followed by Stephen Wanhill's contribution on location marketing which has a strongly supply-side focus. Wanhill examines the range of government incentives offered to the tourism private sector by government and private investors, focusing on the general economic principles in their use. The presence or absence of such incentives is rarely a purely economic assessment, however, and the chapter recognises the wider political and social context in which policy in this area is made. An important practical outcome of the chapter is the guidance it provides in assessing the impact and implications of various incentive options.

Eric Laws and Stephen Hiemstra both look at pricing issues in tourism. Laws' concern is at a macro level and has a strong marketing dimension. He homes in on the UK package holiday or fully inclusive market and assesses the impact of pricing policies which squeeze margins for destination suppliers to a minimum. The chapter examines the nature and evolution of low-price offers by individual companies and argues the case for viewing holiday pricing in a holistic manner. The approach of the chapter is designed to assist holiday companies and those involved in the packaged holiday supply chain to increase prices and, therefore, profitability.

Stephen Hiemstra's chapter, by contrast, looks at the micro context of hotel room pricing and looks at pricing methods which can address the high fixed cost attributes of the hotel sector. The key response is through methods akin to yield management, although this term is deemed restrictive. Rather than assuming market segment homogeneity in terms of price sensitivity and consumer behaviour, Hiemstra demonstrates an approach which can accommodate diversity in the market place.

The final chapter in Part II is Michael Stabler's application of the cost-benefit analysis (CBA) framework to environmental aspects of tourism. CBA, to be truly effective, is multidisciplinary in character even if its tools draw substantially on economic theory. This application is frequently political in context and this may account for its limited use in assessing the relationship between tourism development and its host natural and man-made environment. CBA, in this context, has the potential to make a significant contribution to the sustainability debate in tourism, particularly at a policy level.

REFERENCES

Baum, T., 1997, Themes and issues in comparative destination research: cases from the North Atlantic. Paper presented at 1st TOLERN meeting, London

10 Assessing Local Income and Employment Effects of Tourism: Experience Using the Nordic Model of Tourism

MARJA PAAJANEN

INTRODUCTION

Interest in the effects of tourism on the economy and on employment has grown gradually as the role of tourism as an industry has become emphasised. The economic contribution of tourism is not, however, a new field of research, as both the demand and supply sectors of the industry have been under scrutiny during the past few decades. Although the scope of tourism has developed and grown immensely, the structure of investigation has remained largely unchanged. The links between tourists and tourism enterprises constitute the mainstay of the economic impact analysis of tourism.

The present chapter depicts the empirical research into the economic effects of tourism on the economy and on employment from a methodological point of view. The focus is on a research method, the Nordic Model of Tourism, that has been used extensively in the Nordic countries since the early 1980s (e.g., Forsberg and Johansson, 1980; Rosef, 1981; Jyvälä, 1981, 1988; Holopainen, 1981; Sairanen, 1988a, b, c; Vuoristo and Arajärvi, 1988; Kauppila, 1989; Malinen, 1989; Kettunen, 1990; Havas, 1991; Kemppainen, 1991; Tekoniemi-Selkälä and Södervall, 1993; Raiskinmäki, 1994). Empirical illustrations given here use data from the empirical studies carried out in two Finnish municipalities, Virrat and Espoo (Pitkänen, 1990; Vuoristo and Paajanen, 1991). The studies constitute classical examples of the use of the Nordic Model in field performance and are thus well fitted to the present task of highlighting the merits and drawbacks of the research method.

The chapter continues with a concise delineation of the Nordic Model of Tourism. The methodological core of the Nordic Model is portrayed by a

Economic and Management Methods for Tourism and Hospitality Research.
Edited by Thomas Baum and Ram Mudambi © 1999 John Wiley & Sons Ltd.

brief step-by-step empirical study design. The strengths and weaknesses of the Nordic Model are further discussed by depicting the scope of analyses, data requirements and the availability of data. In this context, previous discussions (Vuoristo and Arajärvi, 1990) on the use of the method are acknowledged. The chapter concludes with an evaluation of the Nordic Model in field performance and points out some innovations developed in the most recent studies.

THE NORDIC MODEL OF TOURISM

In the late 1970s, the Nordic Council of Ministers took the initiative to create a research method for the economic impact analysis of tourism. The resultant outcome, the Nordic Model of Tourism, was designed to lend itself to various kinds of economic and administrative environments. The structure of the model was made flexible and simple enough to support follow-up studies – a facet that would enhance long-range tourism development. The Nordic Model of Tourism was not adopted as a new method, rather it was an innovative construction of two methods, the expenditure and income methods, that had been used with success in different parts of the world. In this field of research, the Nordic Model of Tourism can be seen as an equal method with the input-output method (cf. Airola, 1985; Lankola, 1992) and some other methods that use an identical frame of research (cf. Olsson, 1987, 1988; Paajanen, 1993; Smith, 1995: 274–280).

The Nordic Model of Tourism is a research tool for empirical tourism studies investigating the effects of tourism on the local economy and on employment. The method serves to trace the economic contribution of tourism to localities of different size and character. It aims at outlining the state and scope of tourism and its economic repercussions. Localities where tourism is only a marginal business line are as suitable for inspection as areas of intensive tourism. The method lends itself to different patterns of resources, such as time and size of task force, that dictate the design of the study. Because of its flexibility, the method serves equally well in fundamental analyses assisting long-range planning and in more limited purpose-built studies.

As illustrated in Figure 10.1, the economic circulation attributed to tourism initiates from tourists' spending (cf. Vuoristo and Arajärvi, 1990: 155; Paajanen, 1993: 22; FTB, 1984: 4). Three levels of repercussions may be distinguished: direct, indirect and induced effects (cf. Fletcher and Snee, 1989: 223; Mathieson and Wall, 1989: 65; Bull, 1991: 138–144). The direct effects refer to the money flow spent by tourists and received by local enterprises as tourism income. Tourists entering the tourism locality demand accommodation, restaurant meals, souvenirs, entertainment, and other services. As tourists use these services and buy products, money is transferred to the

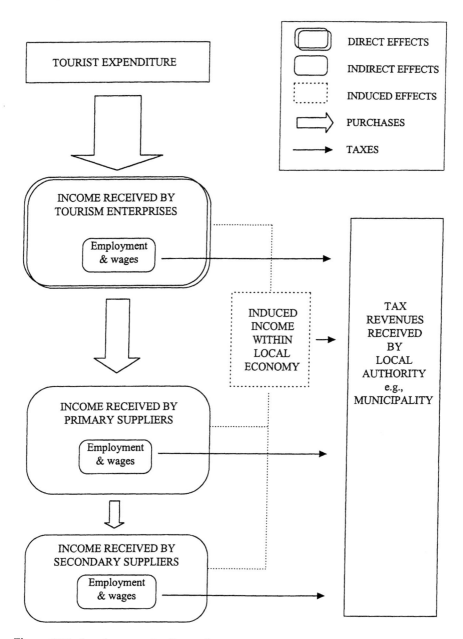

Figure 10.1. Local economic effects of tourism

local enterprises. For some enterprises, tourism constitutes the prime source of income, while for others, tourism is merely a secondary or even an insignificant activity (cf. Smith, 1988, on Tier I and Tier II enterprises). The direct employment effect refers to the employees taken on the payroll to serve tourists, and their wages.

The indirect effect of tourism results from transactions between tourism enterprises (ie, enterprises receiving direct tourism income) and their local suppliers. Tourists are absent from these transactions, although they may constitute the prime motive for such dealings. Analogous to the direct effect, the cash flow received by the suppliers constitutes the indirect income effect. The indirect effect on employment refers to the suppliers' need for personnel. Finally, the induced effects of tourism on the local economy refer to the contribution of the direct and indirect effects to the income levels of the residents. The total economic circulation generated by tourism boosts local household expenditure and thus induces economic activity. From the public sector's perspective, the cash flow spent by tourists stimulates entrepreneurship in the locality and enhances need for personnel at all three levels. This increases the tax revenues of the local authority. The volume of purchases is indicated with arrows of different sizes in Figure 10.1. At the first level (direct effects), the aggregate of transactions is multiple compared to those at other levels.

Figure 10.2 abstracts the stages of an empirical study carried out using the Nordic Model (cf. FTB, 1983; Vuoristo and Arajärvi, 1990: 157). In the initial phase of the study, the key concepts are operationally defined to meet the objective of the study. The operational definitions support the design of data collection. In studies carried out using the Nordic Model, the accuracy of findings largely draws on the use of empirically collected primary data. These data are further supplemented by secondary data, such as tourist and industry statistics.

The application of the income and expenditure methods constitutes the heart of the Nordic Model. These two methods are taken independently of field performance to yield data on the demand and supply sectors of tourism in the locality. The expenditure method investigates the activities of tourists, whereas the income method is used to learn about tourism enterprises (1st business cycle) and their local suppliers (2nd business cycle). Finally, the findings of the two methods are evaluated and synthesised to provide knowledge of the local economic effects of tourism. The contents of Figure 10.2 are examined in more detail below (Tables 10.1–10.5).

Table 10.1 lists the contents of the operational definitions. The key concepts, such as the geographical limits of the region and time period of investigation, are given operational values. The general definitions direct the data collection throughout the study in order to ensure the intercomparability of the data obtained from different sources. The scope of the study is largely

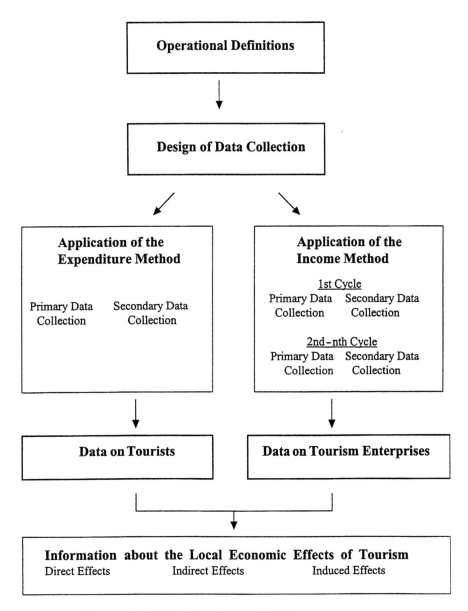

Figure 10.2. The Nordic Model of Tourism: study design

Table 10.1. Operational definitions

General definitions	Definitions attributed to the income and expenditure methods
Geographical study area Time period Units of measure	Types of tourists Types of tourism business lines Activities supporting tourism operations

Table 10.2. Design of data collection

Primary data	Secondary data
Interviews and questionnaires attributed to the expenditure and income methods	Identification of the need for secondary data
Data collections designed to fit the purpose of the study and available resources	Identification of secondary data sources
Recruitment of interviewers and other task force	Identification of potential data blanks

dictated by the depth and purpose of the review, and the availability of resources, such as funds and size of task force. The more ambitious the study plan, the greater the requirements regarding the volume and quality of the data. The types of tourists typical to the index locality are identified for the application of the expenditure method. Correspondingly, for the income method, the business lines immediately and secondarily linked to tourism are identified.

Table 10.2 outlines the need for primary and secondary data. The primary data are produced in a number of personal interviews and questionnaires among tourists, tourism enterprises and their local suppliers. Interviews and questionnaires are designed for each type of tourist under scrutiny, for both domestic and foreign tourists. Additional samples may be formed of other interest groups, such as local households hosting friends or relatives, and non-local households possessing a second home in the locality. Personal interviews tend to yield the most accurate information, as the task force has high control over the material. However, personal interviews are costly and laborious, as they call for trained personnel and a lengthy schedule. Questionnaires are less costly to distribute, as they may be left available at hotels and other facilities or sent by mail. There is, however, a risk with questionnaires that the number of responses remains low.

Statistics and other secondary data are needed to bridge the gaps in the empirically collected data. As the primary data are collected in samples of tourists and tourism enterprises, the secondary data are needed to stretch the data over the whole population. The key sources of secondary data are usually found at the local authority, for example, a municipality, that

Table 10.3. Application of the expenditure method

Primary data collection	Secondary data collection
On-site interviews among tourists	Data on sites and other tourism facilities
Questionnaires delivered to tourists at hotels and other tourism facilities	Data on tourist night and day visits
Other questionnaires	Other supporting data

maintains statistics of tourists at sites, tourists' night and local tourism facilities, and local industries. Secondary data may also be available on the costs of tourism, although they usually are far more complicated to determine. Where such data are available, costs, such as the operative budget of the tourism information office and maintenance of tourism infrastructure, may be observed.

The aim of the expenditure method is to look into the consumption patterns of tourists in the index locality. The quality of the empirically collected data depends on the efficiency with which the activities of tourists are examined and recorded during their visit. In interviews, individual tourists representing their party are asked to list the total purchases made so far and estimate their future purchases in the locality. The duration of stay, mode of transport, type of accommodation and other key details of the visit are also requested. The interviewers may use cards and other material to assist the respondents in recalling their purchases. An identical frame of inquiry is repeated in the questionnaires that are left available to be filled in by tourists by themselves, for instance, at hotels and other accommodation facilities. Arrangements for returning these should be awarded special attention, in order to obtain the highest possible number of replies.

The analysis of the data collected by interviews and questionnaires yields information about the daily expenditure of each tourist type and by each product category. This information is then extended to cover the whole population and the total research period. The calculation entails secondary data on the total number of tourists at hotels, motels and other accommodation facilities, and on day visits. The outcome, the sum total, presents the total (e.g., annual) tourism expenditure made by each type of tourist on services and products provided by different business lines.

The income method constitutes the most challenging part of the Nordic Model of Tourism (Table 10.4). In principle, the aims and rationale of the income method are identical to those of the expenditure method. The major difference between the two methods concerns the area covered by the study. The income method is used in the context of tourism entrepreneurship, whereas the expenditure method, as discussed above, focuses on tourists.

Table 10.4. Application of the income method *1st Cycle*

Primary data collection	Secondary data collection
Interviews among tourism enterprises	Data on businesses and turnover
Questionnaires delivered to tourism enterprises	Data on personnel, wages and taxes

2nd–nth Cycle

Primary data collection	Secondary data collection
Interviews among suppliers	Data on businesses and turnover
Questionnaires delivered to suppliers	Data on personnel, wages and taxes

The challenge of the income method originates from the complexity of tourism as an industry (cf. Leiper, 1979, 1990, 1993; Smith, 1988, 1991, 1993). Unlike traditional service industries, such as finance and transport, tourism cannot be seen as an activity independently responsible for the products and services it provides. Tourism should rather be seen as a conglomerate of businesses marked by a mix of products and services. Tourism is very strongly a cross-industrial economic activity. Tourism acts as an umbrella covering, for instance, transport services, accommodation services, retailing of food and beverages, textiles and gasoline, and various types of entertainment.

Due to this cross-industrial character of tourism, the task force should carefully study the environment of tourism entrepreneurship and identify the lines of business attributed to tourism. The first part of primary data collection, the first business cycle, is targeted at companies immediately serving tourists. Hotels, motels, restaurants, supermarkets and other retail businesses, recreation facilities and travel agencies are typically chosen for this sample. The aim of the personal interviews and questionnaires is to examine the volume of cash flow received by these enterprises from tourists. This cash flow equals the direct income from tourism. The enterprises are also asked to evaluate the pressure of the tourism sales on the need to hire new personnel. These data are used to calculate the direct impact of tourism on employment. The third aim of the inquiry is to list the purchases made by these enterprises from their local suppliers, in order to evaluate the indirect effects of tourism within the locality. Following the geographical delimitation, only local enterprises are observed, omitting income leakages outside the locality. Analogously, personnel residing outside the study area are left out, and only employees who live locally are observed.

Secondary data are collected to trace the base set of the business survey. The total turnover and the total number of employees of these businesses in the locality are obtained. The information received from the sample enterprises is then generalised over the whole enterprise population. Secondary

Table 10.5. Information about the local economic effects of tourism

Direct effects	Expenditure (per day, per year) of different types of tourists on products and services provided by local enterprises, is equal to: Income received by businesses immediately serving tourists Number of tourism-related employees Taxes paid of tourism-related wages
Indirect effects	Purchases of tourism enterprises from their local suppliers, are equal to: Income received by local suppliers Number of employees indirectly attributed to tourism Taxes paid of wages indirectly attributed to tourism
Induced effects	Rise in overall economic activity in the locality

data of taxes are combined with the primary data of paid wages to determine the tax revenues received by the local authority.

The second part of the primary data collection, the second business cycle, is targeted at the local suppliers of the companies receiving direct income from tourism. Wholesale, laundry, cleaning and security services are typically in the picture. Theoretically, a third and even more business cycles could prove necessary in highly self-sufficient economies, where the tourism income circulates efficiently. However, the series of studies have proven that the economic ripple effects of tourism taper off steeply, and repercussions even in large tourism localities are thin.

The amount of money spent by tourists is equal to the cash flow received by tourism enterprises. Accordingly, the information produced using the expenditure method matches the data obtained using the income method. The expenditure method examines the case from the tourists' point of view, whereas the income method has the perspective of the tourism enterprises. To use a metaphor, the two methods show both sides of a coin.

The accuracy of the Nordic Model of Tourism draws on a parallel analysis of the data obtained using the expenditure method, on one hand, and the income method, on the other. Theoretically, the data should look identical and give similar results of the economic impact of tourism. In practice, however, some disparity tends to appear that usually arises from the setting of empirical data collections. The data may be flawed in part by a slip of the memory by the respondents or other human error. Tourists may even be unaware of the distribution of their total spending on different product categories, especially in the case of visitors on a package tour.

The analysis of the primary and secondary data leads to a number of matrices presenting the direct, indirect and induced economic contribution of tourism. The topics are summarised in Table 10.5. The data of the tourists' daily and annual consumption illustrate the importance of different types of tourists. It is very helpful for the decision-makers responsible for local tourism development to be able to identify the types of tourists that are most inclined to use local services. These matrices use data from the expenditure method. The data of the income method, in turn, present the total annual receipts by different business lines, the number of tourism-related personnel and salaries. Valuable insight is thus given into the roles of different business lines as recipients of tourism income.

The total annual purchases from local suppliers by different business lines constitute the basis for the calculation of the indirect and induced effects. The total amount of purchases from the suppliers is equal to the indirect income from tourism in the index locality. Secondary data are needed to determine the number of employees attributed to these purchases, as these enterprises are usually unable to self-determine the causal link between the turnover and the number of employees. Secondary data are also used to determine the potential, yet minimal, contribution of tourism at the successive layers of the supply sector. As empirical study of the concept of the induced impact of tourism is highly complex, the induced effects are generally calculated by multiplying the direct and indirect effects of tourism with a general constant, for example 0.10. In other words, it is generalised that, in addition to the direct and indirect effects, tourism invigorates the local economy an additional 10%.

Finally, the net value of tourism to the local authority, for example a municipality, is calculated. The costs of tourism (discussed above) are subtracted from the total of taxes received by the local authority. Taxes are cross-tabulated by types of tourists and by lines of business showing indisputably and in detail the contribution of tourism from the public sector's perspective.

THE NORDIC MODEL OF TOURISM IN FIELD PERFORMANCE

The qualities of the Nordic Model are evaluated in the light of the two studies that the present author was involved with (Pitkänen 1990; Vuoristo and Paajanen, 1991). The empirical findings of the two case studies, Virrat and Espoo, point out the key features of the Nordic Model of Tourism in field performance. The illustration draws on the composite of the studies and design of data collections. First, the two index localities and the courses of the studies are briefly outlined.

The roots of tourism in Virrat, a smallish town in the lake region in central Finland, date back as far as the seventeenth century (Hokkanen, 1979). Virrat, although a somewhat peripheral tourist attraction, is in the running with its beautiful scenery and small-scale tourism activities. Most of the area is rural and covers vast tracts of wilderness and water. Tourism is heavily concentrated in the summer season, although winter activities have also been developed. Family-type resorts, such as farm tourism, cottages for rent and lake cruises, form the core of the tourism services. There is also some business tourism created by local industrial plants. The role of international tourism is modest, but it is there.

The Virrat study was initiated in the autumn of 1988 and commenced in January 1989. The study was financed by the Tourism Office at the City of Virrat. The motivation for the study sprang initially from the local authority, but also from the local entrepreneurs active in tourism. The Nordic Model of Tourism was chosen as the research method allowing for a holistic study into the economic effects of tourism. A comprehensive study of the state and profile of tourism in Virrat was considered indispensable by the City if it was to be able to conduct local tourism development.

The geographical study area consisted of the municipality of Virrat, the northernmost municipality of the Häme province (Figure 10.3) and 1989 was set as the research period. It was decided that the study should be carried out at a high level of detail and accuracy. Accordingly, the empirical data collections were designed to cover all major tourist groups and the businesses that were known to have either direct or indirect links to tourism. Primary data collections were designed for both winter and summer seasons.

The study of tourism in Espoo, initiated by the City of Espoo, followed a similar plan. This exhaustive analysis, also lasting 12 months, was carried out in 1990–91 to give insight into the state and profile of tourism in the second largest city of the country. The city is situated in the most densely populated part of the country, the Helsinki region. This region is marked by an intensive network of economic, transport and cultural activities that cover the neighbouring cities of Helsinki, Espoo, Vantaa, Kauniainen and Kirkkonummi. An immense growth in population and economic life has taken place in the region over the past few decades.

Espoo as a tourism locality constituted an intriguing case. The profile of Espoo as a tourism locality is highly urban, yet flavoured with its rural origins. The local history constitutes an asset in tourism development. For instance, a number of culturally distinct buildings and the 'King's Road' connecting Stockholm and Vyborg have been highly regarded. A scenic coastline and activities based on the natural surroundings form other important inputs in the marketing of Espoo. However, the majority of tourism services, such as conference facilities, use the image of Espoo as a modern and internationally attractive city by the Gulf of Finland.

Although conducted using the same method, the Virrat and Espoo studies had strikingly different results. The differences between the two studies originated from the dissimilarity of the subjects. As illustrated in Table 10.6, Espoo and Virrat differ considerably in size, character and economic structure. The combination of subjects highlights the potential of the Nordic Model of Tourism to lend itself to various kinds of study environments. The method is as apt in a small town as it is in a large and complex city. However,

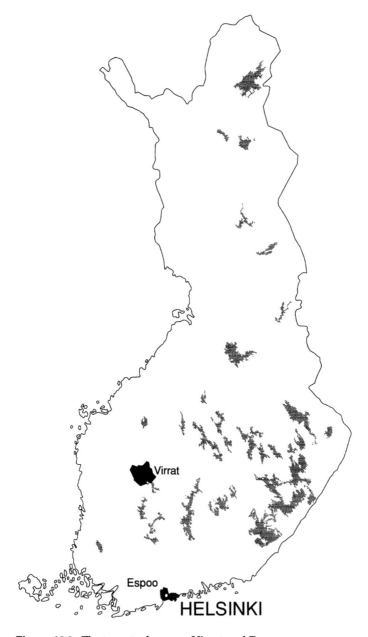

Figure 10.3. The two study areas, Virrat and Espoo

Table 10.6. Virrat and Espoo: municipality profiles

Characteristics	Virrat	Espoo	National average
Resident population	8 879	191 247	11 246
Area (km ^{2})	1 162.7	311.9	699.4
Population/km^2	7.6	613.2	16.8
Degree of urbanisation	50–59.9%	90–100%	80–89.9%
Structure of economy (%)			
agriculture	23.0	0.3	8.6
manufacturing	26.1	16.5	25.3
service	48.3	81.0	63.7

Source: Statistical Yearbook of Finland 1996.

as will be shown below, a large locality presents a number of additional challenges that need to be met precisely in order to attain high accuracy.

The following tables (Tables 10.7–10.10) show how the Nordic Model of Tourism performed in Virrat and Espoo. The aim is to outline the flow of the studies in a nutshell. The intention is to avoid repeating all the details learnt in the studies and to restrict the data to pointing out the critique and recognition that the method gave rise to.

Table 10.7 shows the phases of the empirical data collections that were, despite the dissimilarity of the subjects, to a great extent identical.

Table 10.7. Empirical data collections of the Virrat and Espoo studies

Data collection	Procedure
Expenditure method	
Tourist interviews	Tourists interviewed at major sites and stops Summer and winter samples
Questionnaires at overnight accommodation	Distribution at full coverage: hotels, motels, hostels, camp sites, cottages Summer and winter samples
Questionnaires mailed to households	A sample of local households Early autumn
Questionnaires mailed to non-local holiday cottagers	A sample of non-local residents possessing a second house in the locality Early autumn
Income method	
Business study First cycle	Enterprises directly serving tourists Questionnaires and personal interviews
Business study Second cycle	Suppliers serving enterprises receiving direct income from tourism Questionnaires and personal interviews

Interviewers were recruited and trained for personal interviews. Shopping centres, museums, ski resorts, and other centres of attraction were chosen as sites. Special consideration was shown to motivating visitors to participate in interviews. In Virrat, a lottery was arranged with the cooperation of local enterprises that donated an array of products. The idea was that those interviewed were given a lottery ticket and, if it was a winning ticket, the prizes were personally collected from the local shops. The idea of a lottery was welcomed by the respondents who were, at the same time, drawn to explore the shopping area. In Espoo, an analogous idea was carried out among non-local holiday cottagers.

The empirical data collections were scheduled around the year. Interviews and questionnaires filled in by tourists on site covered both summer and winter seasons. Other questionnaires were mailed soon after the summer to local households and non-locals owning a second house in order to have the most accurate records of visits by friends and relatives (VFR) and cottagers. The business studies among local enterprises were the least sensitive part of the data collection as regards the timing. These data were gradually collected during the study period, as the process entailed careful preparation. As also documented in other studies (e.g., Auvinen, 1965: 22; Kauppila, 1989: 15; Vuoristo and Arajärvi, 1990: 160), entrepreneurs tend to be very reluctant to reveal information about their businesses, even if it is for a good cause.

The flaws of the empirical data collection were, fortunately, largely compensated for by the expertise obtained in dealing with tourists and enterprises during the study period. The data collections in Virrat were generally less complicated because of the smaller size of the area covered. In both studies, personal interviews constituted the most efficient and reliable avenue for obtaining information. However, the tourist interviews in Espoo pointed out a critical flaw that is difficult to overcome. Tourists who had bought a package tour were unable to indicate their total spending and, even less able to divide their spending into different product categories.

Table 10.8 summarises the daily spending and the annual expenditure of each tourist group. The lists sketch the tourist profiles of the localities. In Virrat, boaters were identified as a special group of interest, as their spending appeared different from that of other tourists. Moreover, boaters were taken into consideration by the City, that had recently built harbour services and other infrastructure supporting boat tourism. In Espoo, the day visitors were subdivided into three categories, also because of the dissimilarity of their activities. Most of the visitors at the Vermo trotting racecourse made a short visit but spent a relatively large sum of money. Visitors at the Serena ski resort or water park formed another special group. The daily spending of other day visitors was clearly smaller. The Espoo list does not include

Table 10.8. Daily and annual expenditure of tourists in Virrat and Espoo (expenditure method)

Tourist group	Daily spending FIM/day	Annual expenditure FIM/year (1000)
Virrat		
Tourists in commercial accommodation	123	4 333
Tourists in camping and caravan sites	60	2 015
Boaters	121	382
VFR	56	5 324
Non-local holiday cottagers	59	14 019
Day visitors, tourists passing through	65	16 348
Total	–	42 421
Espoo		
Tourists in commercial accommodation		
(a) business tourists	551*	127 493*
(b) holiday tourists	520*	62 000*
Tourists in camping and caravan sites	72	1 261
VFR	72	120 193
Non-local holiday cottagers	30	11 984
Day visitors		
(a) Vermo trotting racecourse	150	32 298
(b) Serena ski resort and water park	82	4 091
(c) others	45	4 834
Total	–	364 154

*Data based on the income method.

tourists passing through, as it was regarded as being too laborious (and beyond resources) to single out tourists from the other through traffic that is typical of the whole capital region.

The lines of business that were traced as having direct connections to tourism are listed in Table 10.9. The direct income from tourism and the number of tourism-related employees are given as perceived using the income method. The lists are almost identical with the exception that in the Virrat study the state wines and spirits monopoly ALKO was combined with restaurants and cafes. Because of confidentiality regulations individual business data could not be distributed, and the data were to be given in clusters of a minimum of three (today four) enterprises.

A parallel glance at Tables 10.8 and 10.9 highlights the absolute need for symmetry in the use of the expenditure and income methods. The product categories (Table 10.8) introduced to tourists in interviews and questionnaires (expenditure method) need to match the business lines identified using the income method (Table 10.9). Otherwise the two sets of data do not act as counterparts, which undermines the parallel use of the expenditure and income methods. Moreover, these lists of products and business

Table 10.9. Direct effects of tourism on tourism enterprises in Virrat and Espoo: income and employment (income method)

Tourism business line	Income from tourism (1000)	Number of man-year units generated by tourism
Virrat		
Accommodation	4 625	21
Restaurants & ALKO	11 499	15
Groceries	15 992	6
Transport	12 532	36
Retail of textiles	4 311	14
Other retail	6 648	7
Recreation	1 134	5
Other services	2 604	0
Total	59 345	104
Espoo		
Accommodation	155 978	249
Restaurants and cafes	63 860	91
Groceries	42 666	40
Transport	27 365	31
ALKO	4 714	0
Retail of textiles	19 318	10
Other retail	21 140	21
Recreation	56 608	68
Other services	935	3
Total	392 584	513

line categories need to be in accordance with the supporting secondary data.

Table 10.10 combines the sum totals by business lines and determines the inferred tourism income. The conjunction of the expenditure and income methods, introduced by Vuoristo and Arajärvi (1988), provides a means of concluding the total income from tourism, showing the merits and drawbacks met within the course of the study. The inferred tourism income is calculated by evaluating the reliability of the results concerning each business line based on the success of the primary data collections. If both methods seem equally reliable, an arithmetic mean value is calculated. In the event that either the expenditure or the income method proves clearly more reliable with regard to the business line in question, the superior data are chosen as the inferred income.

As shown in Table 10.10, in the Virrat study, the income method was considered more reliable in almost all cases, although the variation between the sums was relatively small (cf. Piirala, 1997: 40). In Espoo, by contrast, the success of the primary data collections was rather more in doubt. The gravest flaw concerns the accommodation sector. The huge gap between the sums is

Table 10.10. Confrontation of the expenditure and income methods: the inferred tourism income (FIM 1000)

Tourism business line	Tourist expenditure	Income from tourism	Inferred tourism income
Virrat			
Accommodation	2 984	4 625	4 625
Restaurants & ALKO	8 749	11 499	11 498
Groceries	11 226	15 992	13 609
Transport	4 602	12 532	12 532
Retail of textiles	4 973	4 311	4 311
Other retail	7 018	6 648	6 648
Recreation	1 745	1 134	1 134
Other services	1 122	2 604	2 604
Total	42 419	59 345	56 961
Espoo			
Accommodation	41 346	155 978	155 978
Restaurants and cafes	63 860	54 024	63 860
Groceries	32 791	52 540	42 666
Transport	23 294	31 435	27 365
ALKO	2 757	6 670	4 714
Retail of textiles	19 318	6 979	19 318
Other retail	19 127	23 153	21 140
Recreation	32 508	56 608	56 608
Other services	14 523	935	935
Total	249 524	388 321	392 584

explained by the inability of the tourists to specify their outgoings. As noted earlier, this was especially the case with tourists on a package tour. Another serious flaw occurred with the expenditure on hair stylists, medical aid, and other personal services. The tourists obviously used this category to enter the purchases that they were unable to specify in detail. Thus, the income method was considered more reliable.

The process of inferring the total income from tourism has proven most helpful. Where the expenditure and income methods are both carried out successfully, the process lends itself to fine adjustment. This was the case with the Virrat study. If there are serious discrepancies, as was the case in Espoo, the process helps the researchers to pull up the weeds and make the necessary corrections. Therefore no single flaw will undermine the study. Moreover, the process of inferring the total income from tourism is a convenient way of identifying the sum total, using the bulk of information that otherwise may seem too complex to comprehend.

Finally, the flux of the economic effects of tourism may be portrayed by cross-tabulating the direct, indirect and induced effects (columns) and the business lines under scrutiny (rows) (cf. Figure 10.1). The summarising

Table 10.11. The economic effects of tourism: summary (FIM 1000)

Business lines	Direct income from tourism	Direct impact on employment and wages (m.y.u.)		Indirect impact on wages	Induced impact on wages	Total impact on wages	Tax revenues
Accommodation	4 625	21	1 368	172	202	2 221	389
Restaurants & ALKO	11 499	15	478	13	41	453	79
Groceries	15 992	6	399	2	107	1 183	207
Transport	12 532	36	1 074	1	41	452	79
Retail of textiles	4 311	14	409	2	41	452	79
Other retail	6 648	7	356	2	36	393	69
Recreation	1 134	5	364	2	37	402	70
Other services	2 604	0	0	0	0	0	0
Total	59 345	104	4 448	192	464	5 104	893

Note: m.y.u. = in man-year units.

matrix is presented (Table 10.11) using the Virrat data. The presentation abstracts the volume and depth of tourism as it contributes to the local economy. In Virrat, tourism generated FIM 59.3 million of direct income and 104 man-year units. Taking into consideration the circulation within the economy, the total amount of tourism-related wages was FIM 5.1 million. For the City, this meant tax revenues of FIM 893 000.

DISCUSSION

This chapter has focused on the Nordic Model of Tourism and its use in two empirical tourism studies in the Finnish environment. The structure of the Nordic Model of Tourism has been outlined. The courses of the two empirical studies have been briefly presented, highlighting the merits and pitfalls of the method in field performance.

The applicability of the Nordic Model to various kinds of study environments has become evident. The method lends itself to localities of different size and qualities. The holism and flexibility of the method has been well acknowledged. The level of accuracy and detail may be accommodated in the available resources, such as time, funds and size of task force. The method is most effective in small and medium-sized localities that have a relatively simple economy and tourist profile. Virrat was an example of this type. However, as shown by the case of Espoo, large localities may entail highly complex tasks that call for ample resources and special caution with regard to the empirical data collections, especially in studies aiming at high levels of detail and accuracy.

The control of the task force over the quality of the data is relatively high. The potential flaws in the use of the Nordic Model of Tourism are attributed to the quality of the primary and secondary data. As the method is relatively cumbersome, the collection of primary data is time-consuming, laborious and costly. This undermines the use of the method in brief surveys. As to the secondary data, the defects attributed to confidentiality regulations, non-availability and delays in providing statistics appear almost unavoidable. To use the expenditure and income methods in the given study environment entails a number of operational solutions such as, for instance, the identification of the target groups and the amount of data collected. Each study carried out using the Nordic Model of Tourism is thus a unique presentation of the state and profile of tourism in that locality. This, however, impairs the intercomparability of the studies.

While recognising the drawbacks of the method, the utility of the Nordic Model of Tourism has still been acknowledged in a number of studies. The design of the study allows for operational solutions, illustrated by the concept of the inferred tourism income, that enhance the success of the study. Due to its infinite flexibility, the model is open for further methodological development.

REFERENCES

Airola, Kristiina, 1985, Matkailun taloudelliset ja työllistävät vaikutukset Turussa vuonna 1984 (Tourism's impact on the economy and on employment in Turku in 1984), *Publications of the Turku School of Economics* C:3. (In Finnish)

Auvinen, Eero, 1965, *Tutkimus Saimaan alueen matkailusta kesällä 1964* (A study on tourism in the Saimaa region in summer 1964), Hämeenlinna: Finnish Tourist Association

Bull, Adrian, 1991, *The economics of travel and tourism*, Melbourne, Singapore

Fletcher, John, Snee, Helena, 1989, Input-output analysis. In Witt, S.F., Moutinho, L., eds, *Tourism management handbook*, Prentice-Hall, Hemel Hempstead, pp. 223–226

Forsberg, Catharina, and Johansson, Ann-Louise, 1980, Undersökning av turism i Falun/Borlänge-region. Del 2. Ekonomiska och sysselsättningsmässiga effekter av turism (A study on tourism in the Falun/Borlänge Region: Part 2: Tourism's impact on the economy and on employment), *University of Falun/Borlänge*, No. 2/80. (In Swedish)

FTB = *Finnish Tourist Board*, 1983, Matkailun tulo- ja työllisyysvaikutukset kunta/aluetasolla: Tutkimusmenetelmä (Tourism's local/regional impact on the economy and on employment: A research method.), A:36. (In Finnish)

FTB, 1984, Turismens effekter på ekonomi och sysselsättning i landskapet Åland (Tourism's impact on the economy and on employment in Ahvenanmaa), A:46, Helsinki. (In Finnish)

Havas, Kristiina, 1991 *Oulun matkailututkimus 1989* (Tourism in Oulu in 1989), mimeo

Hokkanen, Kari, 1979, *Vanhan Ruoveden historia III:I Virrat* (History of Old Ruovesi III:I Virrat), Virtain kaupunki ja seurakunta

Holopainen, Vappu, 1981, Matkailun vaikutukset talouteen ja työllisyyteen Jyväskylässä 1980 (Tourism's impact on the economy and on employment in Jyväskylä in 1980), *University of Jyväskylä. Economic Research Institute of Central Finland*, No. 49

Jyvälä, Kaisa, 1981, Matkailun tulo- ja työllisyysvaikutukset Kuusamon kunnassa (Tourism's impact on the economy and on employment in Kuusamo), *University of Oulu, Research Institute of Northern Finland*, C:37. (In Finnish)

Jyvälä, Kaisa, (1988) Matkailijat ja matkailutulot Lapin läänissä 1985/1986 (Tourists and tourism income in Lapland in 1985/1986), *Finnish Tourist Board* A:61. (In Finnish)

Kauppila, Pekka, 1989, Matkailun taloudelliset ja työllistävät vaikutukset Kuusamon kunnassa (Tourism's impact on the economy and on employment in Kuusamo), *Nordia Publications*, Series B:3, part I. (In Finnish)

Kemppainen, Juha, 1991, Kuusiokuntien matkailun tulo- ja työllisyysselvitys 1990–1991 (Tourism's impact on the economy and on employment in six municipalities in the Vaasa province in 1990–91), *Centre for Tourism Studies* A:32. (In Finnish)

Kettunen, Tarja, 1990, Vaasan kaupungin matkailun tulo- ja työllisyysvaikutukset 1989 (Tourism's impact on the economy and on employment in Vaasa in 1989), *Centre for Tourism Studies* A:17. (In Finnish)

Lankola, Kristiina, 1992, *Turun kaupungin matkailututkimus 1991* (Tourism in Turku in 1991), TKKK Education, Turku, (In Finnish)

Leiper, Neil, 1979, The framework of tourism: towards definition of tourism, tourist and the tourist industry, *Annals of Tourism Research*, 6: 390–407

Leiper, Neil, 1990, Partial industrialization of tourism systems, *Annals of Tourism Research*, 17, 600–605

Leiper, Neil, 1993, Industrial entropy in tourism systems, *Annals of Tourism Research*, 20: 221–226

Malinen, Rauno, 1989, Kuusamon matkailijatutkimus vuonna 1989 (Tourists in Kuusamo in 1989), *Nordia Publications*, Series B, 3, part II. (In Finnish)

Mathieson, Alastair, Wall, Geoffrey, 1989, *Tourism: economic, physical and social impacts*, Longman, Harlow, Essex

Olsson, Roland, 1987, Besöksnäringens regionala effekter på ekonomi och sysselsättning (Tourism's impact on the economy and on employment), *Swedish Tourist Board*, Rapport, 1987: 7. (In Swedish)

Olsson, Roland, 1988, Besöksnäringens regionala effekter på ekonomi och sysselsättning: Manual för automatisk databehandling (Tourism's impact on the economy and on employment: A handbook of a computer application), *Swedish Tourist Board*, Rapport 1988: 5. (In Swedish)

Paajanen, Marja, 1993, The economic impact analysis of tourism: a comparative study of the Nordic Model and the Tourist Economic Model, *Publications of the Helsinki School of Economics and Business Administration*, W-35

Paajanen, Marja, 1994, The economic interaction between tourists and tourism enterprises, *Publications of the Helsinki School of Economics and Business Administration*, B-142

Piirala, Tapani, 1997, Kainuun kesämatkailija 1996 sekä Kainuun matkailun tulo- ja työllisyysselvitys (Tourists, and the impact of tourism on the economy and on employment in Kainuu in summer 1996), *Kainuun matkailun kehittämiskeskus* A:4

Pitkänen, Marja, 1990, *Virtain matkailututkimus 1989* (Tourism in Finland in 1989), City of Virrat, Virrat, (In Finnish)

Raiskinmäki, Marja-Terttu, 1994, *Keuruun matkailututkimus 1993* (Tourism in Keuruu in 1993), City of Keuruu, Keuruu, (In Finnish)

Rosef, Knut, 1981, Turismens effekter på ökonomi og sysselsetting i Bergen (Tourism's impact on the economy and on employment in Bergen), *Norwegian Tourist Board*. (In Norwegian)

Sairanen, Kristiina, 1988a, Savonlinnan kaupungin matkailututkimus 1987 (Tourism in Savonlinna in 1987), *Centre for Tourism Studies* A:1. (In Finnish)

Sairanen, Kristiina, 1988b, Kerimäen kunnan matkailututkimus 1987 (Tourism in Kerimäki in 1987), *Centre for Tourism Studies* A:3. (In Finnish)

Sairanen, Kristiina, 1988c, Punkaharjun kunnan matkailututkimus 1987 (Tourism in Punkaharju in 1987), *Centre for Tourism Studies* A:4. (In Finnish)

Smith, Stephen L.J., 1988, Defining tourism: a supply-side view, *Annals of Tourism Research*, 15: 179–190

Smith, Stephen L.J., 1991, The supply-side definition of tourism: reply to Leiper, *Annals of Tourism Research*, 18: 312–315

Smith, Stephen L.J., 1993, Return to the supply-side, *Annals of Tourism Research*, 20: 226–229

Smith, Stephen L.J., 1995, *Tourism analysis: A handbook*, 2nd edn, Longman, Harlow

SYF 1996 = Statistical Yearbook of Finland, 1996, Statistics Finland, Jyväskylä

Tekoniemi-Selkälä, Teija, Södervall, Reima, 1993, Lapin matkailijat ja matkailutulo 1992/93 (Tourists and tourism income in Lapland in 1992/93), *Centre for Tourism Studies*, A:38

Vuoristo, Kai-Veikko, Arajärvi, Tarja, 1988, Matkailu-Lohja. Lohjan matkailu-tutkimus 1987 (Tourism in Lohja in 1987), *Publications of the Helsinki School of Economics*, D-106

Vuoristo, Kai-Veikko, Arajärvi, Tarja, 1990, Methodological problems of studying local income and employment effects of tourism, *Fennia*, **168**(2): 153–177

Vuoristo, Kai-Veikko, Paajanen, Marja, 1991, Espoon matkailututkimus 1990–91 (Tourism in Espoo in 1990–91), City of Espoo, Espoo

11 Strategic Segmentation: An Empirical Analysis of Tourist Expenditure in Turkey

RAM MUDAMBI AND TOM BAUM

INTRODUCTION

Despite the continued dominance of the mass tourism offering in Europe, North America and the Far East, there are clear indicators that more tailored offerings will be required in the future. Differentiated offers, even within the broad context of what might be called mass tourism, are likely to become increasingly important to a consumer marketplace that is ever more sophisticated in its travel experience and expectations (Ritchie, 1991). Tourism operators have an increasingly complex range of supply options at their disposal which they can use to meet specific tourism needs.

It is, therefore, vital that tourism planners and strategists, at all levels from single operator, through multinational lodging or airline businesses, to those with national or regional responsibilities, are able to use all possible information sources and mechanisms in identifying new market potential but also to understand their existing markets better and maximise the yield from their finite marketing budgets. This chapter presents a way to generate strategic insights from national historic arrivals data by examining tourist expenditures on the basis of demographic variables such as nationality, age and occupation, and behavioural variables such as choice of type of accommodation. A better understanding of expenditure patterns can help to clarify the attractiveness of previously identified tourist segments.

The focus is on a scenario where destinations compete to attract tourists. The management decisions that can be supported by the methodology are those of national and regional tourism boards and of corporate officers with destination-specific responsibilities.

In the context of strategic management (see, for example, Porter, 1985: ch. 7), segmentation analysis can be set up as a sequence of steps, the end

Economic and Management Methods for Tourism and Hospitality Research.
Edited by Thomas Baum and Ram Mudambi © 1999 John Wiley & Sons Ltd.

result of which is the choice of the strategic scope of the enterprise. It is therefore seen as a precursor to the formulation of implementable strategies. The
methodology developed in this chapter focuses specifically on two of the
steps within strategic segmentation analysis, that is, the construction of a
segmentation matrix and the analysis of segment attractiveness or profitability within the overall demand pattern for the product. This does not, in and
of itself, result in identifying success factors or strategic scope, but is an
essential prerequisite for such analysis.

Several other approaches to segmentation are possible. Factor-cluster
segmentation (Kendall, 1980: chs 4 and 10) and neural network approaches
(Eberhard and Dobbins, 1990; Smalz and Conrad, 1994) are only two alternative technical methodologies that may be used. However, the strength of
such methods lies in their ability to identify segments, which is not the principal focus of this chapter. Instead, we use segments drawn up from reviewing practitioner materials with the objective of assessing their validity.
Further, we seek to analyse segment attractiveness.

The literature on strategic segmentation in tourism has developed from
wider analysis of consumer behaviour in areas of discretionary consumption. Early classifications of tourists from which segmentation was derived
were largely conceptual and descriptive and, of these, Cohen (1974), Plog
(1974) and Smith (1977) are perhaps the best known. These approaches were
followed by rather more empirical studies of tourist types and tourist behaviour. Examples in this category include Westvlaams Ekonomisch
Studiebureau (1983, 1986), Shih (1986) and Plog (1987). Indeed, the literature
on segmentation in tourism has grown extensively to incorporate a variety of
empirical approaches as well as conceptual consideration of a number of
demographic, lifestyle and psychographic segmentation bases as well as
combinations of these approaches. The extensive literature in this field is
well reviewed in a number of publications, for example by Moutinho (1982),
Brayley (1993), Mazanec (1994), Vanhove (1995), Lawson (1995) and Weber
(1995). Perhaps the main inadequacy of the approaches which are considered
in this body of literature is that, with the notable exception of Plog, they tend
to consider tourism behaviour in relation to specific tourism product types,
whether it is sun, sea or sand; heritage or cultural experiences; or cruising.

The chapter uses Turkey as a case study for the purposes of analysis.
However, the methodology is universally applicable, provided that reliable
and sufficient data are available for the purpose. The proposed methodology
is merely a specific means of analysing the data in the segmentation matrix,
given an underlying segmentation analysis.

Turkey, however, does provide an interesting case study in itself in that
the tourism industry, to the country, is of relatively recent origin and has wit-
nessed rapid growth in the period since 1980 (Cooper and Ozdil, 1992). Data
collection on all aspects of tourism activity, parallel to this growth, has been

rich and detailed and this facilitated the execution of this study. The period of this analysis also straddles a period of considerable volatility in Turkey's tourism performance, influenced greatly by the European recession and the impact of the Gulf War in 1991. This allows the methodology's robustness to regime changes to be demonstrated to good effect.

STRATEGIC SEGMENTATION

Before proceeding further, it is worthwhile to place our methodology in the context of the overall managerial decision process. In the analysis of inter-regional and international tourist flows, destinations are in competition with one another. While the managers in charge of competition strategies in destinations are often government officials, the management principles that underlie their actions are the same as those for more conventional managers.

Classical segmentation analysis in strategic management proceeds through five steps (Grant 1995):

1. Identification of key segmentation variables and categories;
2. Construction of a segmentation matrix;
3. Analysis of segment attractiveness;
4. Identification of key success factors in each segment;
5. Analysis of attractions of broad versus narrow segment scope

In this chapter, we focus on steps (2) and (3). Our basic premise is the segmentation of tourists first by geographic region and second by identifiable subgroup characteristics, as is standard in the strategic management literature (Mintzberg et al, 1995).[1]

In step (1), we use key segmentation variables drawn from a review of practitioner materials. The primary segmentation variable used by many tourism authorities appears to be country of origin, with visitor characteristics used as secondary variables. Baum (1994) provides some evidence of this for Austria and Ireland. Further evidence can be found for Cyprus in CTO (1993), for Taiwan in Tourism Bureau (1994) and for Singapore in Cheong and Khem (1988).

Step (2) of the analysis involves constructing a segmentation matrix. The primary and secondary segmentation criteria are used to construct a two-dimensional matrix. The quantitative estimation is based on an underlying segmentation matrix as shown in Figure 11.1.

Step (3) involves analysing segment attractiveness. Each cell in this matrix represents a distinct market niche and each has profit potential that can be developed. Analysing the matrix should lead to the identification of those segments where the profit potential is greatest from the manager's perspective. This is the main objective of the current chapter.

		COUNTRY OF ORIGIN				
		1	2	3	4	etc.
VISITOR	1					
	2					
	3					
CHARACTERISTICS	4					
	etc.					

Figure 11.1. The underlying segmentation matrix

Once the attractive segments have been identified, step (4) requires the identification of the key success factors in these segments. Step (5) requires assessing the extent to which synergies exist (implying broad scope) or do not exist (implying narrow scope) between segments. The application of this analysis to the results of the estimation reported in this paper, is the next logical stage in the management decision process. Strategies to most effectively develop the segments identified by the segmentation analysis can now be devised and implemented.

DATA AND METHODOLOGY

Data

The paper uses a data set that was assembled from several sources. The major source is the primary archive of foreign visitor data maintained by the Tourism Board of the Government of Turkey. This archive is generated on the basis of in-depth exit questionnaires filled out by approximately 30% of all departing visitors. The number of respondents rises from 1.24 million in 1988 to 1.54 million in 1993. The archive includes exhaustive figures for tourist expenditure and visitor characteristics, categorised for 33 countries and country-groups. (The countries and country-groups in the data set are reported in Table 11.1, along with tourist arrivals data.) Obviously the identity of individual tourists varies from year to year, as would be the case with any panel of consumers. This is typically argued to be a strength, since individual idiosyncrasies can then be averaged out, sharpening the effects of the measurable components (Cook and Campbell, 1979).

These data are augmented by data taken from the *World Development Report* published by the World Bank and from *International Financial Statistics* published by the IMF. The complete data set is assembled for the years

Table 11.1. Tourist arrivals in Turkey–originating countries and regions

Country	Arrivals					
	1988	1989	1990	1991	1992	1993
Australia	27 724	33 428	40 703	29 442	23 752	25 856
Austria	117 568	155 224	181 049	146 559	190 119	193 244
Belgium	36 779	44 502	56 155	56 245	58 204	68 473
Canada	29 637	31 865	34 912	23 163	13 006	17 469
Denmark	29 467	32 636	34 529	48 534	55 416	67 334
Finland	49 628	69 374	102 182	82 099	87 835	83 805
France	225 685	290 401	304 770	233 675	176 039	212 592
Germany	751 598	900 026	927 804	935 667	1 027 757	951 820
Greece	422 742	273 131	230 695	193 113	108 934	109 678
Holland	80 332	106 827	145 920	154 246	178 122	192 786
Iran	248 057	250 397	266 723	187 842	145 559	117 951
Israel	25 838	52 475	44 862	54 118	41 968	82 902
Italy	138 553	155 643	156 261	119 284	107 376	79 484
Japan	29 044	32 415	40 732	34 601	30 988	37 216
Kuwait	14 402	15 097	10 594	8 810	5 525	5 053
Libya	100 034	52 718	25 006	29 484	10 834	8 462
N'Zealand	8 559	9 246	13 579	8 060	5 489	5 975
Norway	21 035	25 785	36 005	37 646	39 650	49 744
Poland	173 824	178 594	198 628	123 988	106 556	43 230
S'Arabia	32 671	30 867	17 986	21 336	15 947	18 732
Spain	50 546	52 471	65 651	42 532	25 847	34 044
Sweden	39 936	70 358	98 383	87 084	123 469	75 392
Swit'land	64 653	77 638	80 265	71 924	64 383	73 159
Syria	84 606	92 429	113 082	111 006	121 023	121 081
UK	459 370	400 344	332 190	336 176	238 961	341 630
USA	164 854	206 098	206 728	145 545	84 646	120 769
Yugoslavia	294 558	200 645	341 316	215 630	148 856	170 173
O/W.Europe	23 355	31 801	35 711	31 406	34 066	29 325
O/E.Europe	118 842	281 102	866 445	1 375 178	2 578 912	1 712 935
O/Africa	106 858	103 905	68 341	69 897	48 799	56 989
O/W.Asia	123 439	135 704	127 501	111 831	133 627	65 563
O/Asia	30 733	50 831	76 736	40 993	10 040	44 346
S.America	21 636	33 261	37 818	24 241	13 623	21 246

1988 through 1993, yielding a 6-year panel. Overall, the resulting data set is unusually comprehensive.

Methodology

The basic objective of the paper is to estimate a quantitative strategic segmentation model to explain tourist expenditures. The primary segmentation variable is the commonly used one of country of origin, based on the fundamental assumption that expenditure propensities are determined in part by socio-cultural factors that may be proxied (perhaps crudely) by nationality.

The assumption itself is not critical, as we are able to test whether it is supported by the data.

Within the primary panel, ten secondary segmentation variables are used. These variables are drawn to represent a wide variety of visitor characteristics. This part of the analysis is based on the assumption that tourist expenditure is representative of demand. Higher expenditures are associated with a greater demand for tourism services, which may be measured either qualitatively or quantitatively. Thus, both a purchase of a greater number of nights at the same hotel and the purchase of the same number of nights at a higher quality hotel would be registered as an increased demand for hotel services. Expenditure then functions as a common denominator. It is hoped that the estimation results will aid in cataloguing visitor characteristics that are associated with high demand.

The basic model to be estimated follows an established procedure in the literature (see Barten, 1977, and Bakkal, 1991) which suggests that utility-maximising expenditure on a particular good or service may be considered to be a function of three factors: sensitivity to relative prices (P); income (I); identifiable subgroup characteristics (X). The expenditure function may therefore be written as

$$E_i = f[P, I, X] \tag{1}$$

where the three entries in the function may be defined as vectors.

This model is based on an argument involving two theoretical steps. The first is the two-stage maximisation process where it is shown that when the utility function is homothetic and separable, selecting a utility-maximising budget is identical to independently selecting subbudgets for commodity groups (see Blackorby et al, 1970). In other words, subject to these conditions, an individual's subbudget for tourism expenditures may be meaningfully estimated.

The second step involves following Barten (1977) and Phlips (1974) in noting that aggregation bias is empirically unimportant. This means that it is possible to aggregate individual tourism subbudgets to obtain a subbudget for a large group of individuals. In other words, the aggregate tourism subbudgets relating to countries and country-groups may be meaningfully estimated. (It must be borne in mind that the aggregation referred to is the aggregation of *single individuals* into identifiable and usable segments.)

The basic exercise involves the estimation of equation (1). We begin by describing the measures used to represent the variables in the theoretical microeconometric specification. We define the following dependent variable:

TRINC = the total expenditure per visitor day, including a fraction of the travel-related expenditure made outside Turkey.

We define the following regressors:

The price proxy (PR): = the percentage of visitors who stated that price was their main consideration for choosing to visit Turkey (rather than another destination). We expect this variable to capture the relative effects of home country prices, prices in competing destinations and prices in the destination chosen (Turkey). (A detailed discussion of the use of price indices in this context is available in Martin and Witt, 1987).

The Income proxy (INC): = the national per capita income as reported by the World Bank. We expect this variable to capture the relative incomes of tourists from different originating countries.

Identifiable subgroup characteristics: This vector is made up of a number of behavioural and demographic variables (most of them normalised for purposes of comparability), defined as below:

NTS   = the average number of nights spent in Turkey during the visit
HOTL = the percentage of visitors who stayed in registered hotels (rather than guest houses, camp-sites etc.)
WCR   = the percentage of visitors who hold white-collar jobs
SEMP = the percentage of visitors who are self-employed
LTOUR = the percentage of visitors who are 'leisure tourists'
BTOUR = the percentage of visitors who are 'business tourists'
AGE   = the average age of visitors
ISDUM = a dummy taking the value of unity for major originating countries which are Islamic.

ESTIMATION AND RESULTS

Estimation

Since we use the countries and country-groups as our primary segmentation variable, we set up a 33-item panel, with a time series of six observations in each stratum. This gives us a total of 198 observations in the panel. We use ordinary least squares (OLS) as our base-line model. This provides us with null hypothesis estimates. These are generated under the OLS assumption that the primary segmentation variable, namely country of origin, has no statistically significant impact on tourist expenditure, once the other variables in the estimating equation (1) are taken into account.

We estimate two panel data models. These are the fixed effects model (FEM) and the random effects model (REM). As is well known (see, for example, Mundlak, 1978) the FEM is based on the assumption that the differences between the strata are captured by different constant terms, while the REM is based on the assumption that strata each have a different additive variance term. In other words, the FEM assumes that the strata differ in terms of their conditional means, while the REM assumes that the strata differ in terms of their conditional variances.[2]

As the countries differ considerably in terms of visitor arrivals and expenditures, the OLS model was tested for heteroscedasticity. The Breusch–Pagan (1979) test yielded a $\chi^2(10)$ value of 19.7973, which is statistically significant at the 5% level. This suggests that heteroscedasticity is a problem. To deal with this problem, both the OLS and panel models are weighted by the number of visitor arrivals. Reapplying the Breusch–Pagan (1979) test to the weighted models indicates that the hypothesis of homoscedasticity may be accepted.

The estimates are shown in Table 11.2. It may be seen that all models fit the data fairly well. However, when we test for panel, that is, country of origin effects, we find that the OLS model which is based on the absence of such effects, is rejected when tested against either the FEM or REM models.

Table 11.2. Total expenditure per visitor per night: regression results

Regressor	OLS estimates	Panel estimates	
		Fixed effects model (FEM)	Random effects model (REM)
Constant	974.74 (4.12)*	–	1069.1 (4.27)*
PR	−7.458 (4.94)*	−4.172 (2.34)*	−4.347 (2.89)*
INC	11.318 (4.37)*	45.446 (5.12)*	11.868 (3.92)*
NTS	26.243 (5.05)*	−4.116 (0.56)	5.862 (0.97)
HOTL	1.194 (0.74)	23.543 (2.15)*	0.473 (0.33)
WCR	−7.645 (3.55)*	−4.604 (1.44)	−7.178 (2.92)*
SEMP	−1.341 (0.84)	2.200 (3.17)*	2.519 (2.55)*
LTOUR	1.901 (1.14)	3.923 (3.07)*	5.290 (2.90)*
BTOUR	3.590 (1.27)	4.201 (2.69)*	4.060 (1.41)
AGE	−15.191 (3.58)*	−14.762 (2.43)*	−19.239 (4.24)*
ISDUM	85.497 (1.61)	−26.011 (0.00)	39.724 (0.52)
Diagnostics			
Adj. R^2	0.6129	0.7479	0.6952
F statistic	32.186	14.912	–
(d.f.)	(10 187)	(42 155)	
S.E. of residuals	156.116	125.989	139.877
Tests for panel effects			
Likelihood Ratio Test:		122.066	–
FEM vs OLS, $\chi^2(32)$; (p value)		(0.00)	
Breusch–Pagan LM Test:		–	25.688
REM vs OLS, $\chi^2(1)$; (p value)			(0.00)
Hausman Test:		37.903	
FEM vs REM, $\chi^2(10)$; (p value)		(0.00)	

't' statistics shown in parentheses.
* Coefficients significant at the 5% level.

Thus we may conclude that we have fairly strong evidence in favour of country of origin effects on tourist expenditure levels. These tests also suggest that the OLS estimates of significant visitor characteristics may be unreliable.

Next we test the panel models against each other, using a Hausman (1978) test. We find that the REM is conclusively rejected in favour of the FEM. Thus, we may conclude that the country of origin effect expresses itself in terms of mean expenditure, rather than in the form of dispersion. We therefore concentrate on the estimates of visitor characteristics obtained from the FEM in Table 11.2. The actual fixed effects are shown in Table 11.3.

Table 11.3. The fixed effects model (FEM) – estimation of fixed effects

Country	α_i	s.e.(α_i)	T STAT
Australia	564.138	373.232	1.511
Austria	1026.470	309.761	**3.314**
Belgium	435.868	366.458	1.189
Canada	399.790	396.221	1.009
Denmark	816.735	372.122	**2.195**
Finland	702.533	328.822	**2.137**
France	376.003	397.825	0.945
Germany	262.456	408.107	0.643
Greece	806.683	317.007	**2.545**
Holland	447.462	376.451	1.189
Iran	1045.650	243.511	0.004
Israel	1069.040	243.511	0.004
Italy	508.212	380.549	1.335
Japan	1270.650	315.730	**4.024**
Kuwait	551.425	243.511	0.002
Libya	969.384	243.511	0.004
N'Zealand	211.644	418.585	0.506
Norway	1161.370	321.985	**3.607**
Poland	345.074	399.885	0.863
S'Arabia	772.983	386.932	**1.998**
Spain	835.884	353.584	**2.364**
Sweden	1178.870	327.112	**3.604**
Swit'land	1263.260	341.837	**3.696**
Syria	1053.170	243.511	0.004
UK	518.134	393.76	1.316
USA	843.582	290.167	**2.907**
Yugoslavia	498.372	426.253	1.169
O/W.Europe	206.777	383.838	0.539
O/E.Europe	39.626	391.214	0.101
O/Africa	286.083	406.183	0.704
O/W.Asia	−45.43	444.054	−0.102
O/Asia	93.6477	401.069	0.233
S.America	605.658	351.748	**1.722**

Results

We present the most striking results of the estimation below.

- The price proxy is strongly negatively associated with expenditure, lending some support to the idea that the underlying demand is elastic.
- The income proxy is strongly positive, suggesting that the tourists' incomes are representative of the levels in their originating countries. Indeed, income has the strongest effect on expenditure of all the considered visitor characteristics.
- The percentage of visitors staying in registered hotels has a strong and statistically significant effect on expenditure. The magnitude of this effect is second only to that of income.
- The percentage of self-employed visitors has a positive and significant effect on expenditure, albeit a rather small one. The income distribution of self-employed individuals tends to be bi-modal, with a cluster of low-earners and a cluster of high-earners. This suggests that on average, Turkey draws from the high-earner cluster, in contrast to other destinations in the Western Mediterranean.
- Contrary to many claims in the tourism literature, average age is consistently negatively related to expenditure; the effect is strong and significant. This result merits some discussion. The average age of tourists in terms of the primary country of origin segmentation varies from lows in the low 30s to highs in the upper 40s. Thus, the result would seem to indicate that in the case of Turkey, the visitor profiles are dominated by those in their peak earning years and those who are retired, with the former being higher spending. This is in contrast with destinations like Bermuda (Archer, 1992). This has implications for the type of holiday offerings that Turkey should develop and market.
- The percentage of white-collar visitors seems negatively related to expenditure, but the effect is not statistically significant. This variable was inserted to pick up the effects of occupational stability.
- The islamic dummy is insignificant, suggesting that expenditure patterns of visitors from islamic countries are no different from those from non-islamic ones.

Proceeding to the country of origin fixed effects in Table 11.3, we note the following important results.

- Japan and Switzerland seem to have the highest country-specific fixed effects (α_i) in terms of tourist expenditure in Turkey. This reinforces findings from an earlier study of Turkish inbound tourism (Baum and Mudambi, 1996). These countries are followed by Austria, the Scandinavian countries and the US. All of these fixed effects are statistically significant as well. This

means that the tourists from these countries have a significantly higher mean spend in Turkey. Promotional efforts in these countries are likely to yield the greatest return.
• Virtually all large fixed effects are significant. Most of the smaller fixed effects are not. This reflects stability in the overall conditional variance, as would be expected in the FEM, that is, the variability of mean spend is roughly the same for tourists from all originating countries. An exception is Libya, which has a large fixed effect which is not statistically significant. Examining the arrivals data in Table 11.1, this may be traced to the steep decline in Libyan tourist arrivals over the period covered in the sample.

CONCLUSIONS

The objective of this chapter is to illustrate a methodology for analysing the attractiveness of important segments in a country or region's inbound tourist market. While the particular data set used pertains to Turkey, the methodology, in principal, should be applicable to any destination.

The methodology involves setting up a panel data set with originating countries or areas as the primary segmentation variable and then using various visitor characteristics as secondary variables. The precise choice of originating regions or countries and the considered visitor characteristics will depend on the destination chosen and the availability of data. The basic methodology is fairly flexible in this respect. In other words, the construction of the segmentation matrix in Figure 11.1 can be adapted to any destination.

We are able to pinpoint a number of originating countries as important for Turkey in terms of the average daily spend. We are also able to point out some segments, within these countries and country-groups, which are particularly valuable, such as the self-employed, those in the 30–45 age group and those choosing registered hotel accommodation.

We should note that strategic segmentation, even when complete, only provides directional guidance for the manager. For the successful implementation of a given segmenting strategy, the use of more micro level data is necessary. Thus, strategic segmentation based on the methodology described in this chapter must be seen as a precursor to conventional segmentation analysis carried out at the operational level.

Finally, we should contrast our results with the results with those reported in Baum and Mudambi (1996). This earlier work used a smaller data set, relating only to 1989 and 1990. It also used a simultaneous equation estimating procedure, as opposed to the panel approach used here. Our results here reinforce many of the findings of this earlier study. In particular, we find that Japan and Switzerland emerge as important originating markets for Turkey. However, with our richer data set, we are able to uncover several more important originating markets. Further, the Islamic dummy was found to be extremely important in the earlier study. This was primarily based on the data from three countries: Saudi Arabia, Libya and Kuwait. In the post-1990 world, all three have been hard hit by the declining world price of oil. This has caused a considerable decline in the per capita income in Saudi Arabia. In addition, Libya has been affected by sanctions in the wake of the Gulf War, which has also had an impact on Kuwaiti outbound tourism.

As with any statistical technique, the main limitation of this technique is the availability of reliable data. This problem becomes acute in many developing countries, where tourism promotional budgets are small and data is scarce. Further, even when data is available, it will tend to be collected to reflect current tourist flows. For example, in the case of Turkey, all visitors from South America are lumped into a single category, so assessing the attractiveness of the different originating countries on the continent cannot be carried out.

A fruitful avenue for further research would be to proceed from the current results on attractive segments to identifying success factors in individual segments. The next objective would be to address the question of strategic scope in the context of maintaining and enhancing tourist flows.

NOTES

1. This analysis differs from conventional market segmentation analysis only in terms of emphasis. Since the analysis is strategic, the exercise is aimed at identifying success factors and determination of strategic posture (broad versus narrow scope). In contrast, conventional market segmentation analysis is more interested in using the results of the exercise in coming up with a successful marketing plan. Thus, strategic segmentation often has a more macro focus than conventional segmentation analysis.
2. The estimation of the FEM merely involves estimating a partitioned OLS model. Estimation of the REM requires using two step Feasible Generalised Least Squares (FGLS). See Greene (1993).

ACKNOWLEDGEMENTS

We acknowledge the assistance of the Ministry of Tourism, Republic of Turkey, in providing us with the data on which this study is based. We should like to thank Chekitan Dev, Chris Paul, seminar participants at the University of Kent at Canterbury, Cornell University, Purdue University, the Academy of International Business (AIB) meetings at Aston University and at the CHRIE meetings in Washington DC, as well as three anonymous referees for many helpful comments. The usual disclaimer applies.

REFERENCES

Archer, B., 1992, *The economic impact of tourism in Bermuda, 1991*, Department of Tourism, Bermuda, Hamilton

Bakkal, I., 1991, Characteristics of West German demand for international tourism in the Northern Mediterranean region, *Applied Economics*, **23**: 295–304

Barten, A.P., 1977, The system of consumer demand functions approach: a review, *Econometrica*, **45**: 27–51

Baum, T., 1994, The development and implementation of national tourism policies. *Tourism Management*, **15**(3): 185–192

Baum, T., Mudambi, R., 1996, A country-of-origin analysis of tourist expenditure: the case of Turkey, *Tourism Economics*, 2(2): 137–149

Blackorby, C., Lady, G., Nissen, D., Russell, R., 1970, Homothetic separability and consumer budgeting, *Econometrica*, **38**: 468–472

Brayley, R.E., 1993, Psychographic segmentation. In Khan, M., Olsen, M., Var, T., eds, *VNR's encyclopedia of hospitality and tourism*. Van Nostrand Reinhold, New York, pp. 902–909

Breusch, T., Pagan, A., 1979, A simple test for heteroscedasticity and random coefficient variation, *Econometrica*, **47**: 1287–1294

Cheong, W.K., Khem, G.S., 1988, Strategies for tourism in Singapore, *Long Range Planning*, 21(4): 36–44

Cohen, E., 1974, Who is a tourist: a conceptual clarification, *Sociological Review*, **39**: 164–182

Cook, T.D., Campbell, D.T., 1979, *Quasi-experimentation: design and analysis issues for field setting*, Rand McNally, Chicago

Cooper, C.P., Ozdil, I., 1992, From mass to 'responsible' tourism: the Turkish experience, *Tourism Management*, 13(4): 377–386

Cyprus Tourism Office, 1993, *Tourism in Cyprus*, CTO, Larnaca

Eberhard, R.C., Dobbins, R.W., 1990, *Neural network PC tools: a practical guide*, Academic Press, New York

Grant, R.M., 1995 *Contemporary strategy analysis: concepts, techniques, applications*, 2nd edn, Blackwell, Oxford

Greene, W., 1993, *Econometric analysis*, 2nd edn, Macmillan, New York

Hausman, J., 1978, Specification tests in econometrics. *Econometrica*, **46**: 1251–1271

Kendall, M., 1980, *Multivariate analysis*, Charles Griffin, London

Lawson, R., 1995, Demographic segmentation. In Witt, S.F., Moutinho, L., eds, *Tourism marketing and management handbook*, Prentice-Hall, Hemel Hempstead, pp. 306–315

Martin, C., Witt, S.F., 1987, Tourism demand forecasting models – choice of an appropriate variable to represent tourists' cost of living. *Tourism Management*, **8**(3) (September): 233–246

Mazanec, J.A., 1994, Segmenting travel markets, Part 2 of Teare, R., Mazanec, J.A., Crawford-Welch, S., Calver, S., *Marketing in hospitality and tourism*, Cassell, London

Mintzberg, H., Quinn, J.B., Ghoshal, S., 1995, *The strategy process*, Prentice-Hall, Hemel Hempstead

Moutinho, L., 1982, *An investigation of vacation tourist behaviour*, unpublished PhD thesis, University of Sheffield

Mundlak, Y., 1978, On the pooling of time series and cross sectional data, *Econometrica*, **46**: 69–86

Philps, L., 1974, *Applied consumption analysis*, North-Holland, Amsterdam

Plog, S., 1974, Why destination areas rise and fall in popularity, *Cornell Hotel and Restaurant Administration Quarterly*, **14**(4): 55–58

Plog, S., 1987, Understanding psychographics in tourism research. In Ritchie, J.R.B., Goeldner, C.R., eds, *Travel, tourism and hospitality research: a handbook for managers and researchers*, John Wiley, New York, pp. 203–213

Porter, M.E., 1985 *Competitive advantage*, Free Press, New York

Ritchie, J.R.B., 1991, Global tourism policy issues: an agenda for the 1990s. In Hawkins, D.E., Ritchie, J.R.B. eds, *World travel and tourism review*, Vol. 1, CABI, Wallingford, Oxon

Shih, D., 1986, VALS as a tool of tourism market research: the Pennsylvania experience, *Journal of Travel Research*, 24(3): 2–11

Smalz, D., Conrad, J., 1994, Combining evolution with credit apportionment: a new learning algorithm for neural networks, *Neural Networks*, 7(1): 341–351

Smith, V., 1977, *Hosts and guests*, University of Pennsylvania Press, Philadelphia

Tourism Bureau, 1994, *Report on tourism statistics*, Ministry of Transport and Communications, Taipei

Vanhove, N., 1995, Market segmentation. In Witt, S.F., Moutinho, L., eds, *Tourism marketing and management handbook*, Prentice-Hall, Hemel Hempstead, pp. 295–305

Weber, S., 1995, Psychographic segmentation. In Witt, S.F., Moutinho, L., eds, *Tourism marketing and management handbook*, Prentice-Hall, Hemel Hempstead, pp. 316–324

Westvlaams Ekonomisch Studiebureau, 1983, *Toeristische gedragingen en attidues van de Belgische bevolking in 1982*, WES, Brussels

Westvlaams Ekonomisch Studiebureau, 1986, Les Belges en vacances. Comportments et attitudes en 1985, Vol. 5: *Typologie du style de vacances et de vie des Belges*, WES, Brussels

12 The Economic Aspects of Location Marketing

STEPHEN WANHILL

INTRODUCTION

With tourism designated to be one of the major economic 'drivers' in the next century (Boskin, 1996), the world-wide significance of the industry as a mechanism for economic development has meant that it is an investment opportunity that few governments can afford to ignore. However, defining a tourist's journey, whether for leisure or business purposes, is quite complex. The tourist trip has a number of characteristics, namely:

- The trip is not a single product
- It is made up of components supplied by a variety of organisations with different objectives and different economic structures
- Success is the delivering of the right mix of components to satisfy the demands of the visitor
- This delivery requires coordination and cooperation

From this, it may be seen that tourism is a multifaceted product: it includes accommodation, transport, restaurants, shopping facilities, attractions, entertainment, public infrastructure support and the general way of life of the host community. Thus, the essence of successful tourism development is a partnership between the various stakeholders in the activity of tourism to satisfy the requirement to provide a balanced range of facilities to meet the demands of visitors in a sustainable way. Where the line is drawn in this partnership depends on the prevailing economic, political and social policies of the country.

The private sector may have many reasons for investing in tourism: on the one hand, there are foreign tour operators and leisure companies always looking to reap the benefits from the appeal of a new and exciting destination being placed onto the international travel market, while on the other, there

Economic and Management Methods for Tourism and Hospitality Research.
Edited by Thomas Baum and Ram Mudambi © 1999 John Wiley & Sons Ltd.

are many attractions at tourist destinations that have grown out of their owner's special interest or hobby. But in the long run, private operators must be concerned with the viability of their investments through generating an ample surplus to sustain the capital employed. As a rule, the greater the importance of tourism to a country's economy the greater is the involvement of the public sector and the stimulus the government is prepared to give to attract inward investment, to the point of having a government ministry with sole responsibility for tourism. It is often the case that the planning powers with respect to tourism are devolved to local government, while the executive arm of government is transferred to a quasi-public body in the form of the National Tourist Office (NTO).

MARKET FAILURE

The case for public sector involvement in tourism rests on concepts of market failure, namely that those who argue for the market mechanism as the sole arbiter in the allocation of resources for tourism are ignoring the lessons of history and are grossly over-simplifying the heterogeneous nature of the product. The early growth of the seaside resorts during the latter half of the nineteenth century, as, for example, in the United Kingdom, was the result of a partnership between the public and private sectors (Cooper and Jackson, 1989: Cooper, 1992). The local authorities invested in the promenades, piers, gardens and so on, while the private sector developed the revenue-earning activities which enhanced the income of the area and in turn increased property tax receipts for the authorities.

Embodied in the tourist product are goods and services which are unlikely to be provided in sufficient quantity by the market mechanism. The market fails because of the existence of items within the tourist product that everyone can enjoy in common and that are equally available to all, which implies non-rivalry in consumption. These are public goods; their principal feature is that they are non-excludable, due to the lack of, or incompleteness of, property rights. If the good or service is to be provided at all, it may be consumed by everybody without exception, and without charge at the point of use. There are also merit goods, whose consumption the state wishes to encourage because they yield wider benefits that cannot be retained by private businesses themselves and would lead, therefore, to underprovision. The upshot is that the single-minded pursuit of private profit opportunities within tourism may be self-defeating, as many older resorts have found to their cost (Plog, 1973). The outcome may not be the integrated tourism development which distils the essence of the country in its design, but a rather crowded, overbuilt and placeless environment with polluted beaches, that is totally out of keeping with the original objectives set by the country's tourism policy. For example, the major hotel developments that took place in the resorts of southern Spain during the 1960s and early 1970s were completed under laissez-faire expansionism with little consideration given to planning or control. In general, the public infrastructure was overloaded and, since the second half of the 1980s, there has been a continual programme to correct this imbalance and to refurbish the resort centres to give more 'green' space in the form of parks and gardens.

TOURISM POLICY

The precise nature of a country's stance on tourism investment is determined by the kind of development the government is looking for and what role it envisages for the private entrepreneur. In the past, most of the emphasis of Eastern European countries was on social tourism which allowed the population to benefit from subsidised holidays through workers' organisations and central government provision. Currency movements were arranged on a country to country basis through the form of bilateral swaps. The success criteria were based on visitor numbers and most tourist facilities were heavily subsidised. This has now changed, and the influx of Western visitors, as for example in Hungary, has tended to price Eastern European tourists out of the market. African countries have recognised the importance of tourism for conservation. By giving wildlife an economic value, funds are generated to support game reserves, preserve endangered species and help eradicate poaching. Many Caribbean countries have strong views about the wisdom of developing casinos for tourists, because of the possibility of criminal involvement and also on moral grounds.

In most cases, economics forms the basis of tourism development plans. Within this framework there are three objectives which tend to be given the central position:

- Employment creation through spreading the benefits of tourism, both direct and indirect, to as many of the host population as possible
- Foreign exchange earnings to ensure a sound Balance of Payments
- Regional development, notably in peripheral areas which, by their very nature, are attractive to tourists

It is important that governments should not set objectives that may seriously conflict with each other. Too often governments talk of tourism quality yet measure performance in terms of numbers. Common examples of policy objectives which are most likely to be at variance with each other are:

- Maximising foreign exchange earnings versus actions to encourage the regional dispersion of overseas visitors

- Attracting the high-spend tourist market versus policies to continually expand visitor numbers
- Maximising job creation through generating volume tourist flows versus conservation of the environment and heritage
- Community tourism development versus mass tourism

Nevertheless, it must be pointed out that it is no longer considered acceptable in political terms that these objectives should be achieved at a cost to the environment or by adversely affecting the host community. Yet the question of the environment is a difficult one to maintain when it threatens to be a drag on the economy in matters of employment creation. The implementation of policy therefore becomes a process of maintaining the balance between the various objectives as opposed to trying to maximise any single one. Legislation and investment support given by governments for tourism developments are the instruments used to realise the balance of objectives set by the country's tourism policy.

INVESTMENT STRATEGY

To realise the objectives of the development plan governments have to put forward an investment policy which is conducive to developers and investors. Where the social rate of return to tourism projects is greater than the assigned public sector discount rate, but private profit rates are inadequate, governments will need to give financial incentives to investors to encourage the desired pattern of tourism development. The extreme case is where governments themselves set up a Tourist Development Corporation (TDC) and invest directly, perhaps up to 100% ownership in revenue-earning activities such as hotels which are traditionally regarded as the preserve of the private sector. Instances around the world include Egypt, India, New Zealand, Malaysia, Mexico and many African countries. For example, tourism in Mexico began as a totally private sector activity. Its growth was limited in size (largely in the area of Acapulco), the product on offer was generally poor and developments were unplanned. To counteract this, the Government of Mexico, in 1974, created FONATUR for the purpose of developing resorts, and funded the organisation from oil revenues and World Bank loans. Apart from trying to regulate development, the principal reasons for state involvement were:

- Realising potential demand by increasing the number of resorts
- Generating foreign exchange
- Creating employment
- Regional development, in particular moving the jobless from Mexico City to the new resorts and raising regional GDP

FONATUR developed and consolidated six regional resorts, attracting a wide range of international investors. The Government gives FONATUR the development land it requires without charge, the resources to develop a Master Plan and the money to construct the necessary infrastructure, including hotel building. Once complete, the investment is sold to the private sector. The terms for private sector projects are generous: loans for up to 50% of the capital investment, over a period of 15 years. The 'flagship' resort was Cancun on Mexico's Caribbean coast, but this is now mature and issues have arisen about spillover developments outside the original zone and adverse impacts on the environment.

In theory, once the resort has been built, the TDC's function ceases and the assets are transferred to the private sector (at a price) and the local authority. This is the general trend in market-orientated economies, where the rising trend towards greater economic freedom that gathered momentum during the 1980s, led states increasingly to divest themselves of trading operations which could be undertaken by the commercial sector. But in countries where there is a strong degree of central planning, the TDC often maintains an operational role in running hotels and tours.

The counter to increasing market power has been the growing concern for the environment and the concept of sustainable tourism. Given that tourist movements will increase both nationally and internationally, there will be a need for more regulation and improved management of tourism resources to prevent environmental degradation. The current approach is not to reverse the market changes that have taken place, a policy which would now be difficult to implement, as the increasing globalisation of economic activity has reduced the power of national governments to control their destinies, but rather to move towards a more pragmatic approach to intervention and regulation, with an emphasis on international collaboration.

STRUCTURE OF INVESTMENT INCENTIVES

Early work by Bodlender (1982) and Jenkins (1982), and again by Bodlender and Ward (1987), considered the variety of incentives that were available in tourism and made it possible to draw a broad classification along the following lines (Wanhill,1994):

- Financial incentives
- Reduction in operating costs
- Reduction in capital costs
- Investment security

Bloom and Mostert (1995) drew a distinction between incentives that are financial, which may or may not yield cash flow advantages to the business,

Table 12.1. Investment incentives in the European Union tourism industry

Country and tourism	Special to hotels Capital	Financial incentives Operating		Investment security
Austria	Yes, more favourable than manufacturing	Grants and soft loans	Reduced VAT	State loan guarantees
Belgium	Yes	Grants and soft loans	Indirect and direct tax reductions	
Denmark	Yes	Grants		
Finland	No, general schemes only, save for VAT		Reduced VAT	
France	Yes, manufacturing similarly provided for if to do with regional development	Grants and soft loans	Indirect tax exemptions/reductions, special depreciation allowances	
Germany	No, general schemes only			
Greece	Yes, wide range of incentives for tourism	Grants, soft loans and interest rate subsidies	Indirect and direct tax exemptions/reductions, special depreciation allowances	
Ireland	Yes	Grants	Special depreciation allowances	

Italy	Yes	Grants and soft loans	Indirect and direct tax exemptions/reductions, special depreciation allowances
Luxembourg	Yes	Grants	Indirect and direct tax exemptions/reductions Reduced VAT
Netherlands	Yes	Grants and soft loans	
Portugal	Yes, tourism particularly favoured	Soft loans and interest rate subsidies	Indirect and direct tax exemptions/reductions, special depreciation allowances
Spain	Yes	Soft loans principal form of aid but grants also available	Indirect tax exemption
Sweden	Yes, but only for regional development	Grants and soft loans	Reduced VAT
UK	Yes, but only in parts of the UK	Grants principal form of aid; occasionally soft loans	

Source: NTOs and industry departments of Member States

and incentives that are purely fiscal measures. The point here is that in less developed countries (LDCs), due to government budget constraints, benefits in kind, such as site provision at minimal cost, and permissive taxation rules are more likely to prevail than cash grants or 'soft' (cheap) loans, since they exert less pressure on treasury finances. Considerations of risk are also crucial, as pointed out by Baum and Mudambi (1996).

In this chapter, the earlier classification will be used and, as an example, an overview of investment incentives within the European Union (EU) in accordance with this grouping is presented in Table 12.1. It appears that all EU countries provide incentives for inward investment, but not all make any special provision for hotels and tourism and, as a rule, Southern European countries, with their greater dependence on tourism, exhibit more generosity in the terms and the rates at which they support tourist developments. Investment security is not usually questioned within the EU, but in other countries, political and economic uncertainty and a deficient legal framework, particularly in respect of the protection of private property, for example, the lack of bankruptcy laws or provisions against expropriation or nationalisation, are among the main obstacles perceived by investors.

It is to be noted, that over and above the investment support offered separately by the governments of the Union, there is the Pan-European programme of regional aid made available to Member States through the Community's Structural Funds, with the objectives of improving economic convergence and ensuring a better spread of economic activities throughout the territories located within the boundaries of the Union. With the adoption of the Single European Act (1987), with the intention to create one market in Europe and a single currency, there is a commitment by the EU to promote economic and social cohesion through actions to reduce regional disparities and the 1992 Treaty of Maastricht acknowledged, for the first time, the role of tourism in these actions.

Financial incentives

The objective of financial incentives is to improve returns to capital so as to ensure that market potential, which is attractive to developers and investors, may be turned into financially sound projects. Where there is obvious commercial profit potential, the government may only be required to demonstrate a commitment to tourism by, say, marketing and promoting the region, particularly abroad, and giving advice and information to prospective developers. Such circumstances occurred in Bermuda during the early 1970s and so, in order to prevent overexploitation of the tourism resources, the Bermuda Government imposed a moratorium on large hotel building (Archer and Wanhill, 1980).

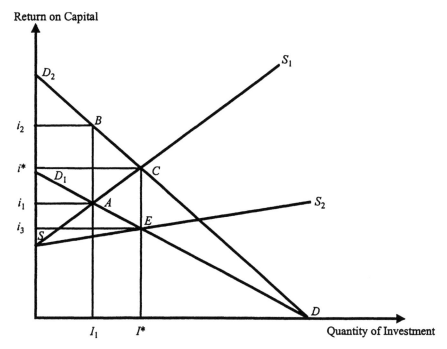

Figure 12.1. Economics of financial incentives

The impact of financial incentives on the amount of investment is illustrated in Figure 12.1. The schedule SS_1 represents the supply of investible funds in the first instance, while D_1D is the schedule of returns to capital employed. D_1D slopes downwards from left to right as more and more investment opportunities are taken up – the declining marginal efficiency of investment. In the initial situation, equilibrium is at A with the amount of investment being I_1 and the internal rate of return i_1. Conditions of market failure imply that the community benefits from tourism investment are not entirely captured in the demand function D_1D. Optimal economic efficiency is where the demand function that includes these externalities D_2D, intersects the supply curve at I^*, yielding a return i^*. To achieve this, the government implements a range of financial incentives which have the effect of raising the private rate of return per unit of capital towards the higher economic rate of return (or social rate, if issues related to the distribution of income are taken into account), by moving the marginal efficiency of investment schedule to D_2D. At i^*, the amount of government subsidy to induce entrepreneurs to invest I^* is the area $i^*CE\,i_3$, and the effective rate of subsidy, say s, is $(i^* - i_3)/i_3$, which implies that $i^* = (1 + s)i_3$ and the total subsidy is sI^*. The private opportunity cost of the investment funds is the area under the supply curve, I_1 AC I^*, while the public willingness-to-pay for correcting the externality is the area I_1 BC I^*: subtracting the two areas gives a net gain represented by the area ABC.

If the amount of investible funds available for tourism is limited at I_1, then the impact of incentives serves merely to raise the return to investors by raising the equilibrium point to B. The loss to the government treasury is the area i_1 AB i_2, which equals the gain to private investors and there is no net economic gain to the community. There is no doubt that many countries have been forced, by competitive pressures to obtain foreign investment, into situations that are similar to those above. Countries can become trapped in a bidding process to secure clients and, as a result, the variety of financial incentives multiplies together with an escalation of the effective rate of subsidy, without evaluating their necessity or their true cost to the economy.

The alternative to stimulating the demand is to increase the supply of investible funds. In Figure 12.1, this is shown by a shift in the supply function to $S\ S_2$, which reduces the cost of capital to the private sector, thus permitting the marginal project to earn an internal rate of return of i_3, and generating the optimal level of investment I^*. Typically, governments attempt to do this by establishing Investment Banks, arranging special credit facilities or, as noted above, constituting TDCs. The economic rationale for this is that governments are usually able to borrow at lower rates than the private sector, since they have ultimate recourse to taxation to cover their debts. In the case of LDCs, finance may be obtained from international banks and multinational aid agencies on favourable terms. The counter arguments to adopting supply-side investment strategies are twofold: first, there is concern that government actions should not displace or 'crowd-out' capital funds from other private investments, which could do equally as well, and second, the wider objectives of governments may generate institutional inefficiencies (and in some cases corruption) in the allocation of investment funds, which will frustrate progress towards I^*. These arguments have found expression in macroeconomic policy through restrictions on government borrowing and the privatisation of state enterprises, but equally beg the question as to the extent to which existing capital market mechanisms are suitable for achieving tourism policy objectives. In practical terms, the implementation of financial incentives is often a combination of demand and supply initiatives.

It is important to note that there are frequent instances where it is gross uncertainty, as in times of recession, rather than limited potential that prevents the private sector investing. In such situations, the 'crowding-out' thesis ceases to hold and the principal role of government intervention is to act as a catalyst to give confidence to investors. Thus public funds are able to lever in private money by nature of the government's commitment to tourism and enable the market potential of an area to be realised.

Capital cost reductions

Incentives to reduce capital costs may include:

- Capital grants
- 'Soft' loans
- Equity participation
- Provision of infrastructure
- Provision of land on concessional terms
- Tariff exemption on construction material.

Capital grants are cash payments which have an immediate impact on the funding of the project as do matching benefits in kind, such as the provision of land or facilities. They are usually preferred by investors because they are one-off transactions involving no further commitment and therefore risk free. From the standpoint of the authorities they are relatively easy to administer.

Soft loans are funds which are provided on preferential terms. At their most simple they may be the granting of interest rate relief on commercial loans. Beyond this the government will normally have to put aside loan funds and create a development agency to administer them. World-wide, the common features of most soft loans relate to generous interest rate terms, extended repayment periods, creative patterns of repayment and usually some restriction of the debt/equity mix so as to ensure that the project is not too highly geared in terms of loan finance. Too much loan capital in relation to owner's funds makes the project vulnerable to downturns in the market. In some instances loans may be tied to specific sources of supply; this is very common in country to country (bilateral) aid programmes. Creative repayment patterns are methods designed to counter the risk profile of the project or the nature of the cash flow over the project's life. Thus a tourist project, such as an attraction, which may be particularly vulnerable in its early stages, may be given a moratorium on all capital repayments, and sometimes interest, for several years. Alternatively, a hotel in which the greater part of the cash flow accrues in the second half of the loan term may be granted 'balloon' financing in which the principal is paid back towards the end of the term so as to ensure greater freedom of operation during the initial years of the investment.

Bodlender and Ward (1987) point out that providing loan funds for tourism is considered often to be more acceptable politically than the provision of grants. The argument in favour of loans rests on the fact that the funds will be recycled and the cost to the government will only be the preference element. This is not a rational argument, as all incentives have a grant element, so it is always possible under conditions of reasonable certainty to prepare a loan scheme which will bestow exactly the same present worth as a cash grant and vice versa.

Consider a soft loan plan whereby a potential investor is offered a loan L for T years on concessionary terms. The latter are a moratorium or 'grace' period for m years followed by a straightforward mortgage repayment at a preferential interest rate of $p\%$ per annum for the remaining years of the loan. Under this scheme the grant element G is the difference between the initial value of the loan L and the present value of the repayment plan. Mathematically this is

$$G = L - \left[\frac{L(CRF)}{(1+r)^{m+1}} + \dots \quad \dots + \frac{L(CRF)}{(1+r)^{T}} \right] \qquad (1)$$

where

$$CRF = \text{the Capital Recovery Factor at } p\% \text{ for } T - m \text{ years}$$
$$= p(1+p)^{T-m}/[(1+p)^{T-m} - 1)]$$
$$r = \text{the commercial cost of capital.}$$

The grant element may be further enhanced if inflation is not adequately accounted for in the repayment plan. G may also be interpreted as a reduction in the cost of capital to the project which serves to raise the internal rate of return. The true cost of capital may be found by calculating that value of r for which $G = 0$. Similarly, equation (1) may be used to calculate the benefit of inter-country loans given as part of an aid programme. Where the loan is tied to the donor country's suppliers it is necessary to adjust for the real value of L. If imports from the donor country cost on average $q\%$ more than world prices, then the real value of L is $L/(1+q)$, thus serving to lower the value of G, other things being equal.

In a world of uncertainty the grant is riskless, while the loan plan becomes part of the risk environment of the project. Any risk premium attached to this environment will differ from project to project, so that the equivalence of the preferential element of the loan and the capital grant can no longer be assured. The instance under which the loan is chosen in preference to the grant would correspond to the situation where the investor is unable to raise the capital funds over and above the grant from elsewhere. This raises the question as to the cause of the inability to secure funds: it may be due to the size of the project raising matters connected with the security of the investment and then it is up to the government to give the necessary guarantees.

Equity participation involves the public sector investing in the commercial aspects of tourism development with the private sector. The case of TDCs has already been referred to, but there are also government sponsored development or investment banks which have the ability to buy equity in a project. As the objective is frequently the encouragement of the private sector, then there are usually restrictions on how much of the equity in a single project such banks can hold (varies from minimal to 30%), with arrangements for selling after 8–10 years, once the project has reached financial stability.

Perhaps more than any other industry, the development of tourism involves the exploitation of real estate. In many countries, the state owns considerable tracts of land and by providing sites on concessional terms the government may be able to attract the investors which best match its tourism policy objectives. The worth of such sites to investors is reinforced by the provision of the necessary construction works, such as access roads, and utilities (water and energy supplies).

Operating cost reductions

To improve operating viability governments may offer:

- Direct and indirect tax exemptions or reductions
- A labour or training subsidy
- Subsidised tariffs on key inputs such as energy
- Special depreciation allowances
- Double taxation or unilateral relief

Indirect tax exemptions and reductions cover such items as waivers on import duties for materials and supplies, exemption or reductions in relation to property taxes, licences and Value Added Tax (VAT). The latter is a tax on labour and payments for capital in use, whether capital is in the form of debt or equity (Wanhill, 1995). Concessions in respect of import duties and other fees are common incentives offered to foreign investors.

As VAT extends itself around the world as the principal form of indirect taxation, then pressure grows to harmonise rates between nations for global industries such as tourism, on the grounds of international competitiveness. A study prepared for the British Tourist Authority (BTA, 1995) identified the UK as having one of the highest VAT rates in Europe. This may be observed from Table 12.2, which compares rates across Member States in the EU according to the components of the tourist product (Browne, 1996). Denmark levies the highest rate of VAT on tourism, a matter which is of continual concern to the Danish tourist industry, due to the belief that this is a key factor in the industry's poor financial performance in a very competitive market. VAT rates also vary within the different categories according to country. Thus for example, the Nordic countries zero rate cultural attractions. Table 12.3 draws a comparison between the standard rates levied by member states and those imposed on the accommodation sector. Only three states, Denmark, Germany and UK, apply the standard rate to this sector, which has invoked protests

Table 12.2. VAT in the European Union tourism industry

Country	Accommodation (%)	Meals Out (%)	Car Rental (%)	Admission: Fun Park (%)	Admission: Museum (%)
Austria	10	10	10	10	10
Belgium	6	21	21	6	0
Denmark	25	25	25	25	0
Finland	6	22	22	6	0
France	5.5	18.6	5.5	0	5.5
Germany	15	15	15	15	0
Greece	8	8	18	8	8
Ireland	12.5	12.5	Exempt	Exempt	Exempt
Italy	10	10	19	19	10
Luxembourg	3	3	15	3	3
Netherlands	6	6	17.5	17.5	6
Portugal	5	16	5	5	5
Spain	7	7	16	16	7
Sweden	12	25	25	25	0
UK	17.5	17.5	17.5	17.5	17.5

Source: Wanhill (1995), updated from Browne (1996).

about unfair competition from hoteliers. It should be noted that those coming from outside the EU can, as a rule, reclaim VAT in relation to shopping purchases, but this is not always arranged in an administratively convenient manner for visitors.

Exemption from direct (income or profits) taxes through 'tax holidays' and

Table 12.3. Comparison of VAT in the European Union

Country	Standard (%)	Accommodation (%)	Difference (%)
Austria	20	10	10
Belgium	21	6	15
Denmark	25	25	0
Finland	22	6	16
France	20.6	5.5	15.1
Germany	15	15	0
Greece	18	8	10
Ireland	21	12.5	8.5
Italy	19	10	9
Luxembourg	15	3	12
Netherlands	17.5	6	11.5
Portugal	17	5	12
Spain	16	7	9
Sweden	25	12	13
UK	17.5	17.5	0

Source: Wanhill (1995) updated from Browne (1996).

special depreciation allowances only have meaning when the project is profitable (hence viable since debt charges are normally deductible), and therefore over the hurdle of initial start-up risks. Tax holidays and reduced profit tax rates are some of the most popular forms of incentives given to new tourism projects and, more recently, are especially noticeable in the packages offered to investors by the expanding Eastern European regions and the Commonwealth of Independent States (CIS): their approach has been to offer tax holidays from 2–5 years after the first year's profits have been recorded, whereas such holidays have tended to be between 5 and 10 years for developments in LDCs. After the expiration of a tax holiday, governments may offer reduced rates of income or profits tax to international firms, depending on:

- The amount of profits invested locally
- How much foreign exchange is generated
- Improved economic linkages through purchases from domestic suppliers
- Staff training undertaken by the firm

Depreciation allowances and tax holidays are often used in tandem, thus a 5-year tax holiday may be followed by special depreciation allowances. The latter may vary from permitting the organisation to write-off its assets to its best advantage over an 8-year period, to providing a substantial initial allowance of 20–30% of the capital cost and a normal 'wear and tear' allowance thereafter. The effect of special depreciation allowances is to defer tax payments, which amounts to an interest-free tax loan from the government (Bloom and Mostert, 1995). This favours longer term investments, because the longer the life of the capital asset, the greater is the present worth value of the tax loan. A further fiscal boost may come from the provision of an investment allowance (also known as a tax or investment credit), which is not merely tax postponement analogous to accelerated depreciation, but a tax reduction through being able to write-off, say, 30% of the initial capital, without affecting the tax value of the asset for depreciation purposes. By this means firms are able to write-off more than 100% of their capital against tax. Investment allowances favour assets that are replaced frequently, allowing the firm to take advantage of the tax savings.

The matter of a labour subsidy is indicative of the employment-creation objective in tourism development. Factor subsidies can alter the choice of technology in the supply process. One criticism of capital subsidies is that they will tend to promote a capital-intensive structure, whereas the emphasis is on generating jobs. A labour subsidy will always improve employment opportunities, but the effects of a capital subsidy may actually reduce employment through switching technologies. As a rule, tourist authorities counter the contrasting effects of subsidising capital by giving priority in funding to employment-creating projects. A ready method of doing this is to tie the amount of support to the number of full-time equivalent (FTE) jobs created. The latter allows for the fact that a good number of tourism jobs are often part-time or seasonal. This presumes an element of discretion in the awarding of incentives, which is not always possible when they have been laid down by legislation and are therefore automatic.

Tourism projects involving hotel developments are high users of energy, particularly where there are climatic extremes, such as in tropical areas where there is a need for air-conditioning or in colder climes where the requirement is for continual heating. In these circumstances, energy use and management becomes a key element in the operating budget of the hotel. Large hotel corporations have always been able to negotiate energy prices with suppliers, but where the energy supplier is a public utility, as is the case in many newly emerging destinations, then the government is able to offer the additional incentive of reduced tariffs to strengthen the profitability of the business.

Double taxation and unilateral relief are country to country or single country agreements to ensure that multinational investors are not taxed on the same profits in different locations. Suppose a company controlled in Country A trades in Country B through a permanent establishment in the latter country; it will pay tax on its trading profits both in Country A and Country B, but if there is a double taxation agreement between these countries, then a tax credit in respect of Country B's tax will be allowed against Country A's tax. If there is only unilateral relief, the company will be entitled to offset its tax liability elsewhere against tax payable in Country B.

Investment security

The objective of providing investment security is to win investors' confidence in an industry which is very sensitive to the political environment and the economic climate. Action here could include:

- Guarantees against nationalisation
- Ensuring the availability of trained staff
- Repatriation of invested capital, profits dividends and interest
- Loan guarantees
- Provision of work permits for 'key' personnel
- Availability of technical advice

To enhance these actions, there is the broader issue of the government's support for tourism. This may be demonstrated by the activities of the NTO, reducing administrative delays, simplifying the planning process, easing frontier formalities, initiating liberal transport policies and so on.

Clearly, without the confidence in the government to set the right economic climate for the tourist industry to prosper, investment incentives on their own may be of limited value in attracting outside funds or mobilising domestic investment in tourism. To counter bureaucratic inefficiency, complicated administrative processes and the lack of transparency in the legislation affecting foreign businesses, together with frequent modifications to the legislation, some governments, notably in countries looking to become new tourist destinations, such as in Eastern Europe and the CIS, have established 'one-stop-shop' agencies to ease the path of foreign investors, as well as including 'grandfathering' clauses in the legislation, which exempt foreign enterprises from unfavourable legal changes for up to 10 years.

IMPLEMENTATION

In implementing a tourism investment policy, the government has to decide to what extent incentives should be legislated as automatic entitlements, as against being discretionary awards. Automatic incentives may give too much money away, when what is required to ensure that the treasury receives maximum benefit from its funds is the application of the concept of 'project additionality'. This concept tries to ensure that the proposed scheme is truly 'additional' by asking the question: 'Would this project go ahead if $xxxx$ amount of investment support was not given?' ... The object is to provide financial support or the equivalent benefits in kind to the point where the developer will just proceed with the scheme (Jenkins, 1982).

The implication of project additionality is an ideal situation where all incentives are discretionary and therefore offered selectively, as is generally true of the incentives given by the member states of the EU (Table 12.1). The legislation would be fairly general, empowering the ministry responsible for tourism to offer loans, grants, tax exemptions and equity investment as it sees fit. As an example, such legislation is embodied in the UK 1969 Development of Tourism Act (House of Commons, 1969). Section 4 of the 1969 Act states that:

4. (1) A Tourist Board shall have power –
    (a) in accordance with arrangements approved by the relevant Minister and the Treasury, to give financial assistance for the carrying out of any project which in the opinion of the Board will provide or improve tourist amenities and facilities in the country for which the Board is responsible:
    (b) with the approval of the relevant Minister and the Treasury, to carry out any such project as aforesaid.

(2) Financial assistance under subsection (1) (a) of this section may be given by way of grant or loan or, if the project is being or is to be carried out by a company incorporated in Great Britain, by subscribing for or otherwise acquiring shares or stock in the company, or by any combination of those methods.

(3) In making a grant or loan in accordance with arrangements approved under subsection (1) (a) of this section a Tourist Board may, subject to the arrangements, impose such terms and conditions as it thinks fit, including conditions for the repayment of a grant in specified circumstances; and Schedule 2 to this Act shall have effect for securing compliance with conditions subject to which any such grant is made.

(4) A Tourist Board shall not dispose of any shares or stock acquired by it by virtue of this section except –

(a) after consultation with the company in which the shares or stock are held; and

(b) with the approval of the relevant Minister and the Treasury.

With general legislation of this kind, the granting of incentives to prospective developers becomes subject to ministerial guidelines. The latter should be regularly reviewed in response to the level of tourism activity and changes in policy. These guidelines may include statements giving priority to certain kinds of tourism projects, that, for example, provide specific benefits to local communities, extend the tourist season, enhance the range of tourist facilities at the destination, offer full-time employment, give access to disabled visitors, attract both domestic and foreign visitors, and preserve the landscape. In sum, discretionary incentives allow tourist agencies to:

● Switch sector priorities with the object of encouraging new developments, modernisation and achieving a balanced development of tourist facilities in specific locations

● Supporting projects which have high income and employment-creating potential

● Selecting projects which have most chance of success, and are socially and environmentally sustainable

● Adjusting the money awarded to oblige the applicant to meet any investment specifications in respect of type, quality and quantity

To have only discretionary incentives, however, is a counsel of perfection. Competition for tourism investment frequently requires countries to legislate for automatic financial help in order to attract investors in the first instance. Some countries may legislate for all the incentives discussed here;

others for a subset of them. Many countries have been guilty of copying the incentive legislation of their neighbours without any real grasp of the meaning of this legislation.

The appropriateness of the various financial incentives available depends on understanding the nature of the business risk and the likely returns of the tourist industry, as well as the ability of the country to afford them. Thus developing countries, as noted earlier, may find themselves in no position to offer grants or cheap loans. It is well known that part of the business risk in tourist projects lies in the fact that services are non-storable (a hotel bed unsold is lost forever) and in demand being generally seasonal. This implies that peak demand determines capacity (unless capacity is regulated by planning legislation in order to preserve amenity value) so that the industry is always facing excess capacity at other times, which inculcates a certain reluctance amongst banks and other financial institutions to lend to the tourism industry, particularly as they often experience difficulty in appraising the financial viability of both tourism products and the managers of projects. As a rule, to control costs, government treasuries are against giving blanket reductions in general taxation, since it is difficult to prevent them applying to 'old' capital as well as new investment. The emphasis on incentives is their ephemeral nature for the purposes of providing the foundation for new projects to establish themselves.

COST STRUCTURES

Not always apparent is the dominant cost structure in the tourist industry. Typically, tourism projects have a high operating leverage, that is a high level of fixed costs arising out of the initial capital investment, and low operating costs, which results in businesses that are very sensitive to variations in demand. The problem is illustrated in Figure 12.2, where it is assumed that there are two projects which have exactly the same revenue line R and break even point BEP. However, one project has a high operating leverage as shown by the cost line C_1, and the other a low operating leverage represented by C_2. The possible outcomes of these two projects are shown by Q_1, Q_2 and Q_3. Suppose Q_3 sales are achieved, then it is clear that the project with the high operating leverage makes substantially more profit than the other. This is represented on Figure 12.2 by the difference between the revenue and cost schedules, where it may be seen that $DF > DE$. On the other hand, if the outcome is Q_1 sales then the project with the cost structure C_1 will make large losses, $AC > AB$. In addition to the above, it has already been indicated that tourism at the destination end is extensive in its use of land and property. This tends to induce elements of real estate speculation, but the non-transferability of assets such as hotels or tourist attractions to other uses

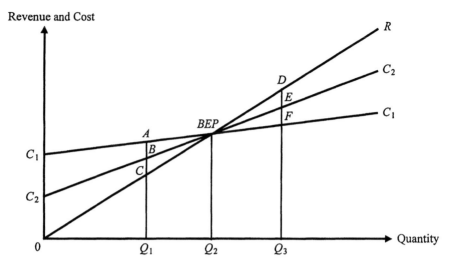

Figure 12.2. Effects of operating leverage

hinders their worth as a property investment. Add to this the seasonality of demand, which produces irregular cash flows and it is not surprising that financial institutions view tourism projects as risky investments.

Risk

As noted previously, it is always possible to structure different incentives so that they each deliver exactly the same benefit to the business under conditions of certainty. It is only under conditions of risk that a priori restrictions can be placed on the type of investment incentive offered. To show this, take the basic business model where profit before tax (Π) is by definition the difference between revenue (R) and costs (C). It is assumed that sales quantity (Q) is a random variable with known mean and variance, and that costs may be broken down into fixed (C_F) and variable (C_V) expenses. From this it follows that the expected value of pre-tax profit is

$$E(\Pi) = E(R - C) \qquad (2)$$
$$= E(R - C_V) - C_F$$

but

$$E(R - C_V) = E(Q)(P - M) \qquad (3)$$

where

$$P = price$$
$$M = marginal\ cost.$$

Thus

$$E(\Pi) = E(Q)\,(P - M) - C_F \tag{4}$$

and

$$\sigma_\Pi^2 = \sigma_Q^2(P - M)^2 \tag{5}$$

Let t be the appropriate rate of company tax, then the expected value of post-tax income is

$$E(\Pi^*) = (1 - t)[E(Q)\,(P - M) - C_F] \tag{6}$$

and

$$\sigma_{\Pi^*}^2 = \sigma_Q^2(P - M)^2(1 - t)^2 \tag{7}$$

From equations (5) and (7) it may be seen that profit volatility is directly proportional to the square of the contribution margin $(P - M)$. In turn, the latter depends on the operating leverage or the ratio between fixed and variable costs. Thus investment incentives must address themselves to improving profitability and lowering the risk inherent in the general cost structure pattern of the tourist industry.

Numerical example

Having established that a high operating leverage, which is so typical of many tourism firms, is a principal source of financial risk, it remains to examine the effect of different kinds of incentives on the risk. The second column of Table 12.4 illustrates a project at operational equilibrium where the expected number of visitors is 400 000 with a standard deviation of 60 000, but with no investment support. The symbols have the same meaning as in the text. The remaining columns in Table 12.4 show three kinds of incentives given to the project under the condition that each delivers exactly the same expected profit after tax:

- A tax holiday: t is set equal to zero such that $E(\Pi^*) = E(\Pi)$
- An input subsidy: a flat rate subsidy (S) per unit of sales is given so as to ensure that $E(\Pi^*)$ is the same as that which would arise from a tax holiday. This can be calculated by solving the relationship

$$(1 - t)[E(Q)\,(P - M + S) - C_F] = E(Q)\,(P - M) - C_F \tag{8}$$

which gives

$$S = M - P + \frac{E(Q)(P - M) - tC_F}{(1 - t)E(Q)} \tag{9}$$

Table 12.4. Project effects of investment incentives

Item	Project + no incentives	Project + grant	Project + input subsidy	Project + tax holiday
P	£3	£3	£3	£3
M	£1	£1	£1	£1
$E(Q)$	400 000	400 000	400 000	400 000
$\sigma_Q{}^*$	60 000	60 000	60 000	60 000
$PE(Q)$	£1 200 000	£1 200 000	£1 200 000	£1 200 000
$ME(Q)$	£400 000	£400 000	£333 333**	£400 000
C_F	£700 000	£633 333	£700 000	£700 000
$E(\Pi)$	£100 000	£166 667	£166 667	£100 000
σ_Π	£120 000	£120 000	£130 000	£120 000
t	40%	40%	40%	0%
$E(\Pi^*)$	£60 000	£100 000	£100 000	£100 000
$\sigma_\Pi{}^*$	£72 000	£72 000	£78 000	£120 000
BEP sales	350 000	316 667	323 077	350 000

* The standard deviation of sales volume is assumed.
** This value is after the input subsidy has been deducted.

and amounts to just under £0.17 per unit. The subsidy reduces the variable costs of operations.
- A cash grant: a lump-sum grant (G) is offered on the same basis as the subsidy. Equation (8) now becomes

$$(1 - t)[E(Q)(P - M) - C_F + G] = E(Q)(P - M) - C_F \tag{10}$$

from which

$$G = \frac{t[E(Q)(P - M) - C_F]}{1 - t} \tag{11}$$

Substitution of the appropriate values gives $G = £66\,667$. The grant reduces the fixed costs.

Inspection of Table 12.4 will show that while all three incentives raise expected post-tax profits by two-thirds, as they are designed to do, their impact on break-even sales is very different. A tax holiday has no effect on the BEP, while the other incentives reduce it, with the grant having the most impact. This arises because the grant acts directly on the source of risk, which is the high level of fixed costs. By lowering the BEP, both the input subsidy and the grant are increasing the probability that the project will more than break-even and thus reducing the downside risk of loss. As Table 12.4 indicates, the grant, by its impact on fixed costs, is superior to the other incentives in lowering the inherent risk in the project.

No statistical probabilistic information about the outcomes can be conveyed until something is known about the distribution of visitors, Q. If it is assumed that Q is distributed with only one mode and is symmetrical about the mean, then it follows that the mean and mode coincide and that the possible outcomes can be determined from knowledge of $E(Q)$ and σ_Q^2 alone. The most common distribution that fits this pattern is the Normal, but the Camp–Meidell inequality (Wanhill, 1986) shows that, under the above assumptions, the probability of an outcome which is greater or equal to a value falling, say, x standard deviations from the mean is $1/(4 \cdot 5x^2)$, from which dispersion probabilities may be calculated, even if the exact distribution is unknown.

Project viability

In practice, the nature by which fixed costs are incurred is important. Projects requiring subvention that have a high level of fixed operating costs will be looking for a renewed subsidy every year. In many tourism projects, a large part of the fixed costs arise from the provision for capital expenditure. Given that variable costs are low, it follows that a 'once-and-for-all' reduction in capital costs at the start of the project should be sufficient to ensure viability. So if the objective is primarily to improve viability, then the preferred form of financial incentives is those which reduce capital costs (Wanhill, 1986, 1994).

In the light of this emphasis on capital costs, the term 'viability' has a distinct role in the financial evaluation of tourism projects and the award of discretionary incentives in the form of equity purchase, soft loans or grants. In the first instance, the scheme must be feasible, in that it is capable of generating a surplus of revenue over its operating costs. Viability, however, has to do with servicing the capital investment: it depends on the interest rate, which can fluctuate considerably by virtue of government policies, the funding package for the capital involved and methods of repayment. These concepts are presented in Figure 12.3. As before, R is the revenue line and C the total cost schedule attributable to running the project in a given year. The line C^* represents the cost of operation excluding the provision for capital recovery. At a level of V_2 visitor days the project is feasible, since it produces a surplus BC over C^*, but it is not viable because there is a gap AB in the funds available to service the capital. To the left of D the project is neither viable nor feasible and conversely for point E. A usual condition to giving investment incentives is that the scheme should become viable, either by moving the C line down to B at V_2 visitor days or reshaping the project to expand the market to V_3 visitor days or some combination of the two.

Revenue and Cost

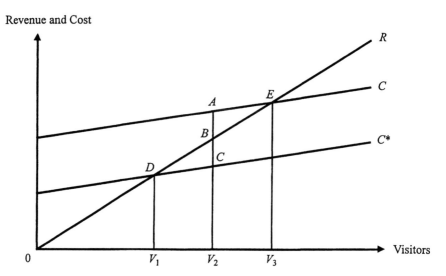

Figure 12.3. Viability of tourism projects

EVALUATION OF INVESTMENT INCENTIVES

Private sector

From the standpoint of the private developer the impact of investment incentives is ultimately on the net cash flow from a project. The various incentives offered are therefore built into the appraisal process. A representative layout is shown in Table 12.5. Capital investment takes place in year zero and year one: K_0 is eligible for a cash grant at a rate of $a\%$, whilst K_1 is given an initial allowance against taxable income of $b\%$. The latter is given to assist investment not qualifying for cash grants. The annual depreciation allowance set by the tax authority is $g\%$ and this is set against the written-down value (W). The latter is an accounting construct laid down by government policy which

Table 12.5. Evaluating the financial worth of investment incentives

Time	Cash outflow	Grant	Initial allowance	Written-down value	Annual allowance	Balancing allowance	Cash inflow
0	K_0	0	0	$W_0 = K_0 - aK_0$	0	0	0
1	K_1	aK_0	bK_1	$W_1\ W_0 + (1-b)K_1$	0	0	V_1
2	0	0	0	$W_2 = (1-g)W_1$	gW_1	0	V_2
3	0	0	0	$W_3 = (1-g)W_2$	gW_2	0	V_3
↓	↓	↓	↓	↓	↓	↓	↓
↓	↓	↓	↓	↓	↓	↓	↓
T	$-S_T$	0	0	$W_T = (1-g)W_{T-1}$	gW_{T-1}	$B_T = W_T - S_T$	V_T
T + 1	0	0	0	0	0	0	0

allows firms to write-off capital purchases against tax on a declining balance basis. The written-down value is defined in most cases on the capital expenditure to date, less grants and allowances. If the initial allowance was a tax credit or investment allowance, bK_1 would not be included in the calculation of the written-down value, thus permitting the business to write-off more than the capital cost.

The project has a time horizon $0-T$, at the end of which the capital assets are disposed of to obtain a scrap value (S_T), which is recorded as a negative cash outflow. The disposal of these assets gives rise to a balancing allowance (B_T) which amounts to the difference between the written down and scrap values at the end of the project's life. This is set against taxable income. If $S_T > W_T$, then there is a balancing charge which is treated as income for tax purposes.

The cash inflow V is defined as the difference between revenue and operating costs. Capital allowances are deducted from V to give taxable income. In Table 12.5, this is taxed at a rate of $t\%$ payable one year after income is accrued, that is, the firm has full use of the current period's income or profits before tax needs to be paid. The last column in the table gives the net cash flow over the life of the project. This is discounted at the going cost of capital to give the net present worth of the project. The net cash flow runs to period $T + 1$ because of the convention that tax is paid in the year following the year of assessment.

The public sector

If substantial amounts of public revenue or the equivalent benefits in kind are put into tourism projects, then it is only to be expected that the benefits of investment incentives should be evaluated. Outlined below is a method for measuring the effectiveness of incentives in which the welfare objective is employment creation. For example, within Europe, the principles governing the bidding process for European Regional Development Fund (ERDF)

| | | | Capital and operating adjustments |
Taxable income	Tax	Net cash inflow	Net cash flow
0	0	0	$-K_0$
$V_1 - bK_1$	0	$V_1 + aK_0$	$V_1 + aK_0 - K_1$
$V_2 - gW_1$	$t(V_1 - bK_1)$	$V_2 - t(V_1 - bK_1)$	$V_2 - t(V_1 - bK_1)$
$V_3 - gW_2$	$t(V_2 - gW_1)$	$V_3 - t(V_2 - gW_1)$	$V_3 - T(V_2 - gW_1)$
$\downarrow$	$\downarrow$	$\downarrow$	$\downarrow$
$V_T - B_T - gW_{T-1}$	$t(V_{T-1} - gW_{T-2})$	$V_T - t(V_{T-1} - gW_{T-2})$	$V_T + S_T - t(V_{T-1} - gW_{T-2})$
0	$t(V_T - B_T - gW_{T-1})$	$-t(V_T - B_T - gW_{T-1})$	$-t(V_T - B_T - gW_{T-1})$

grants for productive investment are:

- An indication of the market outlook in the sector concerned should be given
- The effects on employment should be examined
- An analysis of the expected profitability of the project should be undertaken

In practice, local income and employment generation are the most significant factors affecting project acceptability, since the primary use of ERDF is to correct for regional imbalances. In terms of profitability, project feasibility is the main consideration, namely that the scheme has the capacity to generate revenues above operating costs so that it can support its own running arrangements. Initial project viability is not so significant, because the objective of ERDF is to make up for shortfalls in finance to ensure that the investment will go ahead and has the means to service its capital funding out of its surplus.

The evaluation technique begins from the premise that tourism is a demand-led industry whose influence pervades many different sectors of the economy. There is no single industrial classification called tourism, so the starting point for appraising tourism projects, from the government's perspective, is to measure the economic impact of tourist spending and derive appropriate multipliers, in particular income and employment multipliers. Tourists come to a destination for many reasons, so if the requirement is to establish the worth of a project which has been assisted through public funds, the first step is to draw up the methodology.

Benefit analysis

Suppose that there exists a tourist destination with two attractions and a seaside. Visitors are surveyed both at attractions and on the beach to ascertain what motivated them to come to the destination. Total spending at the destination (T) amounts to expenditure at Attraction X (T_x) plus expenditure at Attraction Y (T_y) plus all remaining expenditure (R). Let the pull factor (reason for visit) for Attraction X be a, for Attraction Y, a value b, leaving $c = 1 - a - b$ as the significance of the beach. It follows therefore that attributable tourist expenditure by drawing power is:

$$\text{Attraction X} = aT$$
$$\text{Attraction Y} = bT$$
$$\text{Seaside} \quad = cT$$

where

$$T = T_x + T_y + R$$

The NTO has put public money into Attraction X and so wishes to evaluate its worth in terms of its contribution to tourist spending and employment in the area. The benefits of Attraction X (B) are the difference between with the project (T) and without the project (T_w). The without situation is

$$\text{Attraction X} = 0$$
$$\text{Attraction Y} = b(T_y + R)$$
$$\text{Seaside} \quad = c(T_y + R)$$
$$T_w = (b + c)(T_y + R)$$

Hence,

$$B = T - T_w$$
$$= T - (b + c)(T_y + R)$$

Expanding T gives,

$$B = T_x + a(T_y + R) \tag{12}$$

Employment effects

The benefits shown in equation (12) are in two parts. The first term on the right-hand side is on-site expenditure and the second, off-site expenditure. The amount of off-site expenditure attributable to the attraction depends on its ability to generate visitors to Attraction Y and the area in general. Hence, this may be termed the 'visitor additionality' factor. The simplified model has been structured to show each attraction and the seaside mutually supporting each other, so the one generates business for the others. Given that the evaluation is undertaken ex post, these mutually supporting actions are contained within the overall tourist spending at the destination, thus the total worth of all the facilities is the sum of their individual contributions, less the benefit contribution each facility bestows on the others, so as to avoid double counting of the additionality effects. The application of employment multipliers per unit of tourist spending to equation (12), either on an FTE or employment headcount basis, will give the gross employment (E) generated by the project. These multipliers are calculated so as to measure the direct employment effects of the project, the indirect effects arising out of intermediate purchases made by the project and the induced effects on the local economy as a result of the respending of local incomes derived from the project, and similarly for off-site expenditure. Thus:

$$E = T_x e_x + a\,O e_o \tag{13}$$

Where e_x is the employment multiplier appropriate to the attraction, O is the sum of off-site expenditure $(T_y + R)$ and e_o the required employment multiplier.

However, equation (13) ignores any demand diversion from competitors elsewhere in the area: this is termed displacement and in this respect it is important to define the boundary of the project. As observed by Johnson and

Thomas (1990):

> In the case of the economy as a whole it is sometimes argued that all expendi-
> ture, and consequently employment, is diverted and there is in effect a zero-
> sum game. This point is of some importance from the point of view of public
> bodies providing funds. Local authorities and the Treasury for example might
> have very different views on what is the net impact because they are concerned
> with different reference areas.

At a national level, this argument assumes that market forces are moving
the economy towards full employment equilibrium so that public investment expenditure is simply displacing private funds in the capital market.
Similarly, the operation of the project is displacing demand in the same or
related product markets and likewise in the labour and property markets. In
reality, economies do get stuck at a level of Keynesian unemployment dis-
equilibrium and one of the major objectives of regional policy is to 'kick-start'
a demand-deficient economy so as to raise the level of output through the
multiplier process. This discussion does not imply that displacement should
be neglected so that policy decisions are made in terms of the gross effect
only, but merely raises the issue that the logic of the crowding out effect ends
up with a 'do nothing' policy.

If d is the proportion of locally diverted demand (or demand diverted from
other assisted projects) in equation (12), then, from equation (13), net
employment is:

$$N = E - dE$$
$$= (1 - d)(T_x e_x + a Oe_0) \tag{14}$$

Equation (14) forms the core of the basic evaluation model which can be used
to judge in employment terms the return to public funds given to the project
by way of the whole range of incentives discussed earlier.

Numerical example

As an example, consider Table 12.6 which presents a hypothetical example,
drawn from case study material, to illustrate how employment multipliers
may be used to assess job creation (see Surrey Research Group, 1993). The
workings of Table 12.6 are as follows: using visitor expenditure surveys, the
total expected on-site and off-site spending arising from the project is estimated at around £22 360 000. It is at this point that the concept of 'visitor
additionality' is invoked: on-site expenditure by visitors is attributable
absolutely to the attraction as the customers have demonstrated their preferences through their willingness-to-pay, but this is not the case with off-site
spending. The extent to which off-site spending may be attributed to the
attraction depends on the importance of the attraction in the customer's

Table 12.6. Employment impact of an attraction

	On-site expenditure	Off-site expenditure
Markets		
Stay	£1 970 000	£11 535 000
Day	£2 200 000	£1 965 000
Local residents	£3 415 000	£1 275 000
Total	£7 585 000	£14 775 000
Visitor additionality		
Stay	Not applicable	15%
Day	Not applicable	90%
Local residents	Not applicable	100%
Displacement		
Stay	0%	0%
Day	35%	35%
Local residents	100%	100%
FTE multipliers per £10.000		
Direct	0.0995	0.0816
Indirect	0.0535	0.0508
Induced	0.0077	0.0077
Total	0.1607	0.1401

decision to visit the location. This can only be ascertained by surveying visitors and asking about their motivations for coming to the destination.

Suppose that surveys have shown that only 15% of staying visitors have come to the destination because of the existence of the attraction. But, as is to be expected, a much higher percentage is recorded for day visitors and local residents, because they normally make a specific decision to go to a place, an event or an attraction. Using the visitor additionality factors in Table 12.6 to account for attributable off-site expenditure, the gross expenditure benefits (B) from the attraction are:

$$B = £7\ 585\ 000 + (0.15 \times £11\ 535\ 000) + (0.9 \times £1\ 965\ 000) + (1.0 \times £1\ 275\ 000)$$
$$= £12\ 358\ 750$$

Implementation has shown the attraction to create 101.5 full-time equivalent (FTE) jobs directly on-site, and so the required additions to this number will be the indirect and induced employment resulting from on-site spending. Using the appropriate FTE multipliers shown in Table 12.6, this figure comes to $(0.0535 + 0.0077) \times £7\ 585\ 000/£10.000 = 46.4$ FTE jobs. Off-site jobs amount to $0.1401 \times £4\ 773\ 750/£10.000 = 66.9$ FTE jobs. Hence, the gross employment generated (E), in terms of FTEs, is:

$$E = 101.5 \text{ FTEs} + 46.4 \text{ FTEs} + 66.9 \text{ FTEs}$$
$$= 214.8 \text{ FTEs}$$

So far the analysis has only estimated gross FTEs generated by the attraction. The net figures have to account for displacement, which is factored into

Table 12.6. It is estimated that a negligible number of staying visitors have been taken from competitors; the attraction is providing more to 'see and do' at the destination and the tourists' budgets have sufficient margin of flexibility. For day visitors, it is calculated that 35% have been displaced from other attractions, while for local residents a conservative assumption is made that all expenditure has been displaced from elsewhere in the local economy. The latter assumption is overly pessimistic in practice, for household budgets are not that inflexible, but it is a working assumption that has been used in the appraisal of tourism projects in applications for assistance from the European Structural Funds.

Weighting the displacement factors in Table 12.6 by the different categories of visitor spending, gives an overall displacement value of 0.4919. Thus, the estimated net employment (N) created by the attraction is:

$$N = 214.8 - 0.4919 \times 214.8 = 109.2 \text{ FTEs}$$

It is this number of FTEs that may be used to evaluate the project's worth in public policy decision-making in respect of the amount of investment support granted. The same model may be used prior to giving investment support as well as afterwards. Further case examples of this model can be found in Johnson and Thomas (1992) in their study of Beamish Museum in the North of England and in Lowyck and Wanhill (1992), which looks at the assessment of the New Theatre development in Cardiff, South Wales, for ERDF funding.

The obvious performance measures in terms of ranking projects relate to factors such as the number of FTEs created, job patterns in relation to educational attainment and skill levels, male/female ratios, the amount of part-time and seasonal work balanced against year-round full-time employment, and so on. In addition, a number of financial indicators have been used in respect of the capital investment (K). The most common is the capital cost per job (K/N) but others include the grant cost per job (G/N), the private capital cost per job $((K-G)/N)$ and the grant leverage effect $((K-G)/G)$.

ADMINISTRATION OF INVESTMENT INCENTIVES

Organisation

It will be appreciated that for an investment policy to be effective, it must be situated within an appropriate administrative framework. Where incentives apply to all sectors of the economy, their administration is commonly placed within the development or investment division of the Ministry of Industry and Commerce (or its equivalent), or in a separate Development Agency.

Specific incentives for tourism are normally to be found within the Ministry of Tourism, a TDC or the NTO. A tourism development organisation or division can only have truly operational involvement if it is given funding to engage in projects with the private sector and implement training programmes and activities. If this is not the case then it can only take on a coordinating and strategic role. The former is achieved by acting as a 'one-stop-shop' for prospective developers, through intermediation to obtain planning permission, licences and any financial assistance or incentives from the relevant authorities. In a strategic role the development division will acquire the planning functions, but it is better to separate these activities. The reason for this rests on the fact that an operational development division is likely to be too heavily involved in day-to-day project management to be able to incorporate long-term development planning. The latter is a research activity and therefore best located in the unit equipped for this task. The ability to offer planning services is an important addendum to the role of an NTO, in that it seeks to capitalise on the expertise of the organisation to provide advice and even undertake studies for the private sector and other public bodies, for example, drawing up tourism plans for local communities.

Promotion

An important aspect of any investment agency or division is the promotion of its product. This may be undertaken through trade missions and exhibitions overseas, as well as seminars and briefings for domestic investors and financiers. Collateral material can be simply an investment prospectus listing the incentives available and contact points or, more extensively, a tourism development manual. The contents of such a manual could include:

- Introduction: this should be about the manual and who to contact in the agency
- Map of the country: to show the tourist resources of the country and the regions
- Description of country and tourist regions
- Registration and Planning Procedures: investors need to know about the details of registration, how the planning process works, land ownership, any regulations governing the construction, shape and style of buildings, and what designs the applicant must submit
- Planning Policies: the government's views on tourism, types of accommodation and recreation activities the government wishes to encourage, the use of natural resources and concern for the environment
- Transport and Communications: information on road, rail and air transport connections and telecommunications
- Tourism Trends and Prospects: profiles of the different tourist segments of

the market according to their demographics, attitudes to the tourist product offer, their activities and spend potential
- Investment Incentives and Financial Assistance: it is helpful to include here, details of the banking system, the kind of finance that can be made available, the situation as to the procurement of international funds and what projects are eligible for support
- Taxation: the tax system should be seen by investors to be simple to apply, easy to administer, transparent (therefore leaving little to discretion in tax collection), stable and robust to inflation. Firms should be able to make project decisions with a proper understanding of the likely returns to investment
- List of Development Sites: items to be considered here are – the nature of the development envisaged, size, location, whether planning consent has been given, water, power, drainage, who to contact about the site, comments on the geography of the site, access and so on
- List of Available Buildings: the contents of this section would include – whether the building is redundant or of historic value, who is the owner, its condition and the potential envisaged for it, for example, an hotel, self-catering units, a craft workshop, an activity or visitor centre.

Project support

This section draws on the author's experience as a Board Member for the Wales Tourist Board, an NTO within Britain, in order to give a case example of the nature of the process of awarding discretionary incentives (Wanhill, 1996). As observed in the Implementation section of this chapter, within the terms of the Development of Tourism Act (House of Commons, 1969), the Wales Tourist Board is permitted to take equity shares, give grants or offer loans in support of tourism projects. In practice, grants have been the main form of support and all sums awarded are discretionary, namely that the amounts are related to the type of project, its desirability in accordance with the overall development strategy and the need for assistance.

Under the statutes of the 1969 Act and internally provided Ministerial Guidelines, every project should be submitted separately to the Board for approval. Significant schemes going before the Board will have an appreciation or project report prepared by the officers of the Board's Development Division. Smaller projects will have similar appraisals, but are dealt with under officer-delegated powers and are matter of report to the Board.

At any one time, summary pro formas will be available giving the current status of projects likely to come forward for approval. These are in the manner of the layouts shown in Tables 12.7–12.9, namely:

- Preparatory questionnaires that are initial enquiries
- Current applications with missing information
- Current applications for approval

Table 12.7. Summary pro forma for preparatory questionnaire results

PQ No.	Project name	New capacity or upgrade	Category	Capital cost	Grant requested	On-site FTE jobs created	Grant cost per job	Project description
7025	Top Food, Barry	Upgrade	Restaurant	£70 000	£20 000	4.50	£4444	Upgrade kitchen, lounge and toilets
7026	Castle Hotel, Aber	New capacity	Serviced accommodation	£250 000	£55 000	7.25	£7586	Additional 8 bedrooms

Table 12.8. Summary pro forma for current applications with missing information

Project No.	Project name	New capacity or upgrade	Category	Capital cost	Grant requested	On-site FTE jobs created	Grant cost per job	Missing information
6451	Glyncorrwg Golf, Llanrug	Upgrade	Activity	£45 000	£15 000	1.50	£10 000	Funding and marketing information
6917	Town Walk Plaques, Caenarfon	New capacity	Visitor amenity	£6500	£2500	Nil	Nil	Cost & additionality statement

Table 12.9. Summary pro forma for current applications for approval

Project No.	Project name	New capacity or upgrade	Category	Capital cost	Grant requested	On-site FTE jobs created	Grant cost per job	Project description
6923	Llandwin Beach Amusements, Cardigan	New capacity	Attraction	£800 000	£200 000	9.00	£22 222	Roller coaster ride
6924	Sunquest Travel Club, Swansea	New capacity	Caravan	£20 000	£6000	1.25	£4800	Development of 20 new touring pitches

The examples shown in the tables are fictitious and are only for illustrative purposes. The classifications, new capacity, upgrade, visitor amenity and infrastructure support are those which would have been agreed in the 5-year development plan.

Project reports

The format of the project report is structured under the following headings:

- General
- Management
- The Project
- Financial Appraisal
- Marketing
- Tourism Impact
- Recommendations

At each stage there are likely to be officers' comments for guidance.

The heading 'General' includes a brief introduction, followed by the project name, its location, description, delegated authority as necessary, who the applicants are, project priority – say, historic town or rural community in accordance with the Board's development strategy – and a note on any previous application or assistance given, together with summary monitoring data. The 'Management' section will include details of the experience of the applicants, their qualifications and those of key staff, any training needs deemed necessary, and details of the existing business in which the project will be placed. Next follows a description of the project and the costs involved. Under the heading 'Financial Appraisal', the project funding package, detailing the shortfall where support is necessary, profit and loss projections for up to five years, and the balance sheet of the enterprise, are discussed, in order to ascertain feasibility and the need for public sector moneys. The 'Marketing' part of the report looks at what is being done to market and sell the product and what may need to happen in the future. 'Tourism Impact' gives consideration to:

- On-site job creation, analysed by full-time, part-time and casual employment
- On-site grant cost per job, this being a key performance indicator for the Board
- The average wage
- Multiplier effects
- Displacement effects
- Any visitor additionality issues

By the time a project comes before the Board for approval, the 'Recommendations' should normally be favourable, though conditions may be imposed on the applicant in respect of training, marketing, requirements to reveal all sources of finance, revisions as to costings, which will entail the Board putting in its own quantity surveyor, various legal matters and so on. But projects are pressed through to Board-level decision, by applicants, which may have to be rejected on grounds of the need for the project, its priority and quality, as well as economic criteria. All aspects of the project are considered, but, ultimately, the accountability for public funds lays stress on the economic sustainability of the proposal, its ability to create employment, the need for a grant or loan for the project to go forward and its effects on other tourist businesses.

CONCLUSIONS

In many parts of the world governments have intervened to assist and regulate the private sector in the development of tourism. This is because the complex nature of the tourist product makes it unlikely that private markets will satisfy a country's tourism policy objectives to produce a balance of facilities that meet the needs of the visitor, benefit the host community and are compatible with the wishes of that same community. Investment incentives are policy instruments that can be used to correct for market failure and ensure a development partnership between the public and private sectors. The partnership approach has particular significance for regional development, particularly in peripheral areas, due to the existence of many small communities, lack of resources, areas in decline and the fragmented nature of the supply by tourist establishments. Here there is often the need for the tourist agencies to provide leadership, direction and coordination, as well as business support through investment incentives that are carefully tailored to the economic structure of small businesses, so as to ensure that tourism can deliver its development potential.

The extent of public involvement depends on the economic philosophy of the government, the type of development being sought and the role it envisages for the private sector. The trend towards pure market-led economics, emanating from the 1980s, led to a clawback of state involvement and the questioning of incentives as mechanisms more likely to lead to market distortions. This is in total contrast to the concept of sustainable development which, especially in tourism, challenges the ability of private markets to improve the distribution of income and protect the environment. The baseline scenario for sustainable development is the alleviation of poverty and the replenishment of the resource stock so that at a minimum no one generation is worse off than any previous one. The spillover benefits of tourism in terms of income and employment creation are well known, and, more than any other industry, tourism deals with the use of natural and cultural resources, which in outlying regions are often their major asset. The lessons of the past indicate that it is unwise for the state to abandon its ability to influence the direction of tourism development either through the provision of finance or through legislation. The short-term gains sought by capital markets are often at odds with the long-term sustainability of tourist environments. With tourist movements set to increase both nationally and internationally, there will be a need for more regulation, direction and improved management of tourism resources to prevent environmental degradation and implement tourism development plans in a sustainable manner.

REFERENCES

Archer, B., Wanhill, S., 1980, *Tourism in Bermuda: an economic evaluation*, Bermuda Department of Tourism, Hamilton
Baum, T., Mudambi, R., 1996, Attracting hotel investment: insights from principal-agent theory, *Hospitality Research Journal*, **20**(2): 15–30
Bloom, J., Mostert, F., 1995, Incentive guidelines for South African tourism: implications and challenges in the context of developing socio-political trends, *Tourism Economics*, **1**(1): 17–31
Bodlender, J.A., 1982, The financing of tourism projects, *Tourism Management*, **3**(4): 277–284
Bodlender, J.A., Ward, T.J., 1987, *An examination of tourism incentives*, Howarth & Howarth, London
Boskin, M., 1996, National Satellite Accounting for travel and tourism: a cold review of the WTTC/WEFA group research, *Tourism Economics*, **2**(1): 3–11
Browne, T., 1996, *VAT: its impact on European tourism*, Deloitte Touche Tohmatsu International, London
BTA VAT Working Group, 1995, *The economic effects of changing VAT rates on the British tourism and leisure industry*, British Tourist Authority, London
Cooper, C., 1992, The life cycle concept and strategic planning for coastal resorts, *Built environment*, **18**(1): 57–66
Cooper, C., Jackson, S., 1989, Destination life cycle: the Isle of Man case study, *Annals of Tourism Research*, **15**(3): 377–398
House of Commons, 1969, *Development of Tourism Act 1969*, HMSO, London
Jenkins, C.L., 1982, The use of investment incentives for tourism in developing countries, *Tourism Management*, **3**(2): 91–97
Johnson, P.S., Thomas, R.B., 1990, The economic impact of museums: a study of the North of England Open Air Museum at Beamish, proceedings of a conference on *Tourism research into the 1990s*, University of Durham, pp. 388–402
Johnson, P.S., Thomas, R.B., 1992, *Tourism, museums and the local economy*, Edward Elgar, Aldershot
Lowyck, E., Wanhill, S., 1992, Regional development and tourism within the European Community. In Cooper, C., Lockwood, A., eds, *Progress in tourism, recreation and hospitality management*, Belhaven Press, London, pp. 227–244
Plog, S., 1973, Why destinations rise and fall in popularity, *Cornell H.R.A. Quarterly*, November: 3–16

Surrey Research Group, 1993, *Scottish tourism multiplier study*, ESU Research Paper No. 31, The Scottish Office, Industry Department, Vol. 1, p. 124

Wanhill, S., 1986, Which investment incentives for tourism?, *Tourism Management*, **7**(1): 2–7

Wanhill, S., 1994, Evaluating the worth of investment incentives for tourism development, *Journal of Travel Research*, **33**(2): 33–39

Wanhill, S., 1995, VAT rates and the UK tourism and leisure industry, *Tourism Economics*, **1**(3): 211–224

Wanhill, S., 1996, Local enterprise and development in tourism, *Tourism Management*, **17**(1): 35–42

13 Package Holiday Pricing: Cause of the IT Industry's Success, or Cause for Concern?

ERIC LAWS

INTRODUCTION

Technological and socio-economic developments underpin the growth of tourism in the second half of the twentieth century, but the success of the packaged holiday sector can also be explained in part by an emphasis on low prices. Low prices have expanded the market, but have also resulted in problems which are increasingly causing concern within the industry and to other interest groups. In particular, concern has been expressed about unsustainably low profit margins and about the effects on destination communities of rapid and insensitive expansion of their tourism sectors. The policies which led to the growth of the inclusive holiday industry now require re-evaluation if it is to continue to extend into new origin markets and destinations.

This chapter discusses the pricing policies commonly adopted by tour operators and retail travel agencies to manage their revenue flows and their market share. It examines the nature and evolution of low-price holiday offers by individual companies, and focuses attention on the consequences for all organisations in the holiday industry, arguing that the analytical and policy focus should be the entire industry. The objective of this chapter is to focus attention on low prices as a significant factor constraining the holiday industry's ability to function systematically as a network of long-term business relationships in creating the types of holiday products and experiences which are enjoyable for clients, rewarding for entrepreneurs and staff, and welcomed by destination area residents, local businesses and politicians. It argues that the appropriate level of analysis for tourism policy-makers should be the industry, rather than its component elements.

Economic and Management Methods for Tourism and Hospitality Research.
Edited by Thomas Baum and Ram Mudambi © 1999 John Wiley & Sons Ltd.

PRICE SETTING AND THE DEVELOPMENT OF THE INCLUSIVE HOLIDAY INDUSTRY

During the second half of the twentieth century tourism has become one of the major industries in the world. Three technological developments – jet aircraft, telecommunications, and computerised reservations systems – have enabled tour operators to increase the range of destinations offered, as well as to hold or reduce the cost of producing holidays in real terms (Pearce, 1992; Poon, 1993; Moutinho et al, 1996). In combination with improved standards of living, especially higher discretionary income, longer paid holidays, and changing demographics and patterns of work, this has resulted in much wider social access to holidays. These developments have also coincided with greater general awareness of overseas travel resulting from the widespread ownership of television, and attractive media coverage of wildlife, archaeology, heritage, ecology and other place-related topics.

The marketplace appeal of tourism is illustrated by the proportion of United Kingdom population who have ever taken an overseas holiday. This doubled in two decades, rising from 34% in 1970 to 70% in 1990 (BTA, 1992). Packaged holidays (also referred to as inclusive tours because they combine the main elements of journey and accommodation during a resort stay) are one component in an industry which includes business travel and leisure travel of all forms, but they are particularly significant in the main destination areas around the Mediterranean and for long-haul holidays. In 1979, 51.6% of all overseas holidays from the UK were inclusive tours (ITs), reaching 54.4% in 1995 (CSO, 1996). In a study of the European leisure holiday market, O'Brien (1996) demonstrated that the ratio of ITs to population was 0.26 in Britain, only the Netherlands and Switzerland having a higher participation rate (0.36 for both, in 1994–95). The total number of package holidays sold was highest in Germany (18.4 million), Britain recording the second highest number (15.16 million). Germany, Britain and the Netherlands together accounted for two thirds of the packaged tours sold in Europe. However, it should be noted that opportunities for international leisure travel are still confined to a small proportion of the world's population, mainly residents of the industrialised nations. 'On a world scale, fewer than 4% of the world's population take international holidays and 80% of international demand is generated by less than 20 countries' (Archer, 1989).

From the perspective of destinations, the inclusive holiday industry can be understood as consisting of a network of competing but interdependent businesses linking a resort with the countries from which its tourists originate. Operating as they do from a base in tourists' origin countries, with specialised knowledge of channels of communication and distribution, and a good understanding of local buying behaviours, travel retailers and tour operators are usually more effective than destinations in reaching potential holidaymakers with advertising designed to influence their decision to purchase holidays in distant countries.

While smaller tour operators specialise in particular destinations (or types of holiday) the nature of mass market tour operators' business is to organise holidays for large numbers of clients. The particular destinations they serve are a lower order of business objective than achieving high usage ratios with ground handling agents, hotel groups, and particularly charter air carriers. Tour operators and the retailers who sell packaged holidays therefore stimulate demand for inclusive holidays by a variety of marketing practices. Their techniques have three main thrusts:

1. advertising images and descriptions of place evoking appeals such as culture, climate, scenery, or opportunities for activities such as snowboarding;
2. appeals based on service style, and a particular level of quality;
3. offers emphasising low prices.

There are several rationales for low prices, including the major companies' wish to defend (or to increase) market share. However, packaged holidays share the characteristics of services, particularly the inability to store inventory (Cowell, 1986): many price-based offers reflect the increasingly urgent need as departure date approaches for holiday companies to sell any remaining capacity they have contracted on flights and in hotels. Economies of scale enable travel retailers and tour operators to sell packaged holidays at an inclusive price which is often below the cost of the various components if purchased direct, even without the uncertainty and the transaction costs incurred by an independent traveller dealing with many separate and distant service providers. The nature of inclusive tours is such that it confers many benefits on holidaymakers, the main being simplicity, convenience, and security in purchasing the complex array of services which comprise an overseas holiday (Laws, 1997a). All major components of the holiday (the return journey, accommodation, meals and so on) are purchased in one transaction, and purchase of an IT also relieves the holidaymaker of making the detailed logistical arrangements for the holiday.

THE SIGNIFICANCE OF HOLIDAY INDUSTRY PRICING POLICIES

The approaches which an organisation adopts to pricing its services should be evaluated in the context of its overall aims, as McCarthy and Perreault (1988) have pointed out, 'Managers develop a set of pricing objectives and policies in the context of the company's objectives. The policy explains how flexible prices are to be, the level at which they will be set over the life cycle of the service, and to whom and when discounts will be allowed'.

Medlik (1993), noting that price competition features strongly in the travel industry, defined this as a 'Market situation in which firms compete on price rather than quality of product or other factors to influence the buyers' choice ... Price competition is sometimes chosen as a deliberate strategy but often is the result of unforeseen market conditions, in which planned capacity or sales exceed actual demand'.

The continuing growth of the British packaged holiday market in the mid 1990s has been ascribed to 'the fierce price competition that has taken place in the last three years between Thomsons, Airtours, and First Choice Holidays, largely at the expense of profit margins' (O'Brien, 1996). Commenting that, together, these tour operators have achieved a 70% share of the UK summer sun market, O'Brien noted that their pricing policy has created a significant problem for the entire industry. 'They have led the public to expect large discounts (up to 15% off brochure holidays) and have engaged in high season discounting to shift unsold product'.

The result of low prices has not only been to stimulate demand for holidays currently on offer, there is also evidence of effects with long-term significance. In the two decades following World War II, organised overseas holidays were mainly taken in the school holiday periods, and by relatively well-off sectors of the community, but low prices have altered the timing of demand, for example by extending the holiday season, and have changed the demographic profile of holidaymakers, to include all age groups and most socio-economic sectors of society. Low prices have also been the locus of power plays between competing companies and between the various organisations in the holiday industry system. Several major companies including tour operators and charter airlines have failed, and there have been many take-overs and mergers between tour operators, travel retailers and charter airlines. Not all of these events can be ascribed to the results of pricing policy, but by putting the customers' focus at the point of holiday purchase on price comparisons rather than alternative destination benefits, these effects have contributed to the commoditisation of holiday products noted and criticised by many analysts of the industry, notably Krippendorf (1987), Urry, (1990), and McCannell, (1992).

PRICING INCLUSIVE HOLIDAYS

The complexity of pricing packaged holiday decisions for a tour operator has been highlighted by Holloway and Robinson (1995). Robinson was the Group Marketing Manager of First Choice, one of Britain's leading tour operators, and the authors noted that the company 'produced some 2300 brochure pages for the summer 1995 season. Most featured a price panel with perhaps 100 separate prices, making a total of almost a quarter of a million prices.' First Choice's pricing was based on a straightforward cost-plus approach, but it also reflected a range of objectives for different products, such as to regain market share in specific resorts. Further adjustments are made to achieve an overall price advantage. 'the brochure price is determined, but so too is the proposed policy on early booking discounts, child discounts, late sales reductions, travel agent commission incentives and the like. This is because the overall profitability target of the programme must be set against the actual sales price likely to be achieved' (Holloway and Robinson, 1995).

In a discussion of pricing issues for the tourism industry generally, Middleton (1991) discussed eleven influences on the prices of tourism products, including high price elasticity in discretionary segments, fixed capacity, high customer psychological involvement, high fixed costs, long lead times between price decisions and product sales, and short-run crisis management. Duadel and Vialle (1994) distinguished between 'spoilage', the underutilisation of resources, and 'spill', selling too cheaply early, with the result that later, higher yielding demand has to be denied. They argued in favour of yield management techniques, using price to balance the market conditions of supply and demand. The principle of price setting for optimum yield management is based on setting various thresholds to segment customers' varying ability or willingness to pay. For holidays, each defined by departure date and airport, duration and resort of stay (Laws, 1997a) the relevant thresholds reflect assumptions about price-related differences in buying behaviour, particularly in respect of seasonal choices, late or early booking habits, and departure airport preferences. These can be modelled by analysis of the company's historic data (Relihan, 1989).

Seasonal pricing

One of the most common ways of setting holiday price differentials is the seasonal banding typical of tour operators' brochures and familiar to all who purchase inclusive holidays, in the form of price and departure date price matrices. This is represented schematically in Figure 13.1. The peak season, when limited discounting is undertaken because many holidaymakers are willing to pay premium prices, is shown as the broad central column, flanked by two shoulders of unequal width representing the early and late seasons. The more restricted nature of demand during the shoulder seasons limits opportunities to charge premium prices, but offers scope to stimulate market demand through a variety of discounting practices. In contrast to the generalised three-season price banding model represented in Figure 13.1, it should be noted that tour operators' brochures typically band their holidays into up to a dozen seasonal prices.

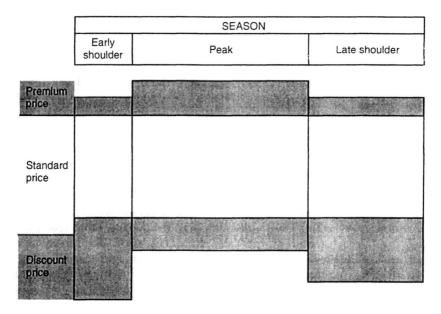

Figure 13.1. A general model of seasonal price handling

Late Booking

Price reductions for late booking are a widespread holiday industry response to its unsold capacity, and typically are promoted by travel agents as well as tour operators shortly before departure. This has proved an effective way to tackle one of the problems characteristic of the services sector, the inability to store inventory (Cowell, 1986). Tour operators consider it advantageous to obtain some revenue for a particular holiday which they have not been able to sell at the price offered in the brochure, and are often able to obtain additional revenue by selling their own clients extra excursions and entertainment after their arrival in the resort. One common approach is to invite clients to pay a stated price, for example £150 per week, for a stated departure and duration, but leaving the hotel and even the resort to the tour operator's discretion. From the customer's perspective, this introduces a higher than normal element of uncertainty (or risk) into the holiday purchase transaction.

Responses to late offers

During the 1960s and 70s, there was a highly publicised annual rush to buy holidays as soon as the next season's brochure was launched. Queues formed outside travel agencies early each new year, to buy holidays for the summer ahead: early purchase gave the clients the highest probability of getting their preference for destination, hotel, duration, and departure date. In contrast, a trend had emerged in the 1990s to delay the purchase of package holidays. This can be understood as representing customers learning the new rules of selling, and adapting these to their own benefit when purchasing holidays. In the case of inclusive tours, the pattern of early booking which formed the basis of buyer behaviour (and consequent price adjustment tactics to shift unsold volume as departures dates approached) has altered under the influence of reduced price offers. Vellos and Becherel (1995) have identified resistance amongst clients to buying holidays early in the belief that a high proportion of capacity will remain unsold, thereby increasing the likelihood of reduced price offers, and of being able to buy a holiday which closely matches that desired.

The benefits for tour operators of increased numbers of clients through the late booking discount mechanism has to be set against difficulties which have resulted. These include customers who did not obtain the quality of holiday which they had hoped for, an apparent shift away from the traditional advanced booking of holidays several months ahead of departure in favour of waiting for these late offers to be made, and approaches to managing both the supply and distribution channels for holidays which have tended to strongly favour the major tour operators and the vertically integrated holiday companies. A travel industry manager commented critically, 'getting a package deal at a knockdown price is now a national sport' (Josephides, 1995). Other criticisms focus on the way that discounting is shifting holiday destination preferences. For example, flat rate holiday discounting (a prominent feature of travel retailer tactics) favours long-haul destinations, because the technique produces a greater cash saving when compared to the typically lower priced European holiday. When combined with seasonal price banding for areas such as the Caribbean, the effect has been to redistribute the peak travel season. A senior manager commented: 'All the hard work done by the tour operator and the hotelier working together in terms of spreading demand across the season is wiped out by the stroke of a felt tip pen in a travel agent's window' (Heape, 1994).

The duration of the interval between clients making a booking and taking their holiday has been important to tour operators, since it provides an opportunity for them to function as 'bankers' benefiting from interest on their clients' deposit. The industry practice is for tour operators to settle their suppliers' invoices at about the time that the client receives services from the charter airline and hotel. The number of clients, and the consequent aggregate value of their deposits, has enabled tour operators to place money on the overnight market (Bull, 1991). This source of income is at risk from the shift towards later bookings. It is partly in response to this threat that tour

Table 13.1. Supplements to fly to Majorca by airport and season of departure

Departure airport	Low season supplement	High season supplement
London/Gatwick	0	£41
Luton	0	£41
Edinburgh	£9	£114
Glasgow	0	£118
Aberdeen	£3	£89

Source: Laws (1997), based on Trend (1994)

operators have recently begun to offer incentives for early booking, including free child places and three weeks for the price of two. Early sale of a holiday also has the advantage of reducing the remaining market open to competitors.

Regional departure supplements

One of the crucial factors for the success of any area functioning as a destination is the ease of access to it from origin points, particularly by direct flights from regional departure airports located close to important secondary origin markets. Charter airlines incur a range of costs when positioning their aircraft away from the main base for these flights, and it might be expected that this will be reflected in the supplements charged by tour operators for regional departures. Other technical considerations, such as the use of smaller aircraft, are also factors increasing regional flight costs (Doganis, 1985, Wheatcroft, 1994). However, as Table 13.1 indicates, setting the price differentials for departures from regional airports represents an opportunity for market price engineering, rather than directly reflecting any extra costs incurred. Table 13.1 also shows how a regional pricing structure further distorts the basic holiday price by the differential application of seasonal price banding to various departure airports.

HIGH AND LOW INVOLVEMENT BUYING BEHAVIOUR

The importance of any category of purchase varies between different customers according to their degrees of interest and 'involvement'. Cohen (1986) defined involvement as 'a state of arousal that a person experiences in regard to consumption related activity'. Involvement is considered likely to be high when the purchase has functional and symbolic significance, and entails some risk (Asseal, 1987). Table 13.2 identifies four features of holidays which make it likely that many tourists will experience a high degree of involvement in choosing their holiday.

Table 13.2. High involvement features of holiday purchases

- Holidays are expensive
- They are complex both to purchase and to experience
- There is a risk that they will not prove satisfying
- The choice of destination (or type of holiday) reflects the holidaymaker's personality

---

The significance of regarding holidays as a high-involvement purchase is the implication that considerable care will be invested by clients in their choice of destination or type of holiday. Thus, the expectation is that the potential tourist will undertake detailed and extended study of brochures, reading and watching holiday advertising, and visiting travel agencies for advice to identify suitable places to visit, given individual interests and the time and budget available.

This rationalist model of holiday destination choice may have much less validity in the conditions which have characterised much of the market for packaged holidays, when tour operators or travel retailers emphasise prices rather than destination attributes in their promotions. This shifts the customers' attention to a comparison of prices rather than of what each destination offers, potentially resulting in a reduced 'commitment' to the resort visited. Under these conditions, there is more likely to be a mismatch between the tourists' holiday expectations, and their destination experiences, resulting in dissatisfaction and complaint. This difficulty is exacerbated by two factors, one internal to the holiday industry, the other characteristic of contemporary society. Discounted, and particularly late offer, holidays often involve relatively low-quality holiday components. These may include inconvenient departure and arrival times, and even unspecified hotel (or other) accommodation. While clients sometimes benefit under these trading terms from accommodation better than they had anticipated, the reverse is often the case. This is partly because those who booked early have opted for the superior accommodation and the better locations within resorts. Another factor is the practice of some tour operators of buying-in extra accommodation close to departure dates for destinations where their charter seat allocation is unfilled. In this case too, the more attractive accommodation will already have been reserved for their own main programme sales or by competitors, relegating late-booking, discounted holiday makers to lower quality, marginal hotel stock.

The industry has regularly experienced a high incidence of complaints about low standards of accommodation, poor resort location and associated difficulties particularly with respect to late-booked holidays. This situation has to be considered in the context of growing consumer-rights awareness (Prus, 1989), and the 'meta-context' of scepticism about the underlying values and institutions of western societies (Hughes, 1993). Thus, the travel retailer also becomes a target of complaint when the client returns, a situation which recent European legislation is likely to accentuate (Rogers, 1993). In response, there is evidence of a growing management emphasis, in tourism no less than other sectors of the economy, on product and service quality (Carlzon, 1991; Normann, 1991; Laws, 1997a).

There is, however, evidence of other problems. The Consumers Association magazine, *Holiday Which* (January, 1997: 12–15) reported a survey of 11 500 members of the consumer organisation asking them to rate the tour operators and countries they had patronised in the year to September 1996. The key criterion was 'whether they would definitely recommend them to a friend who wants to take the same sort of holiday'. Swiss Travel Service was the only operator of the 51 in the survey to gain a 'definitely' or 'probably' recommendation from all Consumer Association respondents who had used the company. Poor accommodation was the main source of dissatisfaction, other concerns related to representatives, brochure accuracy, and changes to the arrangements once booked. At the less recommended end of the scale, several companies were scoring about a quarter of 'probably not' or 'definitely not recommend' ratings. Amongst the major tour operators, the proportion who would definitely recommend a particular tour operator ranged from 48% for Thomsons to 28% for First Choice and 25% for Airtours.

The purchase of a holiday represents a deliberate decision, in which the individual (or a travelling group such as a family) invests part of their limited resources. The price paid for a holiday is constrained by the customer's budget considerations, but for many people the purchase is often treated as a priority expenditure in planning personal or family expenditure. This implies both that the tourist has chosen not to spend money (and time) on alternative products, and that he or she will not be able to visit alternative destinations during that vacation. An exception is that some holidays such as cruising, multi-stop itineraries and coach tours are designed to include a selection of destinations in one holiday. Furthermore, a trend has been noted in several European countries to multiple holiday-taking in any year (O'Brien, 1996), and this enables individuals to patronise several destinations.

PRICE RELATIVITIES AS A SIGNAL OF PRODUCT QUALITY

Kimes (1994) has suggested that consumers seem to accept yield management in the airline sector, where they receive specific benefits if they accept certain restraints. However, she raised the question of how customers react to it in other industries, suggesting that 'a customer who pays more for a similar service and cannot perceive a difference in the service may view the situation as unfair'. Kimes developed her argument on the basis of a reference price, derived from market prices and the customer's previous experience. At a normal (or reference) price, a high standard of service and amenities will please the client, but those same standards will only satisfy clients paying premium rates. Customers enjoying normal or superior standards on a holiday for which they paid low prices will be pleased, or delighted. In contrast, customers receiving normal levels of service in return for high prices will feel at best exploited, and if standards fall further, they are likely to experience (and express) anger. Low levels of service or amenities are likely to provoke negative responses whatever the price paid for them.

Consumer satisfaction is the outcome when expectations are matched by service experience, conversely, dissatisfaction occurs when there is a mismatch, and expectations are not fulfilled by the service delivered (Engel et al, 1986). Aggregate dissatisfaction amongst many consumers is a serious matter to the firm providing a service, as the implication is that customers will take their future business elsewhere. They are also likely to discuss their negative experiences with friends, thereby further undermining the company's market place credibility.

Dissatisfaction can be understood as cognitive dissonance (Festinger, 1957), a psychological condition making it unlikely that the customer will purchase from that supplier in the future. In extreme cases, the customer will complain formally, thereby imposing a burden on the company which will have to respond in a considered way (in case the dispute reaches court or an arbitration process for ultimate resolution). The company may decide (or be ordered) to pay the disappointed client financial compensation. Arbitration involves the travel retailer as the first point of recourse, and this has introduced a new dynamic into the network of organisations contributing to the package holiday industry. Letters to the travel trade press indicate that increasingly, travel retailers are reluctant to act as agents for tour operators which are the subject of frequent complaints by customers. Court cases, or those pursued through the consumer pressure groups and on radio, TV, or press consumer programmes, also attract widespread attention, thereby further threatening the company, and ultimately undermining the credibility and desirability of the industry's products (Rogers, 1993).

REDUCING PRICE LEVELS AND BROADENING MARKET DEMAND

A reduction in price provides increased access to the product. Ideally, the shift from one price band to a lower one occurs after the higher payers have bought, then the lower price has the effect of bringing the product to a new group of potential purchasers, with different behavioural characteristics.

One example of this is the way that cruising holidays are being promoted to a broader market on the basis of reduced prices. In 1995, one tour operator new to the cruising sector claimed to have achieved its aim of gaining around 60% of cruise bookings from clients who have not cruised before. Cooney (1995) reported that the Airtours Marketing Director had said: 'The [newly acquired] ship has been fully refurbished and we have made the product affordable and less formal. We have applied the Airtours sales and marketing formula, so anyone who has enjoyed our other holidays will enjoy our cruises. We have a well thought out formula. The ship is the right size to give us the economies of scale we need to offer affordable fares, which is always the starting point for customers'. Commenting on this, the Director of PSARA (Passenger Shipping Agent Retail Association) remarked that Airtours has a tightrope to walk. 'On one hand, they are telling customers there is no mystique about cruising, it's just a package holiday in which the hotel floats. On the other hand, it must try not to take away the elegance of cruising because they would be selling themselves and the industry short' (Cooney, 1995).

The overall effect of price discounting and the accompanying publicity by tour operators and travel retailers is to focus buyers' attention on the affordability of holidays, thereby widening the customer base but reducing the discrimination shown between alternative destinations. It is sometimes asserted that this has brought 'less desirable' clients into the market. The meaning of this term is generally left unspecified, but two features are apparent. Less desirable clients include low spenders, such as youths, the elderly, or families with lower incomes. The problems which result are that although their presence imposes demands on the resort's infrastructure, tour operators and the resort-based businesses cannot sell low-spending clients the lucrative extras such as souvenirs, excursions and entertainment in the quantities which better-off clients regard as essential elements of their augmented holiday experience. The second suspicion is that people buying the cheapest holiday packages are more likely to indulge in undesirable behaviour on arrival, including heavy drinking and noisy late night carousing. The concern often has another dimension, as it reflects an unproven general assumption that there is a direct link between detrimental client behaviour in a resort, and low-priced access to it through the medium of cheap inclusive holidays.

During the 1990s an increasing number of destinations have indicated that they do not wish to host such groups. Their preferred objectives are to attract clients who will spend more in the resort, and it is often assumed that such clients will be more sensitive to the destination's culture, while less likely to offend local people (or other visitors) by their behaviour. A newspaper report entitled 'Tourists? We only want the cream on Jersey, thank you', illustrates these concerns. Following an attempt to open the Channel Islands to package tourists, hoteliers there refused to reduce their room rates to the level which the tour operator had offered, between £13 and £23 a day, and the island airport declined to offer a 25% reduction on landing charges. Explaining the resistance, an executive of the Jersey Hotel and Guest House Association said: 'Airtours wanted to offer holidays so cheap that you have to wonder whether the people they brought over here would have any money to spend when they arrived ... we don't want to downgrade the island as a cut price destination' (Leith, 1995).

Destination resistance such as this is becoming more common, and overall it implies a limit to the ability of tour operators to price their holidays very cheaply. Some relatively new destinations, such as Dubai, take the view that setting high prices will minimise any social disruption through undesirable behaviour of visitors (Laws, 1995), while some traditional destinations such as Majorca have adopted a policy of moving upmarket (Jenner and Smith, 1993; Morgan, 1991).

Origin market effects

Price-based marketing practices have two consequences for the companies producing and selling holidays in origin markets, achieving shifts in the balance of market power within a sector (one tour operator gaining market share from another through the power of lower prices), or in terms of altering the existing balance of channel dominance between tour operators and retail travel agents. Cooper and his colleagues (1993), have discussed the resultant dynamics, describing how in attempting to increase market share by cutting its price, a company provokes a hostile repricing reaction from its competitors because this is an attempt to take their market share. The overall result may be an increase in the market size as more customers are attracted in by the lower prices, but overall revenue might not be increased. The long-term result is that the market remains unstable due to smaller margins. In this situation a company has to ensure that it has a high volume of business to exceed its break even point, but the rate of collapse of UK tour operators indicates how volatile this is.

Description and analysis of the inclusive holiday industry generally views it from the perspectives of channel management theory originally developed to examine the distribution systems for food, fast-moving consumer goods, or consumer durables (Bucklin, 1967). The issues for channel members are about dominance and control. Retail travel agents have traditionally been regarded as weak because of their small size relative to the tour operators, and their reliance on the tour operator for products to sell, although they are developing ways of gaining influence, for example by refusing to rack the brochures of tour operators paying low commission, or those about which many complaints are received. An aspect of competition leading to changes in channel dominance is the effect of discounting in favouring the larger companies, particularly the multiple-branch retail travel agents. 'Discounting advantages are quickly negated by competitive response, but then there is no doubt that multiples take bookings from independent agents. Through acquisition of extra retail outlets and through heavy discounting, the major multiples are steadily increasing their share of business' (Heape, 1994). Discussing the advantages of larger companies, Heape also pointed to the fact that the tour operators who own retailers do not pay extra commission on the sales made by their retail partners. 'Therefore their products can be priced very competitively compared to other operators'.

Price discounting causes structural changes in the packaged holiday industry by undermining the profitability of some companies to the point where it is no longer viable for them to stay in the industry. Sheldon (1986), discussing the relationship between industry structure and pricing policy, noted a polarisation in the industry, with a few large firms, and many small ones, and pointed to the relatively short lives of many small companies. However, several large tour operators have also failed, and many mergers or acquisitions have been recorded in the industry. Traditionally, economists have considered that incumbent firms in a market gain advantages from insurmountably high fixed costs barring entry to a market. Baumol and Willig (1981) defined entry barriers as 'anything that requires an expenditure by a new entrant into an industry, but requires no equivalent cost upon an incumbent'. Another feature of contestable markets is particularly relevant to the inclusive holiday industry. Exit costs are minimal as other businesses, incumbents or new entrants, will be willing to buy the business assets of companies ceasing operation. A Director of Airtours reported that 'I have about 20 proposals a week land on my desk from companies who want us to purchase them because they know we have lots of money and are ambitious' (Skidmore, 1995).

Destination effects

More attention must be focused on the fact that pricing decisions by tour operators and travel retailers have consequences not only for the companies which take them, but also for their industry partners, the hotels and destinations which are the principal suppliers of the holidaymakers' experiences. The rapid growth of the industry during the 1960s and 1970s resulted in a proliferation of hotel developments, particularly in the Mediterranean resorts. Many of these hotels were built to low design criteria, and they were often aesthetically unappealing in the context of idyllic settings. As the hotel stock grew, and as more destinations became accessible, oversupply enabled tour operators to drive contract room rates down. The cumulative effect of repeated seasons of low contract rates paid by tour operators to hotels has eroded their ability to improve standards of service or invest in upgraded facilities, but this period has coincided with a period of increasing consumer awareness (Morgan, 1994; Vellos and Becherel, 1995). More effective deployment of consumer rights has alerted media attention to the dissatisfaction and complaints arising from low standards in holiday accommodation. Hoteliers have responded by showing a preference to deal with tour operators who do not exert such severe cost controls, notably those from other European countries. This has given rise to the phenomenon of one set of guests in a hotel being afforded preferential treatment in terms of better rooms or a more varied dinner menu, further exacerbating the dissatisfaction.

Hoteliers have also responded by adopting overbooking policies (Lamnert et al, 1989), because the slender margins on room revenue lead to a need to sell all available capacity and to take the maximum advantage of the additional sources of revenue from clients, such as bar sales. Overbooked hotels result in the need for tour operators to switch their clients, often after arrival in the resort, to alternative hotels, and this results in complaints or claims for compensation by disgruntled clients.

DISCUSSION

This chapter has noted the rapid growth of the packaged holiday industry in the second half of the twentieth century, capitalising on technological developments, and the tour operators' and travel retailers' marketing policies which emphasise low prices. The benefits of the resultant increased market size, economies of scale and competitive advantage improve their negotiating position with charter airlines and destination-based suppliers, and enable the strongest companies to consolidate their dominant market position through mergers and acquisitions.

A number of problems have been identified, including a tendency to produce low-quality holiday products to the detriment of consumer satisfaction, and perhaps more significantly, to commoditise the concept of a foreign holiday, reducing the significance to consumers of the destination in their choice of holiday location. Both of these factors have the potential to undermine the future prospects for the inclusive holiday industry by increasing the incidence of disappointment with holiday experiences, and by reducing the interest of mass market holiday takers in the specific character of places they visit.

Cooperation in the holiday system

The problems noted above are the consequence of short-term and self-interest-based policies which, although rational for particular companies, do not have a systematic regard for the long-term development of the industry at heart.

Space limitations do not permit the detailed discussion of alternative approaches in this chapter, but valuable insights into the complexity and the dynamics of relationships between inclusive holiday industry participants can be gained by adopting the theoretical perspectives of network (Gummesson, 1987) or relationship (McKenna, 1994) marketing, and by viewing the holiday industry systematically. Systems theory emphasises the interdependency of the elements which together make up the industry, notably the tour operators, travel retailers, airlines, hotels, and destination organisations and communities (Mill and Morrison, 1985; Leiper, 1990; Laws, 1997a). Systems analysis also focuses attention on the consequences for all stakeholders of the way the system functions, and of any policy or operational changes. These approaches highlight as critical issues for examination the mutual dependency of all organisations in a holiday system, and the environment within which the industry operates, rather than the legitimate but lower order issue of competition between individual member companies.

CONCLUSION

This chapter has reviewed the pricing practices of tour operators and travel retailers against the background of growth and competition which has characterised origin markets in recent decades. It has pointed to changes in package holiday buying behaviour in response to low-price and late-sales offers, and has examined the causes and consequences of consumer disappointment which may result from decisions taken.

The combined effects of relatively low levels of service, overbooking and rowdy behaviour have reduced the attractiveness of budget holidays, and these might ultimately undermine the viability of this type of product. It should be a matter of concern to the industry that heavily discounted holidays distort the market by creating unsustainable long-term price expectations, since the low rates do not provide a sound basis for investment in the upgrading of hotel or resort facilities.

REFERENCES

Archer, B., 1989, Trends in international tourism. In Witt, S.F. and Moutinho, L., eds, *Tourism marketing and management handbook*, Prentice Hall, London, pp. 593–597.
Asseal, H., 1987, *Consumer behaviour and marketing action*, Kent Publishers, Boston
Baum, T., Mudambi, R., 1994, A Ricardian analysis of the fully inclusive tour industry, *Service Industries Journal*, 14(1), 85–93
Baumol, W., Willig, R., 1981, Fixed costs, sunk costs, entry barriers and sustainability of monopoly. *Quarterly Journal of Economics*, 46, 405–431
BTA, 1992, *Annual report*, British Tourist Authority, London

Bucklin, L., 1967, The economic structure of channels of distribution. In Mallen, B.E., *The marketing channel*, John Wiley, New York

Bull, A., 1991, *The economics of travel and tourism*, Longman, Cheshire, London

Carlzon, J., 1989, *Moments of truth*, Harper & Row, New York

Cohen, J.B., 1986, Involvement, separating the state from its causes and effects. Quoted in Wilkie, W.L., *Consumer behaviour*, John Wiley, Chichester

Cooney, M., 1995, Airtours plots a course for a growing market, *Travel Weekly*, March, p. 6

Cooper, C., Fletcher, J., Gilbert, D., Wanhill, S., 1993, eds, *Tourism: principles and practice*, Pitman, London

Cowell, D., 1986, *The marketing of services*, Heinemann, London

CSO, 1996, *Annual abstract of statistics*, Central Statistical Office, London

Doganis, R., 1985, *Flying off course, the economics of international airlines*, Allen & Unwin, London

Duadel, S., Vialle, G., 1994, Yield management: applications to air transport and other service industries, Institut du Transport Aerien, Paris

Engel, J.F., Blackwell, R.D., Miniard, P.W., 1986, *Consumer behaviour*, Dryden Press, Chicago

Festinger, L.A., 1957, *Theory of cognitive dissonance*, Stanford University Press, Palo Alto, CA

Gummesson, E., 1987, *Marketing, a long term interactive relationship*, Anderson Sandberg Dhein, Gothenburg

Heape, R., 1994, Outward bound, *Tourism Society Journal*, **83**: 4–5.

Holloway, J.C., Robinson, R., 1995, *Marketing for tourism*, 3rd edn, Longman, Harlow

Hughes, R., 1993, *Culture of complaint*, Warner Books, New York

Jenner, P., Smith, C., 1993, *Tourism in the Mediterannean*. EIU Research Report, London

Josephides, N., 1995, More to it than meets the eye, *Travel Weekly*, 14 September, p.11

Kimes, S.E., 1994, Perceived fairness of yield management, *Cornell H.R.A. Quarterly*, February

Krippendorf, J., 1987, *The holiday makers*, Heinemann, London

Lamnert, C.U., Lambert, J.M., Cullen, T.P., 1989, The overbooking question, a simulation, *Cornell H.R.A. Quarterly*, August

Laws, E., 1995, *Tourist destination management: issues, analysis and policies*, Routledge, London

Laws, E., 1997a, *Managing packaged tourism: relationships, responsibilities and service quality in the inclusive holiday industry*, Thompson International Business Press, London

Laws, E., 1997b, *The inclusive holiday industry: relationships, responsibility and customer satisfaction*, Thomson International Business Press, London

Leiper, N., 1990, *Tourism systems*, Massey University Press, Palmerston North

Leith, E., 1995, The holiday's over, *Mail on Sunday Review*, October, pp. 6–8

MacCannell, D., 1992, *Empty meeting grounds, the tourist papers*, Routledge, London

McCarthy, E.J., Perreault, W.D., Jr., 1988, *Essentials of marketing*, Irwin, Homewood, IL

McKenna, R., 1994, *Relationship marketing: successful strategies for the age of the customer*, Addison-Wesley, Reading, MA

Medlik, S., 1993, *Dictionary of transport, travel and hospitality*, Butterworth Heinemann, Oxford

Middleton, V.T.C., 1991, Whither the package tour? *Tourism Management*, **12**(3), September

Mill, R.C., Morrison, A.M., 1985, *The tourism system*, Prentice-Hall, Englewood Cliffs, NJ

Morgan, M., 1991, Dressing up to survive: marketing Majorca anew, *Tourism Management*, **12**(1), March

Morgan, M., 1994, Homogenous products: the future of established resorts. In Theobald, W., ed., *Global tourism: the next decade*, Butterworth Heinemann, Oxford

Moutinho, L., Rita, P., Curry, B., 1996, *Expert systems in tourism marketing*, Routledge, London

Normann, R., 1991, *Service management, strategy and leadership in service business*, John Wiley, Chichester

O'Brien, K., 1996, *The west European leisure travel market: forecasts for opportunities into the next century*, Financial Times Management Reports, London

Pearce, D., 1992, *Tourist organisations*, Longman, Harlow

Poon, A., 1993, *Tourism, technology and competitive strategies*, CAB International Press, Wallingford

Prus, R.C., 1989, *Pursuing customers, an ethnography of marketing activities*, Sage Publications, London

Relihan III, W., 1989, The yield management approach to hotel pricing, *Cornell H.R.A. Quarterly*, May

Rogers, P., 1993, *A practical guide to the package travel regulations*, Landor Travel Publications, London

Sheldon, P., 1986, The tour operating industry, an analysis, *Annals of Tourism Research*, **13**, 349–356

Skidmore, J., 1995, Airtours plays down need for acquisitions, *Travel News*, April

Trend, N., 1994, Local airport blues, BBC Holidays, July

Urry, J., 1990, *The tourist gaze*, Sage Publications, London

Vellas, F., Becherel, L., 1995, *International tourism*, Macmillan, Basingstoke

Wheatcroft, S., 1994, *Aviation and tourism policies*, Routledge, London

14 Economic Pricing Strategies for Hotels

BACKGROUND

Economists say that prices set in any industry should be determined by the point of intersection where marginal revenues equals marginal costs faced by individual firms (Stonier and Hague, 1953). Prices may be sufficiently high at that point to cover both average fixed and average variable costs. Profits will be maximized, and the amount of these profits will depend upon the slope of the corresponding demand curve. The higher the share of fixed costs, the higher the desired level of output at that point.

One significant problem with using this approach in pricing hotel rooms is the practical difficulty of measuring the necessary demand and cost relationships. As a result, the industry tends to fall back on use of average rather than marginal costs, which are implied in application of the Hubbert Formula and various other rules of thumb related to costs (such as charging $1 in room rate for each $1000 of construction cost per room) (Lewis and Chambers, 1989). Average-cost pricing is economically quite inefficient, especially for an industry which has sizable fixed costs and typically books many of its room reservations far in advance of actual use. In these cases, marginal costs likely depart considerably from marginal costs.

Further, industry practice has ingrained a set of categorical discounts that customers have grown to expect and rely upon. For example, student and elderly discounts tend to reflect the different demand characteristics usually assumed to be associated with these groups. Others, such as corporate discounts, may be only tangentially related to expected differences in demand but may reflect economies of scale, as in the case of negotiated rates with large customers who rent many rooms. But, for the most part, these discounts tend to confuse economic pricing because the categorical basis of the discount does not reflect the conditions of demand and supply that could lead to profit maximization. Categorical discounts that do have a basis in

Economic and Management Methods for Tourism and Hospitality Research.
Edited by Thomas Baum and Ram Mudambi © 1999 John Wiley & Sons Ltd.

economics (as noted above for students and elderly) tend to be misunder-stood as special favors rather than being reflective of a basis for appropriate market segmentation.

INDUSTRY CHARACTERISTICS THAT AFFECT PRICING

There are specific industry characteristics that condition the type of pricing policies that are feasible and appropriate to the hotel industry. These include the following.

Differing demands of customer segments

The lodging industry is faced with a variety of customer segments with quite differing demands associated with their different purposes of travel. These purposes, broadly speaking, include pleasure, transient (business), and attendance at conferences and various other group meetings (groups).

Pleasure travelers tend to be quite price sensitive and are willing to book rooms far in advance in order to secure low prices (Figure 14.1).[1] This segment generally has negative but a relatively elastic price elasticity of demand for rooms.[2] Transient or business travelers with quite variable sched-ules are not able to plan as far in advance as pleasure travelers and tend to book rooms relatively late in the booking cycle (Figure 14.1). But, once identi-fied, their needs to travel may be quite urgent. Therefore, this group is likely to be less sensitive to prices charged than are pleasure travelers. This segment tends to have negative but relatively inelastic price elasticities of demand. The group business combines attributes of both pleasure and business travelers.

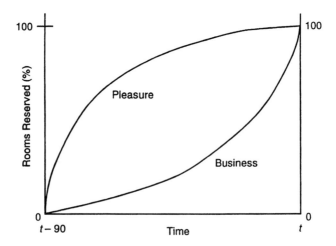

Figure 14.1. Expected booking patterns for pleasure or business travelers

Because of the large number of rooms needed and other special require-ments, groups need to plan far in advance. Also, they tend to be planned by professional meeting planners who are aware of the economies of scale involved, so groups tend to be quite price sensitive. They are expected to fall intermediate between pleasure and business travelers in terms of the nature of their price elasticity of demand.

In concept, there are many demand segments other than the three identi-fied above. These may be associated with different income levels, age group-ings, seasonality, and types of 'pleasure' or business. 'Pleasure' travelers going to say farewell to deceased relatives have much stronger motivations than those taking their vacations or holidays, or those taking a weekend to explore a neighboring city. Business travelers on per-diem or government-reimbursed trips have quite different motivations than high-income execu-tives on unlimited expense accounts. Similarly, groups are not homogeneous in their demands. Some may be business travelers traveling on expense accounts and others may be pleasure travelers spending their own funds.

Variability in demand within segments

Different product offerings also face much variability in the level of demand within customer segments associated with different days of the week, holidays, different seasons of the year, and normal fluctuations in local per-sonal or business situations. This variability causes much noise in forecasting normal room demands for an individual property but also requires that each day of the year be projected and priced individually.

Many rooms are reserved far in advance, which is very useful for planning purposes for a lodging establishment. A large number of transient walk-ins adds to the uncertainty of the business and complicates pricing strategies. Advance reservations aid immensely in managing day-to-day variability in demand. However, different segments are expected to vary considerably in the extent to which they make advanced reservations and in the length of the advance.

Advanced reservations do have a down side, because of the problems caused by those who do not keep their reservations (so-called 'no-shows'). This problem has been alleviated by use of credit card guarantees, but it per-sists to a lesser degree and complicates the objective of maintaining high occupancy levels. Also, the advanced reservations often are made at reduced rates in anticipation of their more price-sensitive demands.

Perishable nature of the product

A room that is not rented for a given day is lost forever as a source of revenue. The room may be rented in the future, but lost revenues can never be retrieved. For this reason, there is a strong incentive to strive for high occupancy rates. (This characteristic also underlies the Ricardian nature of the industry; see chapter 6 in this volume.) This perishability is shared with many other service industries and other segments of the hospitality business such as airlines. (in this connection, see also Masson et al, 1994). Airlines pioneered in the introduction of yield management strategies in part to offer incentives to maintain service levels.

High fixed costs

High fixed costs exacerbate the perishable nature of the business of renting hotel rooms. It means that there is little savings to an organization in not renting rooms. Basic costs associated with building and maintaining the hotel continue regardless of the number of rooms rented. Variable costs associated with the rooms department account for only about one-fourth of total room department income while fixed costs associated primarily with paying for the building and overhead expenses account for a large share of the remaining revenue (Pannell Kerr Forster, 1993). This feature gives strong incentive to rent rooms at relatively low rates rather than leave them vacant. But, fixed costs need to be paid too if a company is going to stay in business for long.

Further, the industry may be reluctant to discount rooms due to the concept of 'rate integrity,' which suggests that once a room is discounted, customers will never want to pay a higher rate in the future.

Fixed capacity

Even though demand may be quite variable and unpredictable, the room supply available in the short run tends to be relatively fixed. It takes a long time to expand a building or build a new one. Adding part-time or seasonal labor may be useful in better serving guests during periods of peak occupancy, but it can add little to available room inventory. As a result, pricing policies are largely restricted to allocating existing supplies among competing demands. This restriction adds importance to appropriate no-show policies.

Differing services offered

Room pricing is complicated by a wide set of product offerings in the form of (A) varying desirability of certain rooms (rooms with a view, those with privacy, those away from noise or other distractions, etc.), (B) differences in number and size of beds, and (C) other variations in levels of service provided. Pricing strategies traditionally assess value to some of these features but not others, and they are difficult to price in an optimum manner because they may be of different value to different customers and they may entail significant variations in costs to the hotel. Adding swimming pools, room service, and meeting space are costly services that must be covered by revenue.

ECONOMIC PRICING PRINCIPLES

Allocating inventory

An appropriate pricing policy involves allocating existing room inventory on the basis of the strongest demands over the reservation cycle for a given room on a given date (Kimes, 1989a; Relihan, 1989). Those guests with the strongest demands are willing to pay the highest room rates. This principle is complicated to follow because the strongest demands are those that are the latest in time to develop. Therefore, one needs to be quite accurate in making projections and saving back a sufficient number of rooms to fill late demands. Errors in projections are costly because rooms not booked late will go unused.

In practice, one needs also to be discrete in holding back inventory to avoid antagonizing customers who may want to rent the room earlier at a low rate. Partly for this reason, hotels never admit to raising or lowering room rates. They only open and close blocks of rooms ('buckets of inventory') in response to expected or actual changes in demand. These rate classes are best kept flexible in 'nested' systems which allow rooms to be moved to different classes in response to changing demand (Kimes, 1989b).

Market segmentation

Secondly, appropriate pricing strategies involve application of market segmentation principles among the various major categories of guests, such as pleasure, business, and group business. As noted earlier, each of these segments involves quite distinct price sensitivities and being able to price differently to the different segments is key to the success of maximizing profits. Just being able to identify different segments is not sufficient. One must be able to market to the different segments individually, without undue overlap, and they must have sufficiently different price elasticities among the segments in order to profit by pricing rooms differently to the different segments.

The appropriate basis for market segmentation tends to be confused in the literature even though the early proponents of market segmentation clarified the concept quite well (Frank et al, 1972). Market segmentation involves the following.

1. *Price Discrimination.*

The economic principle of price discrimination whereby customers in each segment of the market are charged differing prices that relate to that segment's portion of the overall demand curve (Figure 14.2). In the case of perfect price discrimination, there is little or no 'consumer surplus' remaining and sellers maximize profits by selling products at or near the prices indicated by their respective segments of the demand curve (at p_1, p_2, p_3, and p_4 for quantities q_1, q_2, q_3, and q_4, respectively). Customers are satisfied by obtaining the product desired at prices defined by the demand curve, assuming a downward sloping demand curve and prices offered that exceed marginal costs as shown by a supply curve.

Dhalla and Mahatoo (1976) gave a good numerical example of the two-stage process necessary for market segmentation. The first stage involves identification of the segments using situation-specific variables based on various kinds of benefits, or perhaps use of cluster analysis. The second stage involves demand analysis to measure price elasticities in the differing segments of interest to ensure that marginal revenues can be equated to marginal costs in allocating advertising and other marketing costs.

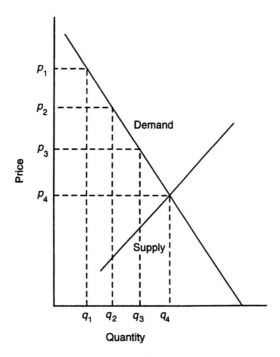

Figure 14.2. Example of first degree price discrimination

2. *Lack of Arbitrage.*

Arbitrage, whereby customers or other market intermediaries in each segment are able to buy in a low-price segment and sell in a higher-priced segment, must be avoided if market segmentation is to be practiced successfully. Airlines do this by requiring advanced ticket sales and Saturday-night stays which are repugnant to business travelers. Hotels and airlines both have an advantage in selling products that cannot be stored; rooms rented on weekends cannot be stored and used the following weekdays.

3. *Additional Costs.*

Costs of serving several segments are normally higher than mass merchandising to a single segment, due to such things as added packaging costs and additional advertising and promotional costs, even if the primary product is physically similar among segments. As a result, higher prices are necessary to at least offset these added costs. In addition, marginal revenues must meet the necessary condition of at least covering marginal costs.

Some authors add various practical rather than conceptual conditions for effective segmentation which include such things as 'measurability,' 'actionability,' and 'substantiality,' that is, being able to reach and market to each segment and serving only those segments that are large enough to be profitable (Kotler, 1994).

Unfortunately, it is not always easy to identify appropriate market segments. For that reason, many authors still use inappropriate methods of identifying segments that have intuitive but not necessarily an economic basis for segmentation, such as those serving different socio-economic or age groups of customers. Benefit segmentation and target-specific procedures are more promising procedures. But even those approaches do not always yield profitable segments (Dhalla and Mahatoo, 1976; Smith, 1989: ch. 3).

Cluster analysis can be used in identifying segments followed by measuring demand relationships within segments to support differences in price responses (and other characteristics) of the segments, as explained by Dhalla and Mahatoo. Multiple regression analysis can be used in calculating demand models based on either time-series or cross-sectional models. If no differences in price elasticities are found among the segments, there likely is no economic basis for the segments.

Even though cluster analysis has identified differences of some kind, those differences may reflect noneconomic relationships which are caused by the use of various criteria in the cluster techniques which are mechanical in nature. However, advertising and promotion themselves may build differing demands for products in a given segment, so demand analysis should follow any such marketing efforts.

Cluster analysis to identify the segments often is followed by discriminant analysis to profile the characteristics of the members of the segment in order to understand preferences and generally to market to them (Weaver et al, 1993). There also may be some practical reasons for subdividing markets, for example geographically or for convenience of the sales force, which are not cost or demand related and they may not affect pricing. But, only by knowing customers' demand relationships can a company classify them into appropriate segments for purposes of economic pricing.

Special features

Finally, one cannot ignore the importance of several special features of hotel room pricing. These include: (A) varying lengths of stay, (B) joint purchases of banquet and other significant foodservice, conventions space, and other major products commonly offered by hotels, (C) underbooking and over- booking problems, (D) variations in basic services offered such as types of room or beds offered or types of foodservice provided, and (E) common forms of categorical discounting used by competitors based on AAA and AARP membership, volume discounts given to large customers, and dis- counts given to government employees and travel agents. The last item may be more important to recognize for public relations purposes than for com- petitive reasons. Hotels with gaming facilities are special cases. The 'special features' in the case of gaming may be the rooms themselves rather than the joint products offered with the rooms.

EXAMPLE OF ECONOMIC PRICING PRINCIPLES

Following is an example for base rate pricing for a single segment of demand for a single date of arrival. Adjustments to these rates must be made for some of the special features enumerated above, such as discounts for length of stay or purchase of joint products, or to implement overbooking strategies, which will be discussed later. This example is far from being a true optimization model, but is indicative of the thought processes involved. Optimization involves a much more dynamic activity than is illustrated here for simplicity.

Determining base room rates[3]

Assume that one of the customer segments, perhaps transient business trav- elers, has a projected reservation path 30 days prior to arrival on date of arrival (t) as shown in Figure 14.3. This example relates to a property dedi- cated to a single segment or can be thought of as a group of rooms dedicated to a single segment in a larger property. In this example, the reservation path

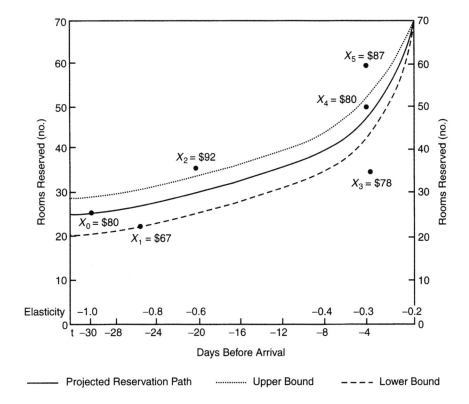

Figure 14.3. Projected reservations and hotel room pricing

has an estimated range or confidence interval of approximately 10% within one standard deviation around the mean. It is not known how representative this particular reservation path is likely to be, but it likely is representative of a transient business segment. The reservation path is upward sloping, particularly during the last 4 or 5 days prior to arrival. On the date of arrival, the expectation is that 70 rooms would likely be rented or 70% occupancy for the 100 room hotel hypothesized. About 20 of those rooms would be expected to be rented during the last three days prior to arrival (The chart is only approximate).

It is assumed for this segment that the price elasticity of demand (ε) for room rental varies from -1.0 at 30 days prior to arrival ($t - 30$) to -0.2 on the day of arrival. This means that 30 days prior to arrival a price decline of 10% would be expected to be associated with an additional 10% of rooms rented whereas on the day of arrival, a 10% cut in prices would have only a 2% increase in number of rooms rented. These numbers are estimates because the author is not aware of any published data on the subject. They reflect the expectation that the price elasticity is more elastic or would have more impact on reservation decisions when price-sensitive, early-reserving guests are making their decisions than near the day of arrival. Late arrivals are more urgently in need of a room and do not have much time or inclination to shop for the best deal.

At point X_0 on Figure 14.3, which is 30 days prior to arrival, about 25 rooms are reserved, and the room rate quoted would be $80. This is the 'rack' rate calculated on the basis of average costs and is the expected average occupancy for that time period for the specified date of arrival. At point X_1, which is 25 days prior to arrival ($t - 25$), the expectation is that 26 rooms would be reserved, but at that time reservations have fallen to only 21. This level is 20% short of expectations and therefore is below the confidence interval of 10%, so prices should be adjusted downward to encourage reservations. The ε on that day has fallen to −0.8, so a discount of 16% (20×-0.8) is warranted, or $13 less than the rack rate of $80 or $67.

This discount brings in a lot of customers, so by $t - 20$ (point X_2) 34 rooms are rented. This level exceeds the 27-room expectation for that day, so prices can again be raised. The ε has fallen to −0.6 on that date so the 26% excess reservations ($34 - 27/27 \times 100$) warrants a price increase of $12 to $92. By time $t - 4$, depending upon whether you are at X_3, X_4 or X_5 will decide whether you drop prices again, return them to the rack rate, or raise them further, respectively.[4] At this time the ε has dropped to the point that it does not warrant much adjustment on the basis of price sensitivity.

Discounts and add-ons

Guests should be encouraged to stay as long as possible and to purchase additional services such as banquets and use of conference rooms. For this reason, quantity discounts should be applied to the basic room rate, particularly when stays are extended over weekends in business-oriented hotels or other low-occupancy periods. Ideally, these discounts should bear a relationship to the value of the additional services purchased, but that may be difficult to determine. In practice, some reasonable rules of thumb should be developed. They would include a minimum length of stay, such as 3 days, for example, beyond which some discount would be applied, perhaps 10% for a 7-day stay. A similar policy would apply to rentals of conference rooms and major banquet sales which are arranged at the time of booking.

Categorical discounts for AARP membership and special rates for government workers and high-volume corporations should be treated as separate segments if the volume generated is sufficient for that purpose. It should be recognized that these groups are more price sensitive and should be accommodated if space is available. However, these segments would receive relatively low priority and not be accommodated when projected occupancy nears full capacity, unless they are contractually based and represent significant shares of business.

Additional services provided in the form of larger sized or additional beds, larger sized or better situated rooms (rooms with a scenic view), or additional persons in a room should result in additional charges either when hotel costs are increased or when the additional service is highly valued by guests. This practice is standard procedure currently in most hotels and should be continued under recommended policies. However, when the services provided have nominal additional costs to the hotel, such as optional king-sized beds or additional persons per room, hotels may want to regard the service as a promotional amenity which adds to the value received by the guests at minimal cost and not make an additional charge. Many first-class properties already take this position.

Overbooking strategies

Overbooking should be avoided when possible because of the additional costs of 'walking' guests, potential illwill, and even legal liability that may be involved. Reservations guaranteed with credit cards or advance payments have greatly reduced the problem, but many hotels still experience 5% no-shows and have a reluctance to charge for guaranteed reservations because of possible misunderstanding. Also, hotels are sometimes forced into an overbooked situation by guests overstaying their reservations.

When hotels have significant problems with no-shows, they should develop overbooking strategies because it is costly to have rooms remain unused when they could be rented with better planning. The first requirement in developing such a policy is to have good historical records of the occurrence of no-shows from which to calculate their probability. These records need to be carefully analyzed to determine seasonality, day of the week, or other patterns with which the practice may be associated. Perhaps there are problems with clarity of reservations that need to be corrected with confirmations or other management practices. The variability in occurrence of no-shows needs to be measured statistically if overbooking is contemplated. One should not plan on overbooking unless the average number of no-shows is projectable into the future with confidence.

Costs associated with overbooking a room must also be determined and compared with the opportunity costs of not renting a room. Overbooking costs include (A) the cost of walking a guest to another hotel plus (B) the cost of the illwill that may be generated as a result of not being able to provide a room to a guest arriving late at night with a reservation. Reciprocal arrangements with nearby hotels in the same quality segment can minimize the direct costs but the cost of the illwill is harder to estimate. The opportunity costs of not renting a room is the lost contribution margin for that room, which is essentially the average room rate less the marginal cost of performing the housekeeping function.

A critical fractile can measure the level of service that should be provided in any service operation by balancing (A) the costs of being out of stock and thereby forfeiting the benefits of lost contribution margin on a sale, with (B) the losses associated with buying or producing excess products (Sasser et al, 1978). The procedure involves calculation of a Markov decision model which measures the risk associated with each alternative and the expected value associated with each increment of additional no-shows. In the case of no-shows, one is measuring the inverse of the level of service that one is wanting to provide, that is, the level of service that a company is not wanting to provide.

$$\text{Critical Fractile} = C_o/(C_o + C_{cm})$$

where C_o is cost of overbooking and

C_{cm} is the opportunity cost of the lost contribution margin

This proportion provides the desired level of service that one prefers to avoid, as measured by the inverse of the probability of no-shows. For example, if the cost of overbooking is $80 for the room cost of a walked guest plus $60 illwill, and the lost contribution margin is $60, the critical fractile is $140/(140 + 60)$ or 0.70. This means that a hotel would want to avoid service equal to 0.3 or 30% of the cumulative probability of the historical rate of number of no-shows.

This information should be incorporated into determination of the economic principles of pricing hotel rooms. It alters the expectation of the occupancy rate targeted for a given hotel segment for a given date. Obviously, this strategy is mute when occupancy is targeted below the 100% occupancy level.

QUESTIONS RELATED TO APPLICATION

This procedure may raise many questions.

1. The most obvious one is how the hotel could possibly make all of these calculations on a timely basis to be able to make all of these price adjustments for each room rate segment and each future arrival date.
2. Is it practical to make accurate forecasts for each segment of the business for each future day?

3. How could you explain the rationale for the changes to your reservation clerks sufficiently that they could relay the information to interested parties that may question the price changes, for example to those reserving earlier who now may learn that the room rate has changed?
4. How could you keep those who had reserved at higher rates from canceling their reservations and making them at new lower rates, if they are lowered?

Calculations

Computers are wonderful gadgets and are quite capable of being programmed to make complicated, repetitive calculations. In fact, there are many yield management programs available that do the necessary calculations. Kimes indicates that linear programming techniques are commonly used in solving airline yield management programs for independent rate classes, but that probabilistic linear programming is necessary for nested rate class problems (Kimes, 1989b).

It is not certain that the programs all proceed precisely as indicated in this chapter because they are proprietary and the developers do not advertise the procedures and coefficients used. Orkin (1988), for example, a well-known consultant in this field, explains his system as maximizing revenue realized in relation to revenue potential, but does not explain how this objective is accomplished. Fortunately, it is necessary for managers only to understand the output, not the inner workings of the programs. But it is useful if they could understand the primary principles involved.

Changing prices frequently is a sizable administrative effort. A sizable property usually designates a manager with the sole responsibility of managing the pricing program, but smaller properties probably do not have this luxury. One needs to compare results with traditional pricing procedures to determine if the benefits outweigh the costs. Some property's pricing programs are more complicated to manage than others, due to the number of market segments that they serve. A small property perhaps serves only one important segment, and may be able to develop tables of coefficients that could be used without making price changes as often or as precisely as would a larger property. Even so, expectations are that these coefficients are quite property specific and need to be developed or at least modified for each property.

Reservation forecasting

Many statistical programs are available for making forecasts of reservations based on projecting past histories. Some of these programs are quite easy to

apply, particularly exponential smoothing. Other simple computer programs are available for this purpose that do not require statistical expertise.
A recent study of alternative projecting procedures was conducted by Zvi
Schwartz (1995). He found that a procedure called 'curve similarity' did the
best job. That procedure involved a comparison of the available part of an
incomplete booking curve to the relevant part of comparable complete
curves.

Schwartz also found that present forecasting procedures do not usually
give good forecasts beyond 45 days in the future. This time horizon is quite
limiting for early stages of the reservation period. While most rooms for the
business segment are booked late in the reservation period, one must make
decisions on prices much earlier for purposes of the more price-sensitive
group business and pleasure travelers.

The main problem in making good forecasts is the lack of complete and
'clean' historical data for several previous years. The procedure is data intensive because each day's actual reservations require a 60–90 day reservation
period of data. The data must be clean in being able to calculate the actual
room rate charged without charges for telephone use, room service charges
of various kinds, and complications of multiple people in a room who may
be paying individually. Further, the reservation history must include the rate
agreed upon and any subsequent changes made to each reservation. In order
to project a reservation history for different guest segments, the further complication of keeping these segments identifiable over time would be
required, which may not be a simple task. At least initially, a property would
likely focus on only a single segment based on all of its guests combined.
Simply tracking each day separately helps in identifying some of the differing segments, such as those that stay on weekends, holidays, and perhaps
offseason.

Reservation clerks

Reservation clerks must be trained to understand the rudiments of the
system so they can explain them when called upon to defend the price
changes. The primary answer is a simple response that prices are adjusted in
line with supply and demand. When reservations are below expectations,
prices are cut slightly to encourage occupancy and when reservations are
strong, prices are increased to ration the rooms to those who need them the
most and are willing to pay for them. One also needs to be practical and not
change prices unduly often, certainly no more than once a week; the airlines
have received a lot of critical publicity by their frequent price changes. There
also may be rules of thumb that price increases cannot exceed a given dollar
amount within a specified period of time, unless something dramatic
happens, like some group that wants to rent half the hotel for a week. The

changes shown in the example were made for expository purposes and likely would not often be that dramatic.

Keeping reservation prices and segments separate

No one can prevent a guest from inquiring later about the price of a new reservation and canceling a previous reservation. Most guests will not ask, but if they do, they should be given any lower rates that are available at the time. Prices are more likely to rise than to decline, because of the expected decline in price elasticity over the reservation period. In that case, the guests will appreciate having made a wise decision to book early. There is no intent or benefit to antagonizing guests.

Keeping pricing segments separate so that prices at a given point in time will be different for differing segments requires more skill and tact. Leading questions must be used to ascertain initially the appropriate segment of a given guest. This may be difficult because many people travel for joint purposes so the delineation may not be complete. However, there should be no intent to hide appropriate prices because they should reflect the market. Low prices are intended to increase bookings but will not have their intended effect if they are hidden from the guests. They will also be angered if charged unduly high prices and the true rates are discovered later.

There is precedent for giving price discounts to corporate travelers, but not for charging businessmen extra. The problem is minimized because of the propensity for pleasure and group travelers to book early and business travelers to book late. Beyond that, any differences can be handled by indicating that pleasure travelers are entitled to a special discount at this particular time. Price differences of many kinds are already commonly offered on the basis of the personal category of which they are a member. Advanced booking discounts can easily be defended. Certainly, group discounts are already common.

CONCLUSIONS

This chapter focuses on the economic principles that relate to pricing strategies for hotels, an important one of which is the principle of price discrimination. This activity is quite legitimate and in common practice, but the terminology is unfortunate in today's concern with avoiding personal or categorical discrimination.

Economic principles underlie many day-to-day decisions currently being made in hotel pricing but reacting to changes in supply and demand is sometimes obscured by the jargon of the trade, such as opening and closing rate segments as a euphemism for changing prices. Surprisingly, some hoteliers and even consultants think and act as though economic principles of supply and demand somehow do not apply to this industry. But, this group likely has diminished in size during the last few years when occupancy rates suffered and price discounts were necessary to fill rooms.

An example of the application of economic pricing principles was provided. This example was rather simplistic and intended mainly to illustrate the concepts involved. The real world is much more complicated, as noted by the discussion of discounts and add-ons and overbooking strategies. Fortunately, computer software programs can relieve us from knowing all of the intricate details that drive the programs, but we should have an appreciation of the basic principles involved in order to apply the results intelligently.

NOTES

1. The booking curve for this segment may almost be an S-curve, depending on how far back in time it begins.
2. Price elasticity is defined as the percentage change in number of rooms rented divided by the percentage change in room rates.
3. The author recognizes the assistance of Radesh Palakurthi, Assistant Professor at the University of North Texas and former graduate student at Purdue University, in the formulation of this numerical example.
4. At X_3, prices would drop to $78, at X_4, prices would return to $80, and at X_5, prices would increase to $87.

REFERENCES

Dhalla, N.K., Mahatoo, W.H., 1976, Expanding the scope of segmentation research, *J. of Marketing*, April, **40**: 34–41

Frank, R.E., Massy, W.F., Wind, Y., 1972, *Market segmentation*, Prentice-Hall, Englewood Cliffs, NJ

Kimes, S.E., 1989a, The basics of yield management, *Cornell H.R.A. Quarterly*, Nov, **30**(3): 14–22

Kimes, S.E., 1989b, Yield management: a tool for capacity-constrained service firms, *J. of Operations Management*, **8**(4): 348–363

Kotler, P., 1994, *Marketing management, analysis, planning, implementation, and control.* Prentice-Hall, Englewood Cliffs, NJ

Lewis, R.C., Chambers, R.E., 1989, *Marketing leadership in hospitality; foundations and practices*, first edn, Van Nostrand Reinhold, New York

Masson R.T., Mudambi, R., Reynolds, R., 1994, Oligopolistic product withholding in Ricardian markets, *Bulletin of Economic Research*, **46**(1): 71–79

Orkin, E.B., 1988, Boosting your bottom line with yield management, *Cornell H.R.A. Quarterly*, Feb, **28**(4): 52–56

Pannell, Kerr Forster, 1993, *Trends in the hotel industry*, Houston, TX 77207

Relihan, W.J. III, 1989, The yield-management approach to hotel-room pricing, *Cornell H.R.A. Quarterly*, May, **30**(1): 40–45

Sasser, W.E., Olsen, R.P., Wyckoff, D.D., 1978, *Management of service operations*, Allyn and Bacon, Boston, MA

Schwartz, Z., 1995, Improving the accuracy of hotel reservations forecasting: curves similarity and parameters processes approach. West Lafayette, IN, unpublished Ph.D. dissertation submitted to Purdue University

Smith, S.L.J., 1989, *Tourism analysis*. Longman Group UK/John Wiley, New York

Stonier, A.W., Hague, D.C., 1953, *A textbook of economic theory*, Longmans, Green, New York

Weaver, P.A., McCleary, K.W., Jinlin, Z., 1993, Segmenting the business traveler market, *J. of Travel & Tourism Marketing*, **1**(4): 53–69

15 Environmental Aspects of Tourism: Applications of Cost-Benefit Analysis

MICHAEL STABLER

INTRODUCTION

As one of the world's most important industries, tourism has a substantial environmental impact in terms of its use of natural and humanmade resources, requirement for specific infrastructures, consumption of productive material and energy resources, and generation of solid waste, polluting emissions and discharges. Accordingly, like any other major market activity, it should attract the attention of environmental economists who are concerned currently with the attainment of sustainable development under which are subsumed hitherto diverse aspects of the subject, such as conservation economics, pollution abatement and the role and value of the environment for productive and amenity purposes, as a life support system, as a sink and as a contributor to a sense of well-being.

It is only since the late 1980s that sustainable development has emerged as a central issue underlined by concerns about global warming, arising from the use of fossil fuels, deafforestation, erosion, and air and water pollution (WCED, 1987; UNCED, 1992). The evolution of the notion of sustainable tourism has followed this wider concept (Inskeep, 1991; Bramwell and Lane, 1993; Goodall and Stabler, 1994; Hunter and Green, 1995; Stabler, 1997a). Tourism's dependence on the quality of natural and humanmade resources, at a local as well as on a global scale, is greater than for many other industries. For example, it uses not only natural environments in the form of beaches, forests, lakes, mountains, rivers and so on but also the built, cultural, political and social environments. Consequently, it would appear to be obvious that national and local governments, destination tourism bodies, the tourism industry, host communities and tourists themselves would have a vested interest in maintaining the resources base by

Economic and Management Methods for Tourism and Hospitality Research.
Edited by Thomas Baum and Ram Mudambi © 1999 John Wiley & Sons Ltd.

promoting sustainability. However, as a fast-growing activity, tourism has interpreted sustainability as viability in the sense of elevating the long-term survival of tourism enterprises as a paramount aim. Thus, attempts to meet the criteria for achieving sustainable tourism have been subjugated to business objectives. This tourism-centric sustainability paradigm emphasises meeting the needs and wants of the host community with respect to improved living standards, satisfying the needs of tourists, and maintaining and enhancing the competitiveness of tourism firms. Although safeguarding the environmental resource base of tourism is perceived as desirable, it currently has been given a low priority.

Many writers abhor the lack of awareness, attitudes and misdirected actions of the tourism industry, arguing that sustainable tourism is a monstrous contradiction (Butcher, 1997; Butler, 1991; McKercher, 1993; Pearce, 1989; Wheeller, 1997). While these criticisms are valid, they do not fully acknowledge the lack of understanding by the tourism industry of the complex interrelationship of the market and natural resources which makes it difficult in practice to pursue sustainability. Here one must, to an extent, indict economics for while it has demonstrated this interrelationship and its consequences in a general context (Pearce et al, 1989; Turner et al, 1994), it has singularly largely ignored tourism as a subject worthy of study, especially its environmental implications. It is only very recently that this has begun to be rectified (Bull, 1991; Fyall and Garrod, 1997; Sinclair, 1991; Sinclair and Stabler, 1997; Slee et al, 1997; Stabler, 1997b).

Currently the economic analysis of tourism environmental issues has tended to be directed towards grappling with the problem of moving from sustainability principles to practice, such as identifying appropriate indicators, the means of measuring the attainment of sustainability and the investigation of feasible policy instruments and their effects, particularly those relating to resource use and pollution. The concentration on these aspects reflects the wider concerns of sustainable development regarding the possible detrimental impact of continued economic growth, as measured by increases in national income, either in aggregate or per capita, on the natural environment. The now well-known Brundtland (WCED, 1987) definition of sustainable development which presupposes the passing on by the present generation of sufficient resources and a natural environment of a quality that the needs of future generations are met, implies that the capital stock, whether natural or humanmade, needs to be maintained or enhanced. A fundamental issue that has arisen is the balance between the natural and humanmade capital stock. Those who take a strong sustainability stance argue that there should be no substitution of humanmade for natural capital, whereas others, taking a weaker stance, allow for such substitution as long as in aggregate the capital stock is not diminished. Without examining in detail the debate concerning the relative merits and demerits of the strong and weak stances, clearly and simply reviewed by Pearce and Turner (1990) and Turner et al (1994), an emerging and more specific issue is the evaluation of the quality of natural and humanmade environments and in turn their contribution not only to the quality of life, an important tenet of sustainable development, but also to continued economic development, as opposed to growth.

This chapter takes up this issue by considering, within an economic analytical framework, tourism's use of and impact on natural and humanmade resources to establish the net benefits or costs it generates and how these might be evaluated. In particular, attention is concentrated on resources which are inputs into the tourism 'product' but which are not normally traded in the market, that is, are not priced. Accordingly, both the technique for appraising tourism activity and the methods of valuing the resources employed are analysed. In doing this the issue of the impact of tourism on these resources and the implications for sustainability are examined. Of especial importance is the possible overuse and degradation of non-priced resources because they are treated as free goods by the industry and tourists. The economic concept of 'market failure' with respect to collective consumption or public goods and externalities is relevant here. This concept is defined in conjunction with the explanation of the appraisal technique, and examples of collective consumption goods and externalities are given in illustrative applications. The chapter includes a significant section on how economics can identify and measure tourism's impact on the economic, cultural, physical and social environments. Examples are briefly examined to indicate the relevance of economic principles and methods to appraising tourism's environmental effects. Finally, an assessment is made of economic methods for appraising tourism activity and projects and a short comment on the prospects of applying these more widely is offered.

TOURISM'S USE OF NATURAL AND HUMANMADE RESOURCES

In order to appreciate fully the use of and impact on resources of tourism activity and how these are incorporated into economic analysis, it is necessary to expand on the outline given above of the nature and characteristics of those which constitute a vital part of the tourism product. A broad distinction can be drawn between the nature of primary and secondary resources.

Primary resources

Primary resources can be both natural and humanmade and constitute the basic product in that they are what attracts tourists to visit specific destinations. Thus natural resources, such as beaches, forests, lakes and mountains, and humanmade resources, for example historic buildings, monuments and whole cities, towns and villages, are either an integral part of the product or act as a backdrop to the holiday experience. Thus, for instance, skiers and walkers make active use of mountains in winter and summer respectively whereas for other, less active tourists, the mountains merely act as an attractive part of the scenery, perceived as characteristic of a particular country, say Austria or Switzerland.

Secondary resources

Many varied resources are required by tourists whether they are active or not. Facilities such as hotels, restaurants, cafés, bars, banks, shops and services (for example car hire, dry cleaners and information centres) are essential components. Also, infrastructural elements, for example airports, ports, railway stations, transport modes, water supply and refuse disposal, need to meet the demands of tourists as well as residents. At specific attractions, visitors demand what they perceive as essential facilities such as toilets, bars, cafés and gift shops.

THE CHARACTERISTICS OF THE TOURISM PRIMARY RESOURCE BASE

Tourism's use of primary resources is of most concern to environmental economics as their characteristics give rise to a number of detrimental effects, threatening both their continued utility as productive inputs and their survival as intrinsically valuable resources. A key feature is that it is very difficult or not possible to exclude access to them as in the case of many goods, such as food, clothing and housing. Being non-excludable, irrespective of whether they are in private or public ownership or are owned by no one, means that no price can be charged for their use. Examples to illustrate this point make clear the notion. In many countries there is an implicit right of access to shorelines or to roam, while in others such rights of access are defined legally. Thus, it is possible for privately owned uplands, mountains, forests and agricultural land to be used for leisure pursuits free of charge. Even where such rights do not exist it may prove so expensive for the owner to, say, erect fences and/or employ people to warden the resources and collect user charges, that any financial return is outweighed by the costs. The same arguments apply to resources in the public domain, including those provided for the general welfare of society, such as defence at a national level and street lighting locally. Some resources, for instance the open sea and oceans and the atmosphere, known as *open access resources*, belong to no-one so are free to all. Economists refer to such resources as *collective consumption* or *public goods*.

In the context of tourism, many natural resources which act as primary inputs – beaches, forests, lakes, mountains and rivers – and humanmade resources – ancient monuments, historic buildings and even infrastructural elements, for instance bridges, railways and harbours – are the rationale for visitors to travel to see and use them. Whether they are in the public or private domain, if exclusion cannot be exercised they may be at risk. This risk is determined by two main factors: the number of visitors and the nature of the use to which they are put. In many instances the use of such collective consumption goods by one person does not deny their consumption by another, for example the pleasure derived from looking at a beautiful landscape or historic building. In economic terms there is non-rival consumption at zero or low marginal cost. From the supply side, the marginal cost of provision is also virtually zero. However, this does not infer that no costs whatsoever are generated; there may be substantial costs incurred by the tourist to get to and stay at or near a particular attraction while the supplier may bear heavy capital and running costs. For example, the provision of a new urban park for the community by a municipality entails significant capital and running costs but, notwithstanding that it was intended for the benefit of residents only, once provided it is available to all. In effect the tourist becomes a *free rider*, enjoying the benefits of a local amenity without directly paying for it through an entry charge. However, should the level of usage increase, it is possible that not only does rival consumption emerge but the provider incurs considerable marginal costs. For instance, remaining with the urban park example, too many visitors may mean that it becomes overcrowded and individuals' enjoyment is adversely affected. The provider may find that it is necessary to employ people to control access, but, perhaps more importantly, that the park suffers from erosion or is damaged. These are examples of *detrimental externalities* generating *social costs*. However, it should not be entirely overlooked that there may be *beneficial externalities* or *social benefits*. The park would almost certainly have been provided on the grounds that it increased the quality of life of local inhabitants. The tourist, if attracted to the area by the presence of such a park, will certainly experience a personal welfare gain but, through expenditure on other facilities and services for which prices can be charged, indirectly increases benefits for local traders and residents. This illustration relates to another economic concept, namely that of the *merit want*.

Because of the inability of would-be suppliers to charge a price, arising from the non-excludable characteristic of collective consumption goods, there is no incentive to make provision. It is thus often necessary for the public sector to step in to make that provision. This can happen with goods and services which are ostensibly private ones, that is where exclusion can be exercised, but the market for which does not operate effectively. In other words, insufficient provision is made either to meet demand fully or to satisfy minimum levels of welfare. This is the reason why there is often state provision of education, health and housing, and even leisure and tourism.

A final aspect of this intervention is that it might occur on grounds of efficiency, both at the level of endeavouring to make provision at minimum average cost or maximising social welfare, that is, social efficiency. To achieve both might justify the existence of monopoly supply because economies of scale can be exploited, particularly where there are high fixed costs and the possibilities of extending markets. Such monopolies are referred to as natural monopolies. Conversely, it is possible for monopolies which do occur as a result of placing them under public control or allowing them to develop in a market context to be inefficient and to reduce welfare.

Market failure

The characteristics of *collective consumption goods* of non-exclusion, no price, non-rival and zero marginal costs of consumption, together with the *externalities* which they tend to generate, whether beneficial or detrimental, are the two most important factors in what is termed *market failure*, meaning that the market fails to take account of such factors rather than ceases to operate. These factors hold implications for the environmental impact of tourism. However, those in the industry have not fully recognised the interrelationship between tourism and the natural and humanmade resources base as inputs on which they depend. Elementary economic analysis not only indicates that any free consumption good, unless it is an inferior one, will result in a higher demand for it than if it were priced, but it also shows that, likewise, a productive input, if it is freely available, will be in greater demand. Figure 15.1 compares the level of demand by the tourism industry for natural and humanmade resources which are priced with those which are not. The demand curve is the conventional marginal revenue product (MRP) curve which relates the demand for the product by consumers and their expenditure on it to the contribution of a specific input to the generation of revenue. The curve falls from left to right on the assumption both that consumers' willingness to pay declines for increasing quantities of the product purchased and that the productivity of the input decreases (under the law of eventually diminishing returns) as more is utilised. When the input is priced (MC shows the supply price at different levels of use of the resource) the quantity demanded is Q_p at P_p price, whereas if the input is unpriced at P_F demand extends to Q_F. In effect $Q_p - Q_F$ can be stated to denote the difference in quantity demanded of natural and humanmade resources if it were priced as opposed to being free. This applies equally to demand by tourists for amenity resources.

As a consequence it is almost certain, in the case of fragile environments, that a higher level of use will lead to degradation by tourists and the industry. There are many examples to demonstrate that this may be so, especially where tourism is concentrated in particular areas, such as on coasts, in ski

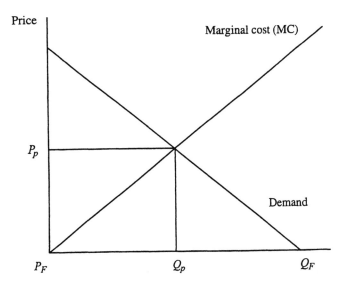

Figure 15.1. The use of natural and humanmade resources: priced and unpriced cases

resors or on small islands. The deterioration in the quality and despoliation of resources is more likely than outright destruction of the physical environment. Overcrowding and extension of holiday seasons are two crucial factors. Tourists, hosts and tourism businesses are seldom aware of the damage being caused, indeed it is often unintentional through ignorance or a failure to identify changes which may be imperceptible in the relatively short run. For example, those managing ski runs may not comprehend that the artificial creation and subsequent compaction of snow can damage plants and eco systems (Tyler, 1989; Smith and Jenner, 1989), the problem being exacerbated in summer months when walking holidays are promoted. Likewise, souvenir hunting and careless mooring of boats can destroy coral reefs (Brierton, 1991). Unthinking management of golf courses using fertilisers, herbicides and keeping grass short in the style of an urban park impoverishes fauna and flora and reduces biodiversity (Tobin and Taylor, 1996). Further examples include the adverse effects on: wildlife and human culture of safari holidays (Sindiyo and Pertet, 1984); Antarctic environments (Erize, 1987); resources for host communities in underdeveloped countries and islands (Romeril, 1989) and national parks, alpine areas and coastal zones (Stanners and Bourdeau, 1995). Many other cases which illustrate the environmental effects of tourism (cultural, economic, environmental, ecological, physical and social) can be found in Hunter and Green (1995), Shackley (1996), Stabler (1997a) and Sinclair and Stabler (1997). They all demonstrate, with few exceptions, a lack of awareness and ignorance of, complacency and indifference to, and failure to act to safeguard, let alone enhance, the environment as defined in its widest sense.

These environmental problems are very likely to increase in the future, not necessarily because tourists and the tourism industry will not change their attitudes and behaviour, but because of the sheer increase in the volume of tourism. International holiday tourism movements alone in the mid 1990s have been expanding at an annual rate of around 5% and total over 500 million (WTO, 1994). In the future increasing numbers will seek to visit not only established destinations but more remote ones with more fragile environments. Domestic tourism is estimated to be 10 times this. If the domestic day visits and use for recreation and sport are added, the pressure on natural and humanmade resources will be immense. For example in the UK, a relatively overcrowded country, it has been estimated that 600 million visits are made to the countryside and coast each year (Lloyd, 1993).

Another aspect of the characteristics of environments forming the tourism resource base, possibly necessitating intervention, which also illustrates the contribution economic analysis can make to explaining the value of resources in different uses, is the issue of their allocation rather than their overuse and degradation. The difficulty with unpriced use of natural and humanmade resources, for both primary and secondary amenity purposes, where primary is defined as sole use and secondary as essentially supplementary or joint use, lies in the lack of an appropriate allocation mechanism. For example, a holiday resort such as a Center Parcs complex would constitute a primary amenity use of resources, while a forest managed for timber production, but within which recreational activities are allowed, would represent secondary use. In the face of competing demand for resources, the market normally allocates them to a specific use by price. This follows the notion of *derived demand*, which posits that the demand for resources is determined by the demand for and prices of the goods and services those resources produce. Clearly, where resources are in private ownership, the highest possible price is likely to be sought, which almost certainly would preclude offering them as primarily for amenity use if other commercial uses would yield a higher return. With open access resources, the amenity demand price will be zero so that the owner has no incentive to make them available. Indeed if as a result of amenity use the resources are damaged there is a negative return. With respect to resources where amenity use is a secondary activity, the owner will only make them available if the returns outweigh the costs or amenity provision is complementary to the other commercial uses. An example of where a commercial use might effectively preclude an amenity one is arable farming, whereas livestock farming is more compatible with amenity use. In general what economics argues is that where unpriced amenity use of resources is in competition with market-based use, the latter will clearly always outbid the former. But even if

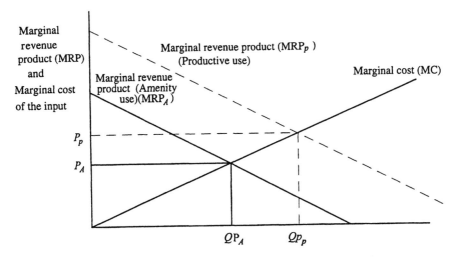

Figure 15.2. The quantity of an input employed and marginal revenue product: amenity and productive uses of resources

amenity use is priced, as depicted in Figure 15.2 where market-based resource use is shown by price P_A where QP_A is supplied, it is suggested that price (P_p) and quantity (Qp_p) are higher for other commercial uses on the assumption that demand for such goods and services commands a higher price and thus the resource, say land, which contributes to producing these, generates a higher marginal revenue produce (MRP$_p$), indicated by the broken line. In effect, for non-amenity use, the MRP$_p$ shifts upwards from and to the right of MRP$_A$. This gives a higher total return to the owner of the resources.

Thus the collective consumption goods characteristics of tourism base resources and the externalities arising from their use confirm the need for intervention to counteract the effects of such market failure. However, while monopoly, another factor which is indicative of market failure, which in tourism does not have a significant effect on the environment, the *intra-* and *intergenerational distribution* of wealth and income, so far not referred to here, does. The term distribution used in economics refers to the *welfare* of a society at a local, regional, national or global level and for international comparative purposes is normally measured in terms of *income per head* using a common currency (usually US dollars). However, increasingly in the context of environmental, particularly sustainability, issues, other measures are advocated (Pearce et al, 1989; Redefining Progress, 1995) including those which attempt to quantify the quality of life using indicators such as the levels of air, water and noise pollution, crime rates, traffic accidents and health. Remaining, in the tourism resource context, wealth can be interpreted as 'capital', whether that is the natural capital or environment or human-made. The distributional factor is an important one for it leads almost directly to a need not only for intervention but also for an analytical frame-work and methods of appraising the impact of a market activity, such as tourism, on the welfare of the current and future generations. Indeed, where unique and irreproducible environments are concerned, the issue is the extent to which the needs, relating to both wealth and income, of the current generation are met (intragenerational distribution). There are horizontal or spatial and vertical variations or inequities in the endowment of and access to resources. The spatial inequities are forcibly demonstrated by the differ-ences in first and third world distribution of income and wealth but there are also vertical differences in both categories of countries.

Understandably, the needs of the current generation tend to assume para-mountcy where sustainable development, and with it sustainable tourism, are interpreted in different ways, indeed perhaps partially explaining the apparent lack of urgency by the tourism industry in safeguarding its resource base. The different sustainability stances which have already been referred to, reflecting the conflicting views of the relationship between natural and humanmade capital, indicated that the strong stance posits that humanmade capital should not be substituted for natural capital. The point being argued, in taking this stance, is that the functions of the environment are vital to the continuation of economic development and human existence and should not be depleted. On the other hand the weak stance, allowing for substitution, asserts that sustainability should still be attainable by future generations.

The relevance of these stances to the intergenerational issue lies in the size and composition of the capital stock which should be passed on to future generations. The debate is not resolved, mainly because of imperfect knowl-edge and uncertainty as to the ultimate effect of current levels and forms of activity and the extent to which future technologies will modify the use of resources, generation of pollution and waste and impact on the environment. Consequently, certainly in the environmental economics field, there is a ten-dency for opinion to favour a strong sustainability stance, adopting what is termed the 'precautionary principle'. This suggests that, given the other market failure factors identified and the evidence of the threats to tourism's resource base that is already occurring, urgent action is required of an inter-ventionary nature. However, given the beneficial, as well as detrimental, effects of tourism activity on its resource base, any intervention needs to be preceded by an appraisal to establish not only the net benefits or costs of the activity before intervention but also after it.

This, therefore, brings the chapter to its core from what has been a long line of argument on the implications of tourism activity for natural and humanmade resources, namely the contribution of economic principles and methods to their evaluation, and decisions on their allocation. Economics stresses the need to place monetary values on such resources, especially if in certain uses they are unpriced, in order to give them proper weighting in the allocation process. Thus, for example, where a market-based use is being considered, whether for agriculture, industry, residences or tourism, there are differences, as discussed earlier, in the price commanded. In a competitive market, allocation will be determined by which use yields the largest returns. In urban economics parlance relating to land, this is referred to as 'the highest and best use', effectively meaning the highest price or rental value. Where a particular use, such as informal amenity, commands no price, the valuation of net social benefits (externalities) becomes crucial in putting all potential forms of use of a specific resource on an equal footing. The implication here of course is that net social benefits in amenity use, as opposed to other uses where there may be a net social cost, would be of an order of magnitude as to show such use as conferring a high value. This is indeed likely to be the case where resources are unique, for example many designated natural and World Heritage Sites, such as the Australian Great Barrier Reef, the Grand Canyon, Stonehenge and Venice.

Within the last 20 years or so, the concentration on the investigation of methods for valuing natural and humanmade resources has been emphasised to such an extent that sight has sometimes been lost of both the purpose and the context within which it should be conducted. Ultimately this valuation is but one aspect of the process of appraisal which should be taken into account if projects involving investment in the development or a change of use of resources is contemplated. Accordingly, in the remainder of this chapter most attention is devoted to considering the application of investment appraisal methods, with especial reference to cost-benefit analysis (CBA), to assess the effects of tourism on its primary resource base. While acknowledging the need to explain the elements of CBA and its variants, and the valuation methods embodied within it, the main emphasis is on reviewing its relevance.

THE ELEMENTS OF COST-BENEFIT ANALYSIS (CBA)

Methods employing discounted cash flows, which signify that the time horizon of the costs and returns generated by a project should be taken account of, have long been advocated as imperative for any large-scale investment in the private sector. The basis of public sector project appraisal, CBA, is the same but, it is argued, should differ essentially in two ways, first by identifying and evaluating costs and benefits which normally do not enter into the purview of business investment appraisal and, second, by considering projects for which no charges are levied and no profits made. In principle, CBA is intended to better inform decision-makers by determining the benefits and costs of proposed projects in monetary terms and presenting them in a form which follows conventionally prescribed decision rules designed to facilitate the allocation of resources and improve the welfare of society, or sections of it. The process of conducting a CBA involves a number of steps which are almost in a strict sequence flowing from a given policy or proposed project.

What is being appraised

Since this chapter is concerned with the natural and humanmade tourism resource base, in short the environment defined in its widest sense to embody the socio-cultural, physical and ecological, as well as the business and economic, CBA is considered in relation to its application to environmental management and protection. This means that the method cannot necessarily be applied prior to a tourism project's initiation, which in an ideal world would occur, indeed being the basic rationale for Environmental Impact Assessment (EIA) which is a European Union (EU) requirement for development proposals likely to have significant environmental effects. The EIA directive identifies a number of leisure and tourism activities in this respect. However, it does not specify that a monetary evaluation of the benefits of a project should necessarily be undertaken; it is essentially concerned with the physical aspects and how adverse impacts will be mitigated.

Most tourism policies and projects do not have an environmental objective, they are more likely to emphasise the creation of income and employment with wider aims of diversifying and developing a local, regional or national economy, considering also the contribution of the activity to foreign currency earnings and the balance of payments. This then is the starting point of a possible CBA for it takes the proposal, say the construction of a holiday complex in a rural area or the conservation of an historic quarter in a city, with a view to developing tourism as an integral part of its projected regeneration, and considers its impact. The two crucial questions, therefore, which a CBA needs to address are what is being appraised and who is affected? However, irrespective of whether the project is in the private or public sector, or both, environmental economics would assert that the appraisal must go beyond the immediate purpose of the project, say its contribution to rural economic development, and consider its ramifications for the wider environment. The issue then becomes how far should the analysis go? How remote or minimal must the impact be before a 'cut-off' point is reached? This issue concerning the scope or boundaries of the exercise is one of the most difficult to resolve, a possible practical but arbitrary solution being that the limits have been reached when the cost of obtaining information exceeds the magnitude of the estimated impact likely to occur.

Accordingly the principal step after determining what is to be appraised is to define its scope.

Definition of the project and the determination of its scope

This can be established by considering the factors on which it is likely to have a significant impact, reflecting the objective of the action. There are five main factors:

1. Allocational, for example a change in the use of land, capital and human resources from agriculture and forestry to leisure and tourism, such as a theme park or holiday centre.
2. Distributional, for example the change in the wealth and income of land-owners, occupiers, employed persons and businesses resulting from leisure or tourism development, for instance a golf course with adjoining hotel.
3. Spatial, which embraces both allocational and distributional factors in the sense that resources both in the immediate area and further afield are affected by the project and likewise local and more distant inhabitants, for example the development of a waterway marina, combined with holiday accommodation and facilities, has allocational implications not only in a change of use of resources where it is located but at a distance because the infrastructure may need to be upgraded to improve access and subsidiary businesses to serve the development may be required. Distributional issues arise if, say, agricultural or horticultural or forestry workers are made redundant and businesses serving these activities are no longer viable and where in extreme cases inhabitants and workers are physically displaced, needing to move in order to find alternative work.
4. Physical/ecological, which is related to all three of the foregoing through the environmental effects of the project, for example the detrimental impact of emission of air pollutants, discharge into water courses of efflu-ents, landfill of solid waste, visual intrusion and noise on the one hand, but perhaps beneficial effects on the other, such as the reclamation of derelict land and buildings or the improvement of a landscape and increased biodiversification.
5. Socio-cultural, which, similar to physical and ecological externalities, may be detrimental or beneficial, are generated by projects, for example its destruction or reinforcement by the introduction of tourism into an area; the social structure and culture of many developing countries has been undermined by Western mass culture but on the other hand tourism has led to the revival of traditional cultures.

There are an increasing number of examples of both specific projects and development of tourism in general which illustrate both the impact and the boundaries with respect to one or more of the factors identified. A recent publication by Shackley (1996) concentrates on wildlife, reflecting in part an earlier emphasis by Hunter and Green (1995), while one by Stabler (1997a) ranges over resort and accommodation development, the creation of cultural holidays, relaunching of traditional seaside centres, and wildlife tourism.

The following two stages not only fall out of the definition and setting of the scope of a project but also, in a kind of feedback, certainly assist their determination by showing what is respectively quantifiable and economically relevant.

Identification of the gains (benefits) and losses (costs)

The identification of the impact of a project's implementation is a key element, particularly if environmental effects are to be given due considera-tion. Basically, the objective is to establish the net effects of the project and therefore what amounts to an inventory of the impacts has to be compiled. This should cover both the construction or initial implementation stage and the operational one. The relevant items can best be identified and explained by taking examples which reflect and typify the approach.

Individual market-based activities in the tourism industry, often without being aware of, or by consciously discounting the significance of the effect, seek to secure the long-term survival of businesses and to make profits. Thus, the direct impact of, say, a holiday complex, of the kind developed by the organisation Center Parcs, is on the land, materials, and labour which is required to build the complex, while its operation will involve the consump-tion of goods and services and energy and the employment of staff. The wider implications, as already identified in step 1, might be the generation of income and employment in subsidiary business serving the complex and the further induced effects. In some senses the well established economic impact analysis, a technique based on regional economics concepts, as exemplified in the studies of tourism multipliers (Archer, 1977), embodying respectively the direct, indirect and induced effects, constitutes a useful foundation for listing the gains of a project which can be feasibly ascertained. However, tourism multiplier analysis does not include the non-market effects nor does it identify the costs. One must adopt a more comprehensive inventory frame-work in order to embody these. In the tourism field Pearce (1989), in exam-ining tourism development, has usefully set out such a framework, largely embracing the general definition of the environment given above, which identifies both the market and non-market benefits and costs. Continuing to examine the case of a holiday complex, the kinds of impacts which need to be taken into account are: the generation of traffic; the increase in the numbers of people attracted to the complex and surrounding area; the increased demand for utilities services – electricity, gas, telecommunications, water supply, sewage disposal, and so on – and local authority services – solid waste disposal, street cleaning, road maintenance, education and training, policing, health, housing and so on.

However, it is in the incorporation of the non-market environmental effects that economists' conceptualisation of collective consumption goods and externalities becomes relevant, but these are more difficult to identify. A number of examples of what might be termed the more intangible and diffuse impacts were given in a different context in the explanation of the previous step concerning spatial, physical/ecological and socio-cultural factors. A leisure complex undoubtedly has similar effects.

In this step it is important to include in the listing all impacts which create changes in the allocation of resources, that is the level and pattern of production, and distribution of income and wealth as indicators of changes in consumer utility or welfare. Ascertaining such changes is known as the *additionality* criterion which refers to the net effects, that is impacts occurring as a result of the project as opposed to those which would have done so even if it had not been implemented; for example it is the additional traffic generated once the complex is operating which is relevant. Conversely, if there is net decrease in some impact, say the adverse effects of the former agricultural use of the land taken for the complex, this should be accounted for. A second and related criterion is that of *displacement*, for which an example was given earlier. In the case of the leisure complex, its development might have displaced an activity which generated more or less income and employment so that again it is the net effect which has to be identified.

What also has to be borne in mind is the net gain or loss of both the quality as well as the quantity of goods and services available to the community, or society at large if the project has such ramifications. Quality enters more prominently into the picture where unpriced environmental impacts assume more importance than priced or market-based ones. Indeed, given the premise stated at the outset that the quality of natural and humanmade environments is a vital component of the tourism product, the benefits and costs attached to them should be of a considerable magnitude. This aspect is now examined.

Evaluation of the gains and losses

Considering the identified benefits and costs in physical terms is not very helpful in reaching a decision on whether a particular project is better than alternatives, even if the listed benefits and the magnitude of each, for instance number of tourists attracted to an area or the number of jobs created, are calculated to be much larger. Therefore, a common unit for measuring the effects is required and since in market economies price is recognised as an acceptable indicator of value, it is used in project appraisal.

However, this is not to assert, unless certain conditions are met, that *market prices* are the correct measure for, as elementary economic analysis shows, they can be inappropriate where, for example, there is imperfect competition, such as monopoly control of a market for a certain good or service or productive input, or taxes are imposed and subsidies granted. A second difficulty is that as projects to which CBA might be applied are likely to be long term, it is necessary to estimate the future prices of the benefits and costs which periodically occur; the relative scarcity of products and productive inputs and rates of inflation being two important determinants. A third complication is that many benefits and costs are unpriced because they relate to the effects of the project not traded in the market. The earlier discussion of collective consumption goods and externalities and the many examples of environmental impacts have made clear the significance of these.

The first two difficulties can be dealt with by making adjustments to prevailing market prices or by deriving *shadow prices*. For example, distortions caused by market imperfections, or government intervention in the form of regulated prices and taxes and subsidies, can be overcome in this way, as can the projection, from current prices, of relative prices in the future, which may be caused by inflation. Inflation, for example, can be dealt with by applying an appropriate index to express prices in real terms, for instance use of the retail price index for consumer goods and services. These issues are not pursued further here as they are adequately explained in many texts, on CBA and environmental economics, of which those by Hanley and Spash (1993) or Turner et al (1994) are respectively sound introductions. The third difficulty is the much more acute one where shadow prices, in the true sense of the meaning of the term of attaching prices to goods and services where none exist, have to be created. It is this aspect to which much attention has been devoted by economists in recent years as environmental problems become more pressing, whether through the increased pressure of demand for resources for productive uses, or amenity, or as a result of greater pollution. Several methods for estimating the value of non-priced resources have been advocated, of which only a few have emerged as the most acceptable to economists in that they reflect the subject's conceptual, theoretical and methodological principles. These are the contingent valuation (CVM), hedonic pricing (HPM) and travel cost (TCM) methods. Others which have been proposed are acceptable but not necessarily suitable for estimating the value of the tourism resource base as opposed to their relevance in environmental economics, especially the abatement of pollution.

The concept of value and the methods used can only be briefly described and reviewed here. Although they make a key contribution to the evaluation of the base in their own right, they are only one aspect of any CBA which should be applied to appraise tourism projects which utilise it. Their importance, therefore, should not be overemphasised.

The concept of total economic value

The concept of consumers' surplus acknowledges that in the market use value can be greater than for all but the marginal consumer as there are many purchasers who are *willing to pay* a higher price than they actually have to pay. The surplus represents the net unpriced user benefit or value which is enjoyed but not embodied in market prices. The notion of willingness to pay has been extended to include the non-use value of unpriced goods or resources, particularly where they are *unique, irreproducible* and where an *irreversible* trend may be initiated if they are overused or degraded, which might result in their eventual destruction. This is certainly true of many natural and humanmade environments forming the tourism resource base. There is some variation in how the willingness to pay for these should be categorised but the following largely embraces the forms of value which make up total economic value:

- Use value:
    direct or exchange value; represented by the price paid
    indirect or net value; represented by the net benefits
- Non-use value:
    option value; the expression of willingness to pay to keep open the possibility of consumption in the future
    existence or intrinsic value; the value placed on retention of goods and resources irrespective of their use to human beings
    bequest value; the value the present generation places on retaining goods and resources for the benefit of future generations (some commentators perceive this as a variant of option value)

Thus total economic value comprises all these and should be included where non-priced environmental resources are under consideration. For most priced goods and services, non-use values would not normally be included for they are not unique, are reproducible and not likely to be subject to irreversibility.

If the concept of total economic value is to be made operational, the question then arises as to which methods capture some or all of its elements; this will be indicated below.

Valuation methods

The principal methods can broadly be divided into those which are *indirect*, revealing preferences, and those which are *direct*, whereby preferences are stated or expressed.

- Indirect methods:
    production function approaches (PFA):
        averting expenditure or avoided cost (AE)
        dose response (DR)
    hedonic pricing (HPM)
    travel cost (TCM)
- Direct methods:
    contingent valuation (CVM)
    Delphi principle (DP)

Explanation of the valuation methods

- Indirect methods.

Production function approaches (PFA)   These are based on the supposition that firms and households respectively combine productive inputs and commodities with environmental services in order to produce a composite good or service. This is aptly illustrated with respect to households who literally become 'holidaymakers' by combining the components of travel, accommodation, services, facilities and natural and humanmade environments to create the tourism product. Thus environments become part of the commodity and acquire value, which is confirmed by the willingness to incur expenditure on them either to change the quantity or improve their quality.

The averting expenditure and dose response methods are of much more relevance to environmental degradation or pollution than tourism, where severe practical problems arise, although in theory it would be possible to apply them. For example, expenditure to improve the built environment in a resort might be undertaken as a substitute for a decline in the quality of its natural environment under an averting expenditure approach. A dose response approach attempts to measure in economic terms the effect of a physical, chemical or biological occurrence. For instance, the deterioration of historic buildings caused, say, by tourism traffic vibration and emissions could be measured in economic terms in so far as it changes the supply production function of those occupying or owning such properties.

Hedonic pricing (HPM)   The method was developed by Rosen (1974) from a theory of demand proposed by Lancaster (1966) to determine the relationship between the attributes of a good and its price. It takes as its starting point that any differentiated product can be viewed as a bundle of characteristics each with its own implicit or shadow price. It has lent itself to the analysis of buildings and their location in determining the contribution individual characteristics make to the total value of properties. For instance, in the context of historic buildings and their value as tourist attractions, it is possible to attribute the impact of location in a tourism area as opposed to virtually identical buildings which are not so located.

There are a number of studies in the heritage and amenity field which have applied HPM. Illustrative examples are those by Asabere et al (1989) who considered the impact of architectural styles on value while Garrod and Willis (1991) used it to explore the effect on property prices of proximity to forest and of location near waterways (Willis and Garrod, 1993). In the former it was found that location near a forest raised property values by 5% while properties near water had values 7% above similar ones which were not. These kinds of studies, however, did not, and indeed cannot, isolate the extent to which tourism was generated by the characteristics of properties or environments, nor did they ascertain in turn the contribution tourism made to their values, simply because the purpose of HPM is to explain property values. The attractiveness of historic buildings or locations which generate tourism equally encourages people to occupy such properties or move into an acknowledged tourism area and so enhance values. The method has been applied to the characteristics of holidays to explain price competitiveness (Clewer et al, 1992) but not specifically to establish the contribution of the resource base. Thus to date the HPM has been of limited relevance as it only takes account of its attributes in so far as they enter into product prices or are capitalised into land and property values. Moreover, it does not measure non-use-option, existence and bequest value. Furthermore, although it is a rigorous and highly refined method, it depends on quite restrictive assumptions and requires an extensive and detailed data base.

Travel cost method (TCM)   This approach to valuation, which is also known as the Clawson method because he was instrumental in initiating its development (Clawson and Knetsch, 1966), was devised specifically to estimate the benefits visitors derived from non-priced amenity resources. It takes explicit expenditure on travel to particular areas or sites as a proxy measure of willingness to pay for the visit. By aggregating the travel costs of the number of visitors or the visit rate from specified zones surrounding the site, its valuation is obtained. It has been widely applied in a rural context to estimate the value of sites used largely for informal recreation, such as ancient monuments, forests and country parks, but increasingly it has been applied to more active pursuits, for example hunting and cruising (Loomis et al, 1991; Willis and Garrod, 1990). It is a more problematic method for sites to which access can be gained without incurring travel costs, for instance those in or close to urban areas. In these cases it has been suggested that the implicit cost of travel time could be used, but this then raises the issue of whether on-site time should also be included. There are very few examples of the application of TCM to urban sites. In addition to the rationale of whether implicit costs should be incorporated there is greater difficulty in identifying and separating the purpose for the journey as visits to urban areas are more likely to be multi-purpose. Another problem specifically related to tourists is the proportion of the travel costs from their place of residence, which may be overseas, which should be assigned to particular sites visited, especially if accommodation is taken close to each. In a domestic tourism context it is possible for visitors to take up residence close to a favoured site in order to reduce the explicit and implicit costs of travel. If the frequency of visits does not increase then for such visitors the benefits and therefore the value of a site is lower. The reverse logic of this reasoning is that sites which are distant, involving high travel costs, are more valuable than those which are close by.

There are other conceptual and methodological problems of the TCM, for example whether or not utility is derived from the journey, what the main purpose of the outing is, how to assign values to individual sites when a number are visited on a single outing and how visitors react to congestion. Such issues have been raised and debated over a number of years (Cheshire and Stabler, 1976; Walsh, 1986). The scope of TCM is also limited because it applies only to visitors to specific sites and effectively only measures actual consumption, not demand. Like HPM it does not capture non-user demand.

● Direct methods.

Contingent valuation (CVM)   The CVM is a survey-based approach in which stated preferences are sought by self-completed questionnaire or interview. The respondent can be asked for willingness to pay (WTP) for access to resources currently unpriced or an improvement in their quality, or conversely the willingness to accept (WTA) to forego access or suffer a fall in quality. The method need not be confined to eliciting such responses in actual situations or for specific proposals but can seek likely behaviour in hypothetical cases. Consequently it lends itself to questioning about option, existence and bequest demand.

A number of steps in a defined sequence are required: a hypothetical reason for payment or compensation is set up, perhaps accompanied by information on the subject to assist the respondent to appreciate the issues; the cost of the action; the means of payment or compensation and; lastly, bids are sought which might include a maximum WTP or a minimum WTA. Notwithstanding many misgivings concerning the reliability and validity of CVM (Heberlein and Bishop, 1986; Mitchell and Carson, 1989; Bowers, 1997), it has gained ground as a valuation method because of its potential to cover the whole of a population, its ability to embody use and non-use values and its political acceptability because it can reflect the democratically expressed preferences of society at large.

The CVM has been extensively applied in environmental and recreational fields and there are a number of examples where option values have been investigated (Bateman et al, 1994; Lockwood et al, 1993; Garrod et al, 1994) showing that non-use values accounted for between 20% and 40% of the total economic value. Its application to tourism, while examined in principle, has not yet resulted in any significant studies yielding indications of non-use WTP. Given the acute pressures on the tourism resource base in certain locations, there has certainly not been research to ascertain the WTA by tourists to forego visits to areas under threat of despoliation.

Delphi Principle (DP)   This approach is akin to CVM in that through a survey it employs a panel of 'experts' to elicit their views on an issue. It was developed in the 1950s by the RAND corporation (Dalkey and Helmer, 1963) and was found to be useful in instances where historical data were unavailable or forecasts of possible future trends were sought. Panels should ideally be quite large, consisting of people with knowledge of the topic and with diverse views and valuations. The purpose of the technique is, through a series of stages whereby individual responses are analysed and returned to the panel, to establish whether each member wishes to revise an estimate in the light of others' responses. The process of analysis, redistribution of the results and requestioning continues until an overall convergence of views is achieved. It is a relatively simple exercise to conduct but the selection of an appropriate panel, appropriate briefing and design of the questionnaire may have a crucial influence on the final outcome. Currently it is untested as a valuation method in CBA although it has been referred to as a tourism forecasting tool (Witt and Martin, 1989).

A critique of valuation methods

Of the valuation methods outlined here the HPM, TCM and CVM are currently emerging as the most feasible. However, they are not alternatives, for as shown they focus on different sectors of consumers and types of values. The main drawbacks of the HPM and TCM are their restrictive assumptions, data requirements, danger of omitted variables and their limited coverage of the possible range of respondents; but above all their failure to measure nonuse values is a fundamental failing. This suggests that CVM, not without its own shortcomings, for example, biases arising from strategically under- or overstating WTP/WTA depending on expectations about payment and its form and the hypothetical nature of the method and survey design (Garrod and Willis, 1990), is the most favoured because it possesses the advantages which the HPM and TCM do not. Yet very recently (Allison et al, 1996) the suggestion has been made that the three methods could possibly be additive in certain circumstances in order to cover use valuations by both residents and visitor, and non-use ones by them and society at large. Moreover, these methods, measuring *static* values could be combined with those, such as multiplier and input output analysis, which measure *dynamic* values (Stabler, 1996). The development of other approaches, the Delphi principle for example in relation to CVM, could act both as complementary and external validity checks. What is apparent, however, is that further refinement and empirical testing of the methods for valuing benefits and costs needs to be undertaken. Of especial importance is the need to investigate how appropriate they are in estimating valuations of impacts in the future, given the long-time horizons of projects to which CBA would be applied. This raises the issue of whether a sensitivity analysis might be required where there is uncertainty as to values to be attached to impacts. This analysis entails taking different estimates of benefits and costs, say high, medium and low, so that when discounted different present values are thrown up.

Allied to the valuation of both current and future benefits and costs and sensitivity analysis, is the issue of weighting. This concept recognises that the benefits and/or costs falling on one section of the present generation might be of more importance than those experienced by another section. Thus, for example, in a project to use tourism as a means of diversifying or developing a primary product economy, greater weight may be given to the benefits accruing to unemployed people or a community in a disadvantaged rural area than the redeployment of those already working in an urban area. With respect to the intergenerational impacts of a project, differential weights may be applied to benefits and/or costs falling on the present generation in comparison with those falling on future generations. Thus projects to develop marine tourism, say in the Great Barrier Reef in Australia, or the newly designated World Heritage one bordering the Belizean coast, would attach weight which might impose more costs on the present generation in order to preserve and safeguard coral reefs for future generations. In short, weights can be used to discriminate against or in favour of certain objectives. In effect the magnitude of the benefits and costs is enhanced or diminished, which affects the outcome of the net present value of a project, discussed below.

Discounting benefits and costs and timing

Having conducted the evaluation of benefits and costs in the previous step, in order to establish their present value on which the decision as to whether or not to proceed with a project depends, it is necessary to discount them. That the discounting of benefits and costs should be done is not really in dispute. Positive interest and inflation rates underpin time preferences which suggest that present monetary returns and benefits are more highly valued than future ones. The more important question is what discount rate should be employed. Since it is most often used as an indicator, distortions requiring adjustment notwithstanding, the market rate of interest acts as a datum. This is mainly because it represents the opportunity cost of funds in the private sector, sometimes referred to as the *external rate of return* (ERR) as opposed to the *internal rate of return* (IRR) which tourism businesses would, or should, employ to appraise investment within their enterprises, say in the hospitality or facilities sectors. The IRR is the rate of return (benefits) on the capital invested (cost) expressed as a percentage where the timing and flow of returns and costs is taken account of. In technical terms the IRR is the discount rate which makes the net present value of benefits and costs of a project equal to zero. In CBA which is generally considered as the appropriate appraisal method in the public sector, the use of IRR is not favoured. Objections are based on the premise that public sector projects tend to have high capital costs which are incurred early in their lives while benefits accrue, very likely after a substantial period where none are generated, far into the future over a very long time horizon. The IRR, which might carry a risk premium and also reflect the desire for high and early returns, would discriminate against such projects. This is not difficult to appreciate if a simple example is taken to illustrate the effect of a given discount rate on the present value of a benefit accruing after one year as opposed to five or ten years hence. The present value of £1 million in one year's time at a 10% interest rate is £0.9090909, five years hence it is £0.6209213 million and £0.3855433 million in ten years time. It is equally easy to understand the impact of the effect of the capital cost and longer gestation period of returns on the present value. If a project in the public sector costs £0.5 million as opposed to £0.35 million in the private sector (both incurred in the first year), the present value of the benefit accruing respectively at the end of the tenth and fifth year, will show the public sector project as negative in comparison with the private sector positive one:

Sector	PV costs (£m) (year 0)	PV benefit (£m) (£1 million)	PV of project (£m) (Benefit-cost)
Public	0.5	0.3855433 (10 years)	−0.1144567
Private	0.35	0.6209213 (5 years)	+0.2709213

For the public sector project to be viable the discount rate would have to come down to 7% for the project to produce a positive present value (£1 million at 7% after 10 years equals £0.5083493 million) and $2\frac{1}{2}$% to exceed the present value of the private sector one (£1 million at $2\frac{1}{2}$% after 10 years equals £0.7811984 million, minus £0.5 million equals £0.2811984 million).

Thus the rudimentary example indicates the effect of three variables on the present value: the timing of the benefits and costs; the magnitude of the capital cost and the discount rate. Unfortunately it is not possible here to trace the arguments which have been put forward with regard to what the discount rate to be applied to public sector projects should be. On balance, if only because the risks are lower in comparison with private sector ventures, social time preference rates are likely to be lower than private time preference rates. There is, therefore, a case for lower discount rates to be employed. The use of sensitivity analysis by varying the discount rate rather than the value of the benefits and costs, as shown in the example, does change the present value and this has been advocated as a way of establishing how susceptible certain projects might be to high discount rates. If society deems that projects with respect to the preservation of natural and humanmade environments, with pay-offs well into the future, are worthwhile, then the use of low discount rates will place them in a more favourable position vis-à-vis private sector ones, or if there are a number of public sector projects competing for limited funding resources. This takes the outline and review of CBA to its final step of how to determine which projects to choose and/or in what order.

Decision rules

The ultimate aim of CBA is to select the projects which should be undertaken on the grounds of their efficiency, essentially maximising social welfare. A rather lower order criterion is that the net present value is positive. The first presupposes that projects should be ranked in some way, particularly if resources are limited and insufficient to carry out all desired projects in a given period. The second is merely an accept-reject or yes-no criterion and represents the requirement for a project to be considered. To operate the decision rules the discounted costs and benefits generated over the estimated life of the project are summated. To pass the basic test, the sum of discounted benefits should exceed the sum of discounted costs, that is the net present value (NPV) should be greater than zero.

In order to rank projects, other rules can be applied. A simple one is merely to list them in descending order of the magnitude of the NPV. A more sophisticated approach is to use the benefit-cost ratio whereby for each project the present value of the benefits is divided by the present value of costs and ranked by the resulting ratio. A third alternative is to rank each project by its IRR. However, the IRR has been heavily criticised (see Hawkins and Pearce, 1971, for a very clear and concise exposition) because of the technical anomalies that arise, apart from the observations made on it above.

AN ASSESSMENT OF COST-BENEFIT ANALYSIS (CBA)

In explaining the nature of CBA by tracing the process and its possible application to tourism resource base issues, by means of the six principal steps, it became apparent that the core aspects were the third and fourth, concerning the identification and evaluation of benefits and costs. These steps and the concepts and methods associated with them were considered more fully because the benefits derived from and imposed on the natural and human environments constituting the base are mostly unpriced. More importantly, however, these account for the majority of the total economic value and costs included in a CBA appraisal of tourism projects.

The exposition of CBA offered here largely reflects the widely accepted foundations and development of the method as expounded in the many texts of varying complexity and length published since the 1950s. Early and sound introductions were published by Krutilla and Eckstein (1958) and Prest and Turvey (1966) and examples of more applied studies are those by Dorfman (1965) and Peters (1968). Later contributions combining principles and practice were made by Little and Mirrlees (1974), Sugden and Williams (1978) and Pearce and Nash (1981). In recent years texts have tended to consider CBA in the context of specific problems, particularly traffic and pollution. Good examples are the texts by Pearce (1978, 1986) and Nash (1990); while latterly the method is examined within texts on the environment (Hanley and Spash, 1993; Turner et al, 1994) or sustainability (Pearce et al, 1989).

There have, however, always been dissenting voices about the relevance of CBA to investment appraisal in practice and as a concept. Lichfield (1956), who investigated urban land and development issues and the role of planning, was one of the first researchers to set the development of the method off in a different direction, whereas Mishan (1967, 1971) was very sceptical of the efficacy of the concept, a view which has recently been echoed with respect to its application to environmental problems by Kelman (1986), Sagoff (1988) and Bowers (1997). These two lines of argument are examined as a means of highlighting the 'philosophical' issues surrounding the method, including the difficulties of translating the principles of the method into practice and how it might be adapted and developed. This leads to some concluding observations on the outlook for CBA as a means of appraising tourism's impact on its primary resource base.

Two fundamental issues underlie the whole concept of CBA and are still unresolved. The first, stemming from its foundations in welfare economics, is the distributional debate and the second, related to it to an extent, is the values which should be attached to the benefits and costs identified where they are based on measures of willingness to pay, underpinned by effective demand.

In original conceptions of CBA, the distribution of income and wealth was taken as given, and transfer payments, unless intragenerational redistribution was a specific objective of the project, were to be ignored, mainly because of the desire to establish its net effects, that is whether or not costs falling on one section of society were offset by benefits enjoyed by another section. This is exemplified in what is known as the Kaldor–Hicks test. However, with the increased concern for environmental quality and protection, the intergenerational distribution of wealth (natural and humanmade) has assumed greater importance, which has led to the questioning of the method's basic principles.

The distributional issue has also cast doubt on the superiority of the means in CBA of establishing WTP/WTA as being more objective over the political system based on voting (perhaps through a referendum) or lobbying pressure. The methods used to establish WTP/WTA are underpinned by effective demand and this is determined by the distribution of income and wealth. Thus richer sections of society are more likely to secure the goods and services they want because their WTP/WTA will be higher. Allied to this is the interpersonal comparison issue in demand theory whereby different individuals place different values on goods and services. In the context of tourism resources, one may value the natural environment highly while another discounts it by placing a high value on the human or built environment. These differences cannot be reconciled without measuring the values but this violates current consumer behaviour theory which makes no claims to measure variations in utility between different goods and services of one individual, let alone between two different consumers. Yet another aspect emerges when the intergenerational distributional issue and approaches to valuation are considered. The WTP/WTA of the present generation, conditioned to seeking high economic growth and consumption, may be more anthropocentric, whereas future generations, inheriting a diminished natural environment, fauna and flora, are likely to be ecocentric. Accordingly, the environment is undervalued today to its detriment, therefore constraining the options open in the future. This is the case which is put forward by ecologists. They argue that decisions affecting the environment should not be based on monetary evaluations but on physical criteria, such as maximum sustainable yields for renewable resources and safe minimum standards for pollution, or the precautionary principle where the outcome of an action is uncertain, especially in the face of irreproducibility and irreversibility.

In part, the problems of translating the principles of CBA into practice and the development of different approaches reflect the conceptual debate. Lichfield (1956; 1988) and Lichfield et al (1993) expressly included means for identifying distributional effects and indeed included them as integral parts of the benefits and costs of the appraisal. In his later versions of his approach to CBA he referred to them as Community Impact Analysis (CIA) or Community Impact Evaluation (CIE), the designation reflecting the emphasis placed on the distributional issues. He also accepted in his planning balance sheet analysis (PBSA) that many impacts cannot be evaluated in monetary terms but, however, could be identified and listed (Lichfield,

1956). Bowers (1997) supports this view and, implicitly siding with the ecologists, considers that a physical quantification of impacts can be equally as informing as a monetarised one. Furthermore he asserts that it is impracticable to quantify all benefits and costs but that many of a qualitative nature may nevertheless be important and included.

There are other practical, or even political, reasons for moderating the strict criteria which should be adhered to in conducting a CBA or by looking for other approaches. To conduct appraisals to establish the best of many alternatives ex ante would be hideously expensive, especially for most tourism projects for which it has been shown that they have widespread environmental and socio-cultural repercussions, as well as economic impacts, often on a large spatial scale. There are also regulations in place, albeit as a consequence of increasing concerns over the environmental impact of large-scale and potentially damaging activities, which require appraisals to be in a particular form. The European Union (EU) has instituted Environmental Impact Assessment (EIA) as a response. In seeking planning permission an environmental statement must be submitted which considers the impact of the development on people, socio-cultural structures, fauna and flora, the environment with respect to pollution and the landscape. The statement must include the action to be taken to offset any detrimental effects. The submission must be made available for public consultation and the EIA must be taken into account in reaching a decision. The submission of an EIA is compulsory for many activities with the potential for widespread and adverse environmental effects, such as chemical works, transport programmes and power stations, but it does also cover leisure schemes over a certain size, for example marina developments or large coastal and resort developments. An EIA only covers environmental costs and does not require that all impacts be expressed in monetary terms where the steps to mitigate damaging effects are offered. Thus, although it recognises the importance of taking account of environmental factors, EIA is not a full CBA, particularly in ignoring possible benefits. This omission is important since alternative schemes with the same objectives might have generated more benefits than the particular one submitted, together with its EIA.

The form of appraisal may also be dictated by the conditions to receive funding where projects depend on such support. Thus, for example, the United Nations and World Bank both determine the nature of the project and the appraisal to be carried out (see the reference to multi-criteria analysis below). There are examples in developing countries in which funds to protect the natural or socio-cultural environment have been given which are intended to mitigate or moderate the effects of tourism development (Wilson, 1997). There are also various other organisations, including charities which offer funds on specified terms to protect ancient monuments and artefacts, cultures and fauna and flora which are under threat from tourism activity. For instance, Shackley (1996) gives a number of examples of such problems with regard to wildlife and the action which has been taken to protect habitats and species. Other instances of this interrelationship between tourism and funding arrangements which determine the nature of the appraisal are the EU RECITE programme for urban schemes and the LEADER programme for more rural investment, both of which have tourist elements which can be in conflict with conservation and environmental protection.

Organisations with a remit to achieve certain objectives often see the need to justify their expenditures and therefore conduct an appraisal of their activities. In the UK, for example, the English Tourist Board has justified financial support from the state by trying to show that tourism means jobs. English Heritage recently felt compelled to fund research into the value of conservation (Allison et al, 1996), one aspect being to show that public expenditure on heritage artefacts and buildings was justified. Thus, because of difficulties of applying a full CBA in practice, its cost and the need for organisations to meet regulations or funding conditions or to justify their actions, a number of approaches have been advocated that move further away from the conceptual ideal or its close derivatives, such as Lichfield's versions referred to above.

In circumstances where the decision to proceed with a project to meet a specified objective has already been made a CBA is unnecessary, unless it is considered that an ex post appraisal is of value to guide future decisions on projects. Consequently it has been asserted that a cost-effectiveness analysis (CEA) would be feasible. The point of issue then becomes how best to attain the objective. Hanley and Spash (1993), in concluding comments on their review of CBA as applied to the environment, suggest that if the inputs into a scheme (the outputs having already been determined) are costed at shadow prices reflecting their social marginal costs, then CEA partially meets CBA criteria. Once costed, but not implemented, the project can be assessed on the basis as to whether it is worthwhile. Therefore, for example, if the activities of the English Tourist Board, or English Heritage, or of environmental bodies, such as the Countryside Commission and English Nature, have given objectives, the question can be asked as to whether the several million pounds each receives every year are value for money.

Another type of approach is multi-criteria analysis (MCA) which in an urban environmental context has been developed by Nijkamp (1975), Paelinck (1976) and Voogd (1988). Here the various alternatives are ranked according to criteria thought to be relevant and the 'best' are chosen through calculating the extent to which it outranks others on average. The method is designed to include benefits and costs in monetary terms, as in a CBA, but can also embrace qualitative variables which are identified as environment gains or losses. In this it tends to follow the Lichfield (1956) model of CBA in his 'above' and 'below' the line balance sheet, the former containing the direct monetary benefits and costs and the latter the listing of the indirect quantifiable and qualitative gains and losses. This characteristic of MCA is useful where the cost of conducting an appraisal in order to collect the requisite data is substantial. This is an important factor in its favour, as pointed out earlier with regard to the likely large scale of an exercise to appraise the impact of tourism. The method is also one of those now given the imprimatur of the United Nations and the World Bank. The problem with the MCA, as Buckley (1988) pointed out in an exchange with Voogd, is that unless the best alternative outweighs all the others on all criteria, a weight, explicit or implicit, is being attributed to the attainment of each criterion of each alternative, which creates the danger of subjectivity.

A more mathematical approach to decision-making between alternatives, in the absence of full information, is the Analytic Hierarchy Process (AHP) developed by Saaty (1987). It has been suggested for the evaluation of alternative approaches to conservation by Lombardi and Sirchia (1990).

These major alternative approaches to appraisal have been derived largely to attempt to overcome the technical difficulties of CBA encountered in practice; they do not undermine its principles. Despite the problems of applying CBA, it has powerful attractions for it is well grounded in economic theory and resolves the weighting problem, crucial in sustainability and intergenerational distribution issues, much more objectively than other methods. Also, by expressing outcomes in monetary terms, directly or indirectly from people's stated preferences or behaviour, weights are derived in a systematic way. Furthermore, it is comprehensive and explicit in its embodiment of priced and non-priced costs and benefits and, as stated earlier in the context of natural and humanmade environments with respect to non-priced benefits and costs, this is a fundamental advantage because of their magnitude. To this extent it acts as the datum for the appraisal of projects irrespective of whether that appraisal is actually implemented.

CONCLUSION: COST-BENEFIT ANALYSIS AND TOURISM

Inspection of the applications of CBA in the references cited earlier throws up examples that are mainly concerned with water supply, flood control, pollution abatement, transport and traffic management, airports and urban development and redevelopment. Also, as shown in indicative examples, it has increasingly been applied to wider environmental issues which clearly relate to the quality of the tourism resource base. While it is acknowledged that pollution abatement, particularly reductions in water, air, noise and visual intrusion arising from tourism activity in holiday destinations, and every bit as damaging as normal day-to-day human activity, can yield marked improvements in the quality of the resource base, the extension of studies into the natural environment should do the same. Therefore, appraisals of projects which have an impact on such resources as coasts (especially estuaries), islands, forest, lakes, mountainous areas, rivers and wetlands are equally relevant. Examples of leisure and recreational impacts on these resources abound, but they concern their evaluation, applying principally CVM, HPM and TCM, or combinations of them. In short they relate to methods for valuing the benefits. They are not appraisals which include the costs associated with such use so do not ascertain the net effects. Consequently there are virtually no examples of comprehensive CBA applications directly concerned with the impact of tourism on its resource base.

The nearest that actual schemes have got to full appraisals is with respect to tourism development. There are innumerable and obvious examples of almost haphazard growth in the Mediterranean area with the advent of mass air travel, particularly in Spain and the islands under its jurisdiction, but the most comprehensively planned development was that of the resorts along the Languedoc–Roussillon coast in France. This was conceived nationally and was primarily concerned with regional policy. It, however, paid scant respect, de facto, to the natural environment, as did the many other such developments in the Mediterranean. At the time of its conception in the 1960s, governments and developers were largely complacent about the environmental impact of their respective policies and actions. While the Languedoc–Roussillon development was cognisant of the economic and to an extent the social benefits, it ignored the external social costs. The situation is changing, but very slowly. Governments are beginning to recognise the need for action to safeguard the environment because of the key roles it plays in all forms of economic and social activity. However, two earth summits have yielded only declarations of intent and principles, but virtually no action. If this is the position in general what hope is there for practical moves regarding tourism? Given, on balance, the positive attributes of CBA to contribute to both the appraisal and direction of tourism development and to moderate its impact on its resource base, why has the method or its close derivatives not been adopted? The answer probably lies in the academic failure to promote it and that it has not been appropriately brought to the attention of the tourism industry.

The academic failure stems largely from the subject of economics which, as indicated earlier, has singularly overlooked tourism as a research topic. Although it has moved strongly towards investigating the impact of the agricultural and manufacturing industries, and perhaps urban development, on natural resources, it has not recognised that tourism as a major economic activity and user of resources also has a significant impact. Thus appraisals of the industry and its effects have simply not been undertaken. A second criticism of the discipline is its failure to make CBA comprehensible to practitioners. Geographers have performed better in this respect by modelling tourism development and indicating its consequences. A notable example of how the process of development and its environmental impact can be assessed is the work of D. G. Pearce (1989) who constructed, with admirable clarity, the framework for appraising tourism's impact.

The tourism industry has yet fully to accept responsibility for its actions and effects. Aided and abetted by governments and various international and national organisations, which promote it as a valuable contributor to economic growth and development, the full implications of unrestrained expansion are only just being realised. To an extent, as it is a fragmented and diverse industry, the slow response to the threats to its resource base are unsurprising. Moreover, those representing the industry understandably perceive the problems of making a comprehensive and coordinated action as being beyond their capabilities and purview. It is also not necessarily unfair to assert that most effort has gone into improving the quality of the project, the standard of service and in improving the management and marketing structure of the industry. Furthermore, a lack of awareness of the more strategic approach to appraising tourism projects and the methods that can be employed is another explanation. The introduction of regulations, such as Environmental Impact Assessment (EIA), and the greater role played by planning authorities, has started to improve the situation.

Thus, currently, a convincing case for using CBA as a suitable appraisal method to assist better decision-making in tourism has yet to be made. At the moment it remains as a potentially valuable tool to governments and public authorities, as well as the industry. A closer relationship between economists and practitioners in devising a theoretically and methodologically sound version of CBA, but one which can be inexpensively and simply applied, needs to be encouraged. However, this liaison and the implemention of benchmark studies will almost certainly have to be triggered by public sector funding, backed by longer term, perhaps mandatory, arrangements, to build up a database of projects.

REFERENCES

Allison, G., Ball, S., Cheshire, P.C., Evans, A.W., Stabler, M.J., 1996, *The value of conservation: a literature review of the economic and social value of the cultural built heritage*, English Heritage, London

Archer, B.H., 1977, *Tourism multipliers: the state of the art*, Occasional Papers in Economics, No. 11, University of Wales, Bangor

Asabere, P.K., Hachey, G., Grubaugh, S., 1989, Architecture, historic zoning and the value of homes, *Journal of Real Estate Finance and Economics*, 2: 181–195

Bateman, I., Willis, K.G., Garrod, G., 1994, Consistency between contingent valuation estimates: a comparison of two studies of UK National Parks, *Regional Studies*, 28(5): 457–474

Bowers, J., 1997, *Sustainability and environmental economics: an alternative text*, Addison Wesley Longman, Harlow

Bramwell, B., Lane, B., 1993, Sustainable tourism: an evolving global approach, *Journal of Sustainable Tourism*, 1(1): 1–5

Brierton, U.A., 1991, Tourism and the environment, *Contours*, 5(4): 18–19

Buckley, M., 1988, Multicriteria evaluation: measures, manipulation and meaning, *Environment and Planning B: planning and design*, 15(1): 55–64

Bull, A., 1991, *The economics of travel and tourism*, Pitman, Melbourne

Butcher, J., 1997, Sustainable development or development? In Stabler, M.J., ed., *Tourism and sustainability: principles to practice*, CAB International, Wallingford, Oxon

Butler, R.W., 1991, Tourism, environment and sustainable development, *Environmental Conservation*, 18(3): 201–209

Cheshire, P.C., Stabler, M.J., 1976, Joint consumption benefits in recreational site surplus: An empirical estimate, *Regional Studies*, 10: 343–351

Clawson, M., Knetsch, J.L., 1966 *Economics of outdoor recreation*, Johns Hopkins University Press, Baltimore, MD

Clewer, A., Pack, A., Sinclair, M.T., 1992, Price competitiveness and inclusive tour holidays in European cities. In Johnson, P., Thomas, B., eds, *Choice and demand in tourism*, Mansell, London

Dalkey, N., Helmer, O., 1963, An experimental application of the Delphi method of the use of experts, *Management Science*, 9(3): 458–467

Dorfman, R., ed., 1965, *Measuring benefits of government investments*, Brookings Institute, Washington, DC

Erize, F., 1987, The impact of tourism on the Antarctic environment, *Environment International*, 13(1): 133–136

Fyall, A., Garrod, B., 1997, Sustainable tourism: towards a methodology for implementing the concept. In Stabler, M.J., ed, *Tourism and sustainability: principles to practice*, CAB International, Wallingford, Oxon

Garrod, G., Willis, K.G., 1990, *Contingent valuation techniques: a review of their unbiasedness, efficiency and consistency*, Countryside Change Unit Working Paper 10, University of Newcastle, Newcastle

Garrod, G., Willis, K.G., 1991, The environmental economic impact of woodland: a two stage hedonic price model of the amenity value of forestry in Britain, *Applied Economics*, 24: 715–728

Garrod, G., Willis, K.G., Saunders, C.M., 1994, The benefits and costs of the Somerset levels and Moors ESA, *Journal of Rural Studies*, 10(2): 131–145

Goodall, B., Stabler, M.J., 1994, Tourism environment issues and approaches to their solution. In Voogd, H., ed., *Issues in environmental planning*, European Research in Regional Science, Vol. 4, Pion, London

Hanley, N., Spash, C.L., 1993, *Cost-benefit analysis and the environment*, Edward Elgar, Aldershot

Hawkins, C.J., Pearce, D.W., 1971, *Capital investment appraisal*, Macmillan, London

Heberlein, T., Bishop, R., 1986, Assessing the validity of contingent valuation: three experiments, *Science of the Total Environment*, 56: 99–107

Hunter, C., Green, H., 1995, *Tourism and the environment: a sustainable relationship?* Routledge, London

Inskeep, E., 1991, *Tourism planning: an integrated and sustainable approach*, Van Nostrand Reinhold, The Hague

Kelman, S., 1986, Cost-benefit analysis: an ethical critique. In Van De Veer, D., Pierce, C., eds, *People, penguins and plastic trees: basic issues in environmental ethics*, Wadsworth, Belmont, CA

Krutilla, J.V., Eckstein, O., 1958, *Multiple purpose river development: studies in applied economic analysis*, Johns Hopkins Press, Baltimore, MD

Lancaster, K.J., 1966, A new approach to consumer theory, *Journal of Political Economy*, 84: 132–157

Lichfield, N., 1956, *Economics of planned development*, Estates Gazette, London

Lichfield, N., 1988, *Economics in urban conservation*, Cambridge University Press, Cambridge

Lichfield, N., Hendon, W., Nijkamp, P., Ost, C., Realfonzo, A., Rostirolla, P., 1993, *Conservation economics*, The International Council on Monuments and Sites (ICOMOS), Sri Lanka

Little, I.M.D., Mirrlees, J.A., 1974, *Project appraisal and planning for developing countries*, Heinemann, London

Lockwood, M., Loomis, J., De Lacy, T., 1993, A contingent valuation survey and benefit-cost analysis of forest preservation in East Gippsland, Australia, *Journal of Environmental Management*, 38: 233–243

Lombardi, P., Sirchia, G., 1990, Il quarterre 16 IACF di Torino. In Roscelli, R. ed., *Misurare nell'incertezza*, Celia, Turin

Loomis, J.B., Creel, M., Park, T., 1991, Comparing benefit estimates from travel cost and contingent valuation using confidence intervals from Hicksian welfare measures, *Applied Economics*, 23: 1725–1731

Lloyd, N., 1993, *Rural policy and research*, Action with Communities in Rural England, Cheltenham

McKercher, B., 1993, The unrecognised threat to tourism: can tourism survive sustainability? *Tourism Management*, 14(2): 131–136

Mishan, E., 1967, *The costs of economic growth*, Staples Press, London

Mishan, E., 1971, *Cost-benefit analysis*, Allen and Unwin, London

Mitchell, R.C., Carson, R.T., 1989, *Using surveys to value public goods: the contingent valuation method*, Resources for the Future, Washington, DC

Nash, C.A., ed., 1990, *Appraising the environmental effects of road schemes: a response to the SACTRA Committee Institute for Transportation Studies*, Working Paper 293, University of Leeds, Leeds

Nijkamp, P., 1975, A multicriteria analysis for project evaluation: economic-ecological evaluation of a land reclamation project, *Papers of the Regional Science Association*, 35: 87–111

Paelnick, J.H.P., 1976, Qualitative multiple criteria analysis, environmental protection and multiregional development, *Papers of the Regional Science Association*, 36: 59–74

Pearce, D.G., 1989, *Tourism development*, 2nd edn, Longman, Harlow

Pearce, D.W., ed., 1978, *The valuation of social cost*, Allen and Unwin, London

Pearce, D.W., 1986, *Cost-benefit analysis*, Macmillan, Basingstoke

Pearce, D.W., Nash, C.A., 1981, *The social appraisal of projects: a text in cost-benefit analysis*, Macmillan, Basingstoke

Pearce, D.W., Turner, R.K., 1990, *Economics of natural resources and the environment*, Harvester Wheatsheaf, London

Pearce, D.W., Markandya, A., Barbier, E.B., 1989, *Blueprint for a green economy*, Earthscan, London

Peters, G.H., 1968, *Cost-benefit analysis and public expenditure*, 2nd edn, Eaton Papers 8, Institute of Economic Affairs, London

Prest, A.R., Turvey, R., 1966, Cost-benefit analysis: a survey. In American Economic Association and Royal Economic Society, *Surveys of Economic Theory: Volume III, Resource Allocation*, Macmillan, London

Redefining Progress, 1995, *The genuine progress indicator: summary of data and methodology*, Redefining Progress, San Francisco

Romeril, M., 1989, Tourism and the environment: accord or discord, *Tourism Management*, 10(3): 204–208

Rosen, S., 1974, Hedonic prices and implicit markets: production differentiation in pure competition, *Journal of Political Economy*, 82(1): 34–55

Saaty, R.W., 1987, The analytic hierarchy process: what it is and how it is used, *Mathematical Modelling*, 9: 161–176

Sagoff, M., 1988, *The economy of the earth*, Cambridge University Press, Cambridge

Shackley, M., 1996, *Wildlife tourism*, International Thomson Business Press, London

Sinclair, M.T., 1991, The economics of tourism. In Cooper, C.P., ed., *Progress in tourism, recreation and hospitality management*, Vol. 3, Belhaven, London

Sinclair, M.T., Stabler, M.J., 1997, *Tourism economics*, Routledge, London

Sindiyo, D.M., Pertet, E.N., 1984, Tourism and its impact on wildlife in Kenya, *Industry and Environment*, 7(1): 14–19

Slee, W., Farr, H., Snowdon, P., 1997, Sustainable tourism and the local economy. In Stabler, M.J., ed., *Tourism and sustainability: principles to practice*, CAB International, Wallingford, Oxon

Smith, C., Jenner, P., 1989, Tourism and the environment, *Travel and Tourism Analyst*, 5: 68–86

Stabler, M.J., 1996, Are heritage conservation and tourism compatible? An economic evaluation of their role in urban regeneration: policy implications. In Robinson, M., Evans, N., Callaghan, P., eds, *Managing cultural resources for the tourist*, University of Northumbria, Newcastle

Stabler, M.J., ed., 1997a, *Tourism and sustainability: principles to practice*, CAB International, Wallingford, Oxon

Stabler, M.J., 1997b, An overview of the sustainable tourism debate and the scope and content of the book. In Stabler, M.J., ed., *Tourism and sustainability: principles to practice*, CAB International, Wallingford, Oxon

Stanners, D., Bourdeau, P., 1995, *Europe's environment: the Dobris Assessment*, Office for Official Publications of the European Communities for the European Environment Agency, Luxembourg

Sugden, R., Williams, A., 1978, *The principles of practical cost-benefit analysis*, Oxford University Press, Oxford

Tobin, R., Taylor, R., 1996, Golf and wildlife, *British Wildlife*, 7(3) (February): 137–146

Turner, R.K., Pearce, D.W., Bateman, I., 1994, *Environmental economics: an Elementary introduction*, Harvester Wheatsheaf, Hemel Hempstead

Tyler, C., 1989, A phenomenal explosion, *Geographical Magazine*, 61(8): 18–21

UNCED (United Nations Conference on Environment and Development), 1992, *Agenda 21: a guide to the United Nations Conference on Environment and Development*, UN Publications Service, Geneva

Voogd, H., 1988, Multicriteria evaluation: measures, manipulation and meaning: a reply, *Environment and Planning B: Planning and Design*, 15(1): 65–72

Walsh, R.G., 1986, *Recreation economic decisions: comparing benefits and costs*, Venture, State College, PA

WCED (World Commission on Environment and Development), 1987, *Our common future*, Oxford University Press, Oxford

Wheeller, B., 1997, Here we go, here we go, here we go, eco. In Stabler, M.J. ed., *Tourism and sustainability: principles to practice*, CAB International, Wallingford, Oxon

Willis, K.G., Garrod, G., 1990, *Valuing open access recreation on inland waterways.* Countryside Change Unit Working Paper 5, University of Newcastle, Newcastle

Willis, K.G., Garrod, G., 1993, *The value of waterside properties: estimating the impact of waterways and canals on property values through hedonic price models and contingent valuation methods,* Countryside Change Unit Working Paper 44, University of Newcastle, Newcastle

Wilson, D., 1997, Strategies for sustainability: lessons from Goa and the Seychelles. In Stabler, M.J., ed., *Tourism and sustainability: principles to practice,* CAB International, Wallingford, Oxon

Witt, S.F., Martin, C.A., 1989, Demand forecasting in tourism and recreation. In Cooper, C.P., ed., *Progress in tourism, recreation and hospitality management,* Vol. 1, Belhaven, London

WTO (World Tourism Organisation), 1994, *Global tourism trends,* World Tourism Organisation, Madrid

Index

Aaker, D.A. 5
Additionality
  cost-benefit analysis 247
  investment incentives 175–6, 185–6, 187–8
Age factors
  segmentation 151, 152, 154
  utility analysis 108–9, 113
Aggregation bias, segmentation 150
Airline industry, transactions analysis 43–4
Airola, K. 124
Ajami, R.A. 45
Allison, G. 253, 260
Allocation mechanisms, environmental impacts 240–3, 245
Almost ideal demand system (AIDS) 52
Alwang, J. 27
Analytic hierarchy process (AHP) 261
Arajärvi, T. 123, 124, 126, 136, 138
Arbitrage, market segmentation 221
Archer 198
Archer, B. 69, 71, 154, 166
Archer, B.H. 7, 11, 30, 246
Archer-Owen multiplier model 11
Asabere, P.K. 251
Ashworth, J. 30
Asseal, H. 204
Austria
  behavioural model of tourism 55–8
  investment incentives 164, 171
  VAT 171, 172
Auvinen, E. 136
Average-cost pricing, hotels 215
Averting expenditure (AE) 250
Avoided cost 250

Bagehot, W. 12
Bakkal, I. 150
Balloon financing 169
Barten, A.P. 150

Base theory models 9
Bateman, I. 253
Baum, T. 36, 68, 72, 119, 147, 154, 155, 166
Baumol, W. 210
Becherel, L. 203, 211
Behavioural models 5, 47–65
  almost ideal demand system 52
  assumptions about variables 60–2, 65
  assumptions for specification 59–60, 65
  basic form 50, 53–4
  Cochrane-Orcutt procedure 58, 64
  Cook's D 63
  cost variables 54, 57
  data time periods 50–1
  dfbetas 63
  diagnostics 62–4, 65
  discriminant analysis 52
  distance travelled 54
  distributed lag models 48
  distributional factors in CBA 258
  Durbin-Watson test 58, 64
  error terms 57–8, 62–4
  exchange rates 56, 57, 58
  expenditure data 51, 52
  for explanatory purposes 48, 64–5
  for forecasting 48–9, 65
  heteroscedasticity 63
  Hildreth-Lu procedure 64
  income variables 54, 56, 58
  inflation variables 50
  interpretation 55–8
  irrelevant variables 59, 60
  log-linear 51, 52
  logistic models 52
  Martin and Witt model 53–4, 55–8
  measurement errors 60
  multicollinearity 57, 58, 60–2
  omitted variables 59–60, 64
  ordinary least-squares 50, 51, 52
  polynomial form 51–2
  price variables 54–5, 57, 58

Behavioural models (*continued*)
  residual analysis 62–3, 64
  ridge regression 62
  seasonality 48
  semi-log form 51
  serial correlation 58, 63–4
  specification 52–5, 59–60, 64
  studentized residuals 63
  time-series models compared 47–9,
    64–5
  tolerance 61
  utility theory 49–50
  variance inflation factor 61
  'what if' uses 49, 65
Belgium
  investment incentives 164, 171
  VAT 171, 172
Benefit analysis, investment incentives
  184–5
    see also Cost-benefit analysis
Bermuda 68–72
  government policy 166
  Ricardian analysis 74–83
Bermuda Department of Tourism 69, 70,
  71, 74
Bermuda Hotel Association 70
Bishop, R. 252
Blackorby, C. 150
Bloom, J. 163, 166, 174
Board, J. 31, 32, 33, 34
Bodlender, J.A. 163, 169
Boey, C.K. 25
Boskin, M. 159
Bote Gómez, V. 30
Bourdeau, P. 239
Bowers, J. 252, 257, 259
Bramwell, B. 233
Brand position analysis 5, 85–95
  classes of travellers 87
  competitive sets 86, 95
  data analysis 88–91
  data collection 87–8
  determinant attributes 87
  marketing implications 94–5
  multidimensional scaling 90–1, 96–7
  objective position 86
  perceptual maps 88–94, 95
  positioning statements 86–7, 95
  relative market positions 91–4
  subjective position 86
Brayley, R.E. 146

Breusch, T. 152
Breusch-Pagan test 152
Brierton, U.A. 239
British Tourist Authority (BTA) 172, 198
Brown, W.C. 69, 70–1
Browne, G. 171, 172, 173
Buckley, M. 261
Buckley, P.J. 26, 40, 45
Bucklin, L. 209
Bull, A. 4, 124, 203, 234
Butcher, J. 234
Butler, R.W. 234
Buying behaviour, involvement 204–6
  see also Behavioural models; Utility
    theory

Campbell, D.T. 148
Camp-Meidell inequality 181
Capital grants 169, 170, 176, 180–1, 182,
  191
Carlzon, J. 206
Carson, R.T. 252
Casson, M. 40
Central Statistical Office (CSO) 198
Chambers, R.E. 215
Channel Islands 208–9
Channel management theory 209–10
Cheong, W.K. 147
Cheshire, P.C. 252
Clawson, M. 251
Clawson method 251–2, 253–4
Clewer, A. 251
Cluster analysis 221, 222
Coase, R.H. 4, 39–40
Cochrane-Orcutt procedure 58, 64
Cognitive dissonance 207
Cohen, E. 146
Cohen, J.B. 204
Collective consumption goods 236–7,
  238, 240–1, 247
Commoditisation 200, 211
Commonwealth of Independent States
  (CIS) 173, 175
Competitive markets, Ricardian analysis
  67, 73
Competitive sets, branding 86, 95
Conrad, J. 146
Consumer decision-making,
  involvement 204–6
    see also Behavioural models; Utility
      theory

Consumer satisfaction, package
  holidays 205–6, 207, 211
Contingent valuation method (CVM)
  252–4, 258
Cook, L. 71
Cook, T.D. 148
Cook's D 63
Cooney, M. 208
Cooper, C. 160, 209
Cooper, C.P. 146
Copeland, T.E. 100
Cost-benefit analysis (CBA) 121, 243–63
  additionality 247
  adoption of 262–3
  allocational factors 245
  alternatives to 260–1
  assessment of 256–61, 263
  averting expenditure 250
  Clawson method 251–2, 253–4
  contingent valuation 252–4, 258
  decision rules 256
  Delphi principle 253, 254
  determining scope of 244–6
  direct valuation methods 249–50,
    252–4, 258
  discounting benefits and costs 254–6
  displacement 247
  distributional factors 245, 257–9
  dose response method 250
  ecological factors 245
  evaluating benefits and costs 247–54,
    257, 258–60
  externalities 247
  funding arrangements and 259–60
  generational distribution 254, 258
  hedonic pricing 250–1, 253–4
  identifying benefits and costs
    246–7
  indirect valuation methods 249,
    250–1, 253–4
  internal rate of return 255, 256
  market prices 248
  net present value 256
  non-use value 249
  physical factors 245
  production function approaches 250
  rates of return 255, 256
  sensitivity analysis 254, 256
  shadow prices 248
  socio-cultural factors 245
  spatial factors 245
  theory-practice translation 257,
    258–61
  total economic value 249
  tourism development 262
  travel cost method 251–2, 253–4
  use value 249
  weighting 254
  what to appraise 244–5
  willingness to accept 252, 253, 258
  willingness to pay 252, 253, 258
Cost-effectiveness analysis (CEA) 260
Cost structures, tourist industry 177–83
Cost variables, behavioural models 54, 57
Country of origin of tourists see
  Nationality of tourists
Cowell, D. 199, 202
Crouch, G.I. 54
Crowding-out thesis 168, 186
Cruising holidays 208
Cumberland 21
Curve similarity procedure 228
Cyprus Tourism Office (CTO) 147

Dalkey, N. 253
Davé, V. 45
Dawe, D. 26
Deaton, A. 52
Delphi principle (DP) 253, 254
Demand forecasting 5
  hotel pricing 217, 219, 228
  Ricardian model 67, 68, 75–83
  utility analysis 114
Demand instability see Earnings
  instability
Demand models see Behavioural models
Demand strategies, investment
  incentives 167–8
Denmark
  investment incentives 164, 171
  VAT 171, 172
Depreciation allowances 173–4
Derived demand, environmental
  impacts 240
Development of Tourism Act 176, 191
Dfbetas 63
Dhalla, N.K. 220, 221
Diagnostics, behavioural models 62–4,
  65
Discriminant analysis
  behavioural models 52
  market segmentation 222

Displacement
  cost-benefit analysis 247
  investment incentives 186
Distribution factors 241–2, 245, 257–9
Dobbins, R.W. 146
Dodswell, D. 71–2
Doganis, R. 204
Dorfman, R. 257
Dose response (DR) method 250
Duadel, S. 201
Dunning, J.H. 43, 45
Durbin-Watson (DW) test 58, 64
Dwyer, L. 45

Earnings instability 25–6
  portfolio models 26–35
    advantages 35
    basic premise 27
    bounded 29, 32, 33–5
    earnings maximisation 33–5
    earnings-instability efficient frontier
      29
    instability minimisation 32–3
    multi-area 30, 32
    objective function constraints 28–9,
      31–2, 33
    specifying the model 28–30
Eastern Europe
  investment security 175
  tax incentives 173
  tourist policy 161
Eberhard, R.C. 146
Eckstein, O. 257
Economic aspects of location marketing
  see Public investment in tourism
Economic impact estimation 7–11
  ad hoc models 10–11
  Archer-Owen model 11
  base theory models 9
  direct effects 8, 124–6, 131–2, 138,
    139–41
  general equilibrium 7–8, 11
  indirect effects 8, 124, 125, 126, 131,
    132, 139–41
  induced effects 8, 9, 124, 125, 131, 132,
    139–41
  input-output analysis 7, 11–23
    computer software 22–3
    data requirements 20
    environmental impact analyses
      20–1

  model construction 14–17
  table construction 12–14
  underlying assumptions 17–20
  uses 21–2
  Keynesian approach 9–10
  Nordic Model of Tourism 120, 123–4
    advantages 141–2
    applications 141
    data analysis 129, 131–2
    data collection 128–9, 130–1, 135–9,
      141
    direct (first-round) effects 124–6,
      131–2, 138, 139–41
    empirical studies 132–41
    expenditure method 126, 129,
      131–2, 136–9
    flaws 141
    history 124
    income method 126, 129–32, 137–41
    indirect effects 124, 125, 126, 131,
      132, 139–41
    induced effects 124, 125, 131, 132,
      139–41
    study design 126–8, 136–7
  partial equilibrium 7–8, 11
Economies of scale, input-output
  analysis 18
Employment
  economic impact estimation 9
  government incentives 174, 184–9
  Nordic Model of Tourism 125, 126,
    130, 140, 141
  transactions analysis 40
Employment status of tourists 151, 152,
  154
Energy prices 174
Engel, J.F. 207
Environmental Impact Assessment
  (EIA) 244, 259
Environmental impacts of tourism 20–1,
  233–43
  access to resources 236–7
  allocation mechanisms 240–3, 245
  analytic hierarchy process 261
  collective consumption goods 236–7,
    238, 240–1, 247
  cost-benefit analysis 121, 243–4
    adoption of 262–3
    alternatives to 260–1
    assessment of 256–61, 263
    decision rules 256

determining scope of 244–6
discounting 254–6
distributional factors 245, 257–9
evaluation methods 247–54, 257,
    258–60
identifying benefits and costs 246–7
project definition 245–6
theory-practice translation 257,
    258–61
what to appraise 244–5
cost-effectiveness analysis 260
derived demand 240
despoliation examples 239
displacement 247
distribution 241–2, 245, 257–9
externalities 237, 238, 241, 243, 247
fragile environments 238–9, 240
free riders 237
generational distribution 241–2, 254,
    258
government policy 162, 163, 194
humanmade capital 234–6, 242
market failure 238–43
merit want 237
monopolies 238
multi-criteria analysis 260–1
natural capital 234–6, 242
open access resources 236–7
precautionary principle 242, 258
primary resources defined 235–6
primary use of resources 240–1
public goods 236–7, 238, 240–1, 247
secondary resources defined 236
secondary use of resources 240–1
sustainable tourism 194, 233–5,
    241–2
volume growth 240
Equity participation 170–1
Error terms, behavioural models 57–8,
    62–4
European Union
    environmental protection 244, 259,
        260
    investment incentives 164–5, 166, 171,
        172, 176, 184
    Regional Development Fund 184
    VAT 171, 172
Exchange rates, behavioural models 56,
    57, 58
Expenditure by tourists
    behavioural models 51, 52

investment incentives 185–8
Nordic Model of Tourism 126, 129,
    131–2, 136–9
segmentation 145, 149–55
Externalities, environmental impacts
    237, 238, 241, 243, 247

Factor-cluster segmentation 146
Festinger, L.A. 207
Financial incentives for investment 163,
    166–8
Financial risks of investment 178–81
Finland
    impacts of tourism 132–41
    investment incentives 164, 171
    VAT 171, 172
Finnish Tourist Board (FTB) 124, 126
Firm organisation 4–5, 39–41, 43–4
Fiscal investment incentives 166, 171–5,
    177, 180–1, 183–4
Fixed effects model (FEM),
    segmentation 151–3, 154–5
Fletcher, J. 124
Fletcher, J.E. 7, 20, 22
FONATUR 162–3
Forsberg, C. 123
Forsyth, P. 45
France
    environmental impacts 262
    investment incentives 164, 171
    VAT 171, 172
Frank, R.E. 219
Free riders 237
Fyall, A. 234

Gabszewicz, J.J. 72
Garrod, B. 234
Garrod, G. 251, 253
General equilibrium models 7–8, 11
    see also Input-output analysis
Generational distribution 241–2, 254, 258
Germany
    behavioural models 55–8
    investment incentives 164, 171
    package holiday growth 198
    VAT 171, 172
Geyikdagi, N.V. 26
Geyikdaki, N.V. 45
Goeldner, C.R. 100, 108
Goodall, B. 233
Governance structure 44

Government investment *see* Economic
  impact estimation; Portfolio models;
  Public investment in tourism
Grant, R.M. 147
Grants 169, 170, 176, 180–1, 182, 191
  Greece
  investment incentives 164, 171
  VAT 171, 172
Green, H. 233, 239, 246
Greene, W. 156
Grimmeau, J-P. 30
Gummesson, E. 212
Gunadhi, H. 25

Hague, D.C. 215
Hamilton, D. 68
Hanley, N. 248, 257, 260
Hausman, J. 153
Hausman test 152, 153
Havas, K. 123
Heape 203, 210
Heberlein, T. 252
Hedonic pricing (HPM) 250–1, 253–4
Helmer, O. 253
Heng, T.M. 3
Heteroscedasticity
  behavioural models 63
  segmentation analysis 152
Hick, J.R. 49
Hiemstra, S.J. 48
Hildreth-Lu procedure 64
Hokkanen, K. 132
Holiday complexes 240, 246–7
Holloway, J.C. 200–1
Holopainen, V. 123
Hotels
  balloon financing 169
  positioning analysis 85–95
    classes of travellers 87
    competitive sets 86, 95
    data analysis 88–91
    data collection 87–8
    determinant attributes 87
    marketing implications 94–5
    multidimensional scaling 90–1,
      96–7
    objective position 86
    perceptual maps 88–94, 95
    positioning statements 86–7, 95
    relative market positions 91–4
    subjective position 86

  pricing 215–30
    add-ons 225
    advance bookings 217, 228
    allocating inventory 219
    average-cost 215
    business travellers 216, 217, 229
    calculations 227–8
    categorical discounts 215–16, 225,
      229
    computer programs 227, 228
    curve similarity 228
    customer segment demands
      216–17, 229
    demand forecasting 217, 219, 228
    discounts 215–16, 224–5, 229
    example 222–6
    fixed capacity 218
    fixed costs 218
    groups 217, 229
    marginal costs 215, 220
    market segmentation 219–22
    no-shows 217, 218, 225–6
    overbooking 211, 225–6
    package holidays 208–9, 210–11
    perishability 217–18
    pleasure travellers 216, 217, 229
    rate integrity 218
    reservation clerks 228–9
    Ricardian analysis 67–8, 72–5,
      79–82, 83
    separating pricing segments 229
    services provided 218–19, 222,
      225
Ricardian analysis 67
  assumptions 72
  Bermudan data 74–5
  Bermudan environment 68–72
  competitive markets 67, 73
  demand forecasting stage 76–8
  forecast analysis 78–82
  market perceptions 82
  methodology 75–6
  the model 72–4
  oligopolistic markets 67–8, 72–4,
    83
  quality 80–2
  seasonality 82
  withholding strategies 67–8
transactions analysis 43
Hughes, R. 206
Hunter, C. 233, 239, 246

Impact analyses *see* Economic impact
   estimation; Environmental impacts
   of tourism; Nordic Model of
   Tourism
Inclusive holidays *see* Package holidays
Income from tourism *see* Economic
   impact estimation
Income variables
   behavioural models 54, 56, 58
   strategic segmentation 151, 152, 154
Indifference curves, utility analysis
   100–2
   age factors 108, 113
   inflation 107–8
   interest rates 106
   leisure time allocation 105
   two period consumption 102–4
Inflation
   behavioural models 50
   utility analysis 107–8, 113, 114
Information, transactions analysis 40–1
Input-output analysis 7, 11–23
   computer software for 22–3
   data requirements 20
   environmental impact analyses 20–1
   for impact assessment 22
   model construction 14–17
   Nordic Model of Tourism 124
   table construction 12–14
   underlying assumptions 17–20
   uses 21–2
Inskeep, E. 233
Instability of earnings *see* Earnings
   instability
Interest rates
   cost-benefit analysis 255–6
   tourism consumption and 100, 103–4,
      105–7, 109–13, 114
Internalisation, transactions analysis
   39–41, 44–5
Intriligator, M.D. 48
Investment allowances 174
Investment in tourism *see* Economic
   impact estimation; Portfolio models;
   Public investment in tourism
Investment by tourists, utility analysis
   99–100, 102–4
   interest rates 105–7, 109–13, 114
   leisure time 104–5
Involvement, package holiday pricing
   204–6

Ireland
   investment incentives 164, 171
   VAT 171, 172
Islamic dummy, segmentation 151, 152,
   154–5
Island tourism 68
   Bermuda 68–72
   Ricardian analysis 74–83
Ismail, J.A. 48
Italy
   investment incentives 165, 171
   VAT 171, 172

Jackson, S. 160
Jenkins, C.L. 163, 176
Jenner, P. 209, 239
Jersey, holiday pricing 208–9
Johannsen, N. 12
Johansson, A-L. 123
Johnson, P. 30
Johnson, P.S. 186, 188
Joint production, input-output analysis
   19
Jones, P. 68
Josephides 203
Jyvälä, K. 123

Kahn, R.F. 12
Kauppila, P. 123, 136
Kelman, S. 257
Kemppainen, J. 123
Kendall, M. 146
Kettunen, T. 123
Keynes, J.M. 12
Keynesian multiplier model 9–10
Khem, G.S. 147
Kimes, S.E. 206–7, 219, 227
Kleinbaum, D.G. 110
Knetsch, J.L. 251
Knudsen, O. 25
Kotler, P. 221
Krippendorf 200
Krutilla, J.V. 257
Kundu, S.K. 45

Labour services
   Bermudan hotels 71
   government subsidies 174
   transactions analysis 39, 40
   see also Employment
Lamnert, C.U. 211

Lancaster, K.J. 250
Lane, B. 233
Lankola, K. 124
Laws, E. 199, 201, 206, 209, 212
Lawson, R. 146
Legislation, investment incentives 176,
    177, 191
Leiper, N. 130, 212
Leisure time allocation, utility analysis
    104–5, 106–7
Leith, E. 209
Leontief, W. 12
Levy, H. 27, 100
Lewis, R.C. 86–7, 215
Lichfield, N. 257, 258, 260–1
Lieberman, W.H. 68
Litteljohn, D. 3
Little, I.M.D. 257
Little, J.S. 25
Lloyd, N. 240
Loans, government 169–70, 176
Location marketing see Public
    investment in tourism
Lockwood, A. 68
Lockwood, M. 253
Loeb, P.D. 25, 54
Logistic models, behaviour 52
Log-linear behavioural models 51, 52
Lombardi, P. 261
Loomis, J.B. 251
Love, J. 26
Low, L. 3
Lowyck, E. 188
Luxembourg
    investment incentives 165, 171
    VAT 171, 172

Mahatoo, W.H. 220, 221
Malinen, R. 123
Marginal costs, hotel pricing 215, 220
Marginal rate of exchange (MRE), utility
    analysis 101–2, 103–4, 105–6, 107–8,
    113
Marginal rate of substitution (MRS),
    utility analysis 101, 103, 104, 105
Market prices, cost-benefit analysis 248
Market segmentation 156, 219–22
    additional costs 221
    arbitrage 221
    cluster analysis 221, 222
    discriminant analysis 222

price discrimination 220
    see also Strategic segmentation
Marketing strategies
    hotel positioning analysis 85–7, 94–5
    input-output analysis 21–2
    utility analysis 114
    see also Package holidays, pricing;
        Strategic segmentation
Markets
    employment creation 186
    failure 160–1, 167, 238–43
    package holiday pricing 209–10
    Ricardian analysis 67–8, 72–4, 82, 83
    transactions analysis 39–40
Markowitz, H.M. 27
Marshall, A. 49
Martin, C. 151
Martin, C.A. 31, 49, 53–4, 55–6, 253
Masson, R.T. 72, 74, 218
Mathieson, A. 124
Maurice 100
Maurice, S.C. 99
Mazanec, J.A. 146
McCannell, D. 200
McCarthy, E.J. 199
McIntosh, R.B. 100, 108
McKenna, R. 212
McKercher, B. 234
McQueen, M. 43, 45
Medlik 200
Mendenhall, W. 63
Merit want 237
Mexico 162–3
Middleton, V.T.C. 201
Mill, R.C. 212
Mintzberg, H. 147
Mirrlees, J.A. 257
Mishan, E. 257
Mitchell, R.C. 252
Monopolies, natural 238
Morgan, M. 209, 211
Morrison, A.M. 212
Mostert, F. 163, 166, 174
Moutinho, L. 146, 198
Mudambi, R. 36, 72, 154, 155, 166
Muellbauer, J. 52
Multicollinearity 57, 58, 60–2
Multi-criteria analysis (MCA) 260–1
Multidimensional scaling (MDS) 90–1,
    96–7
Multidisciplinary methods 119–21

see also Cost-benefit analysis; Nordic
  Model of Tourism; Pricing
  strategies; Public investment in
  tourism; Strategic segmentation
Multipliers 7–11
  ad hoc 10–11
  Archer-Owen 11
  base theory 9
  general equilibrium 7–8, 11
  in impact assessment 22
  Keynesian 9–10
  partial equilibrium 7–8, 11
  portfolio analysis 31–2
  see also Input-output analysis
Mundlak, Y. 151

Nash, C.A. 257
Nathan, R.R. 9
Nationality of tourists
  portfolio analysis 30–5
  segmentation 147, 148, 149–50, 151–3,
    154–6
Natural monopolies 238
Net present value (NPV) 256
Netherlands
  investment incentives 165, 171
  package holiday growth 198
  VAT 171, 172
Network marketing 212
Neural networks, segmentation 146
Nijkamp, P. 260
Nordic Model of Tourism 120, 123–4
  advantages 141–2
  applications 141
  data analysis 129, 131–2
  data collection 128–9, 130–1, 135–9, 141
  direct effects 124–6, 131–2, 138, 139–41
  empirical studies 132–41
  expenditure method 126, 129, 131–2,
    136–9
  flaws 141
  history 124
  income method 126, 129–32, 137–41
  indirect effects 124, 125, 126, 131, 132,
    139–41
  induced effects 124, 125, 131, 132,
    139–41
  study design 126–8, 136–7
Normann, R. 206

O'Brien 198, 200, 206

Oligopolistic markets 67–8, 72–4, 83
Olsson, R. 124
Operating costs, investment 163, 171–5,
  180–2
Operating leverage, investment 177–9
Ordinary least-squares models 50, 51, 52
  segmentation 151, 152–3
Organisation of firms 4–5, 39–41, 43–4
Originating country of tourists *see*
  Nationality of tourists
Orkin, E.B. 68, 227
Owen, C. 11
Ozdil, I. 146

Paajanen, M. 123, 124, 132
Package holidays 198–9
  benefits 199
  growth 198
  pricing 120–1, 197–212
    broadened market 207–9, 211
    channel management theory 209–10
    cognitive dissonance 207
    commoditisation 200, 211
    complexity 200–1
    consumer satisfaction 205–6, 207, 211
    cooperation 211–12
    cruises 208
    desirable clients 208–9
    destination effects 210–11
    early booking 202–3, 204, 205
    entry barriers 210
    exit costs 210
    industry structure 210
    influences on 201
    invoice payment 203–4
    involvement 204–6
    late booking 202–4, 205–6
    long-term effects 200, 209–11, 212
    network marketing 212
    objectives 199, 201
    origin market effects 209–10
    overbooking 211
    quality 205–7, 211, 212
    regional flights 204
    seasonal 201–2, 203, 204
    significance 199–200
    spill 201
    spoilage 201
    systems theory 212
    yield management 201, 206–7
  transactions analysis 42, 43

Paelinck, J.H.P. 260
Pagan, A. 152
Pannell Kerr Forster 218
Papadopoulos, S.I. 45
Parnes, A. 25
Partial equilibrium models 7–8, 11
Pearce 198
Pearce, D.G. 30, 234, 246, 263
Pearce, D.W. 234, 235, 241, 257
Perceptual maps 88–94, 95
Perreault, W.D., Jr. 199
Pertet, E.N. 239
Pesaran, M.H. 77, 78
Peters, G.H. 257
Phlips, L. 48, 150
Pigou, A.C. 12
Piirala, T. 138
Pindyck, R.S. 59, 64
Pitkänen, M. 123, 132
Plog, S. 146, 160
Poon, A. 198
Porter, M.E. 145
Portfolio models 26–36
  advantages 35
  applicability 36
  basic premise 27
  bounded 29, 32, 33–5
  earnings maximisation 33–5
  earnings-instability efficient frontier
    29
  instability minimisation 32–3
  multi-area 30, 32
  objective function constraints 28–9,
    31–2, 33
  policy implications 35
  in Spain 30–5
  specifying the model 28–30
Portugal
  investment incentives 165, 171
  VAT 171, 172
Positioning analysis 85–95
  classes of travellers 87
  competitive sets 86, 95
  data analysis 88–91
  data collection 87–8
  determinant attributes 87
  marketing implications 94–5
  multidimensional scaling 90–1, 96–7
  objective position 86
  perceptual maps 88–94, 95
  positioning statements 86–7, 95

relative market positions 91–4
subjective position 86
Precautionary principle 242, 258
Prest, A.R. 257
Price mechanisms
  market failure 238
  transactions analysis 40
Price methods, cost-benefit analysis
  247–8
  contingent valuation 252–4, 258
  hedonic pricing 250–1, 253–4
  travel cost method 251–2, 253–4
Price variables
  behavioural models 54–5, 57, 58
  strategic segmentation 151, 152, 154
Pricing strategies
  hotels 121, 215–30
    add-ons 225
    advance bookings 217, 228
    allocating inventory 219
    average-cost 215
    business travellers 216, 217, 229
    calculations 227–8
    categorical discounts 215–16, 225, 229
    computer programs 227, 228
    curve similarity 228
    customer segment demands
      216–17, 229
    demand forecasting 217, 219, 228
    discounts 215–16, 224–5, 229
    example 222–6
    fixed capacity 218
    fixed costs 218
    groups 217, 229
    marginal costs 215, 220
    market segmentation 219–22
    no-shows 217, 218, 225–6
    overbooking 211, 225–6
    package holidays 208–9, 210–11
    perishability 217–18
    pleasure travellers 216, 217, 229
    price discrimination 220
    rate integrity 218
    reservation clerks 228–9
    Ricardian analysis 67–8, 72–5,
      79–82, 83
    separating pricing segments 229
    services provided 218–19, 222, 225
  package holidays 120–1, 197–212
    broadened market 207–9, 211
    channel management theory 209–10

cognitive dissonance 207
commoditisation 200, 211
complexity 200–1
consumer satisfaction 205–6, 207, 211
cooperation 211–12
cruises 208
desirable clients 208–9
destination effects 210–11
early booking 202–3, 204, 205
industry structure 210
influences on 201
invoice payment 203–4
involvement 204–6
late booking 202–4, 205–6
long-term effects 200, 209–11, 212
objectives 199, 201
origin market effects 209–10
overbooking 211
quality 205–7, 211, 212
regional flights 204
seasonal banding 201–2, 203, 204
significance 199–200
yield management 201, 206–7
Production functions
cost-benefit analysis 250
input-output analysis 18, 19
Prus, R.C. 205
Public (collective consumption) goods 236–7, 238, 240–1, 247
Public investment in tourism 4, 159–60
case for 160–1, 193–4
cost-benefit analysis 255–6, 259–60, 262
cost structures 177–83
environmental issues 162, 163, 194, 236–8
extent of 194
incentives
additionality 175–6, 185–6, 187–8
administration 189–93
application process 190–3
benefit analysis 184–5
capital adjustments 183–4
capital costs 163, 169–71, 174, 176, 180–2
capital grants 169, 170, 176, 180–1, 182, 191
classification 163, 166
crowding-out thesis 168, 186
demand strategies 167–8
discretionary 176–7, 190–3
displacement 186

employment creation 174, 184–9
equity participation 170–1
in European Union 164–5, 166, 171, 176
evaluation 183–9
financial 163, 166–8
fiscal 166, 171–5, 177, 180–1, 183–4
implementation 175–7, 190–3
infrastructure 171
investment security 163, 168, 170, 175
land 171, 178
legislation 176, 177, 191
ministerial guidelines 176–7, 191
operating adjustments 183–4
operating costs 163, 171–5, 180–2
operating leverage 177–9
project additionality 175–6
project viability 181–3
promotion 189–90
risk 177, 178–81
soft loans 169–70, 176
supply-side strategies 168
visitor additionality 185–6, 187–8
market failure 160–1, 167
policy objectives 161–2
strategies 162–3
sustainable development 194, 233–4
Tourism Development Corporations 162–3, 168
see also Economic impact estimation; Portfolio models
Pyo, S.S. 51

Quality, package holidays 205–7, 211, 212
Quality management 45

Raiskinmäki, M-T. 123
Random effects model (REM) 151–3
Rao, A. 26
Redefining Progress 241
Regional airports 204
Regional Development Fund 184
Relihan, W.J. III 68, 201, 219
Residual analysis, behavioural models 62–3, 64
Retail travel agents, transactions analysis 42, 43, 44
see also Pricing strategies, package holidays

Ricardian analysis 67
  assumptions 72
  Bermudan data 74–5
  Bermudan environment 68–72
  competitive markets 67, 73
  demand forecasting stage 76–8
  forecast analysis 78–82
  market perceptions 82
  methodology 75–6
  the model 72–4
  oligopolistic markets 67–8, 72–4, 83
  quality 80–2
  seasonality 82
  withholding strategies 67–8
Ridge regression 62
Riley, C.W. 69, 70–1
Risk, investment in tourism 178–81
Ritchie, J.R.B. 145
Robinson, R. 200–1
Rogers, P. 206, 207
Romeril, M. 239
Rosef, K. 123
Rosen, S. 250
Rubenfeld, D.L. 59, 64
Russo, J.A. 68

Saaty, R.W. 261
Sagoff, M. 257
Sairanen, K. 123
Sarnat, M. 27, 100
SAS Institute 63
Sasser, W.E. 226
Schulmeister, S. 4
Schwartz, Z. 228
Seasonal prices, package holidays
  201–2, 203, 204
Seasonality
  as behavioural model 48
  input-output analysis 18
  Ricardian analysis 82
Segmentation analysis see Market
  segmentation; Strategic
  segmentation
Sensitivity analysis 254, 256
Serial correlation, behavioural models
  58, 63–4
Sessa, A. 100
Shackley, M. 239, 246, 260
Shadow prices, cost-benefit analysis 248
  see also Contingent valuation; Hedonic
  pricing; Travel cost method

Shaked, A. 72
Shamsuddin, S. 25
Shaw, M. 68
Sheldon, P. 210
Sheldon, P.J. 30
Shih, D. 146
Siegel, P.B. 27
Sincich, T. 63
Sinclair, M.T. 26, 30, 234, 239
Sindiyo, D.M. 239
Sirchia, G. 261
Skidmore, J. 210
Slee, W. 234
Smalz, D. 146
Smith, C. 209, 239
Smith, L.J. 124, 126, 130
Smith, S.L.J. 221
Smith, V. 146
Smithson 100
Snee, H. 124
Södervall, R. 123
Soft loans 169–70, 176
Spain
  investment incentives 165, 171
  portfolio models 30–5
  public sector investment 161
  VAT 171, 172
Spash, C.L. 248, 257, 260
Spill, package holidays 201
Spoilage, package holidays 201
Stabler, M.J. 30, 233, 234, 239, 246, 252, 254
Stanners, D. 239
Stonier, A.W. 215
Strategic segmentation 120, 145–56
  age factors 151, 152, 154
  aggregation bias 150
  Breusch-Pagan test 152
  classical segmentation analysis 145–6,
    147–8
  country of origin 147, 148, 149–50,
    151–3, 154–6
  data sources 148–9, 156
  factor-cluster method 146
  fixed effects model 151–3, 154–5
  Hausman test 152, 153
  heteroscedasticity 152
  income proxy 151, 152, 154
  Islamic dummy 151, 152, 154–5
  limitations 156
  literature on 146
  neural network method 146

ordinary least-squares model 151, 152–3
price proxy 151, 152, 154
random effects model 151–3
segment attractiveness analysis 146,
  147, 151–5
segmentation matrix construction 146,
  147, 155
study methodology 149–51, 155
subgroup characteristics 151, 152–3
tourists' employment 151, 152, 154
Turkey 146–7, 148–56
utility-maximising expenditure 150
Studentized residuals 63
Substitution, input-output analysis 19
Sugden, R. 257
Supply policies 5
  Bermudan hotels 70–2
    Ricardian analysis 68, 72–4, 75,
      76–83
Supply-side strategies, government
  investment 168
Surrey Research Group 187
Sustainable tourism 194, 233–5, 241–2
Sutcliffe, C.M.S. 32, 33, 34
Sutton, J. 72
Sweden
  investment incentives 165, 171
  VAT 171, 172
Systems theory 212

Taiwan Tourism Bureau 147
Tax holidays 172–4, 180–1
Tax incentives 166, 171–5, 177
  European Union 164–5
  evaluation 180–1, 183–4
Tax revenues, Nordic Model of Tourism
  125, 126, 132, 140, 141
Tax systems, transactions analysis 40
Taylor, R. 239
Tekoniemi-Selkälä, T. 123
Thomas, R.B. 186, 188
Time-series models, behavioural models
  compared 47–9, 64–5
Tobin, R. 239
Tolerance (TOL), behavioural models 61
Total economic value, cost-benefit
  analysis 249
Tour operators, transactions analysis 42,
  43, 44
  see also Pricing strategies, package
    holidays

Tourism Development Corporations
  (TDCs) 162–3, 168
Transactions cost analysis 39–45
  applications in tourism 45
  brokers 42
  internalisation 39–41, 44–5
  marketing implications 44
  organisational forces 43–4
  quality management 45
  transactions chains 41–4
  transport function 44–5
Transport function, transactions analysis
  44–5
Travel agents, transactions analysis 42,
  43, 44
  see also Pricing strategies, package
    holidays
Travel cost method (TCM), cost-benefit
  analysis 251–2, 253–4
Tremblay, P. 45
Trend, N. 204
Tsegaye, A. 26
Turkey, strategic segmentation 146–7,
  148–56
Turner, R.K. 234, 235, 248, 257
Turvey, R. 257
Tyler, C. 239

United Kingdom
  behavioural model of tourism 55–8
  domestic tourism 240
  environmental impacts 260
  investment incentives 165, 171, 176,
    190–3
  package holiday growth 198
  package holiday price competition 200
  package holiday pricing 208–9
  public sector investment 160
  VAT 171, 172
United Nations Conference on
  Environment and Development
  (UNCED) 233
United Nations projects 259, 261
Urry, J. 200
USA, utility analysis 109–13
Use value, cost-benefit analysis 249
Utility maximisation
  cross-time consumption 102, 104–5,
    108, 113
  definition 99–100, 102
  in strategic segmentation 150

Utility theory 49–50, 99–100
  cross-time consumption 5, 99, 100,
    104–14
    age factors 108–9, 113
    applications 114
    empirical study 109–13
    future research 114
    indifference curve defined 100–2
    inflation 107–8, 113, 114
    interest rates 105–7, 109–13, 114
    leisure time allocation 104–5, 106–7
    marginal rate of exchange defined
      101–2
    marginal rate of substitution
      defined 101
    utility maximisation defined
      99–100, 102
  strategic segmentation 150

Valenzuela, M. 30
Value added tax (VAT) 171–2
Vanhove, N. 146
Variance inflation factor (VIF) 61
Vellas, F. 203, 211
Viability of projects 181–3
Vialle, G. 201
Volatility of earnings see Earnings
  instability
Voogd, H. 260
Vuoristo, K-V. 123, 124, 126, 132, 136,
  138

Wales Tourist Board 190–3
Wall, G. 124

Walsh, R.G. 252
Wanhill, S. 163, 166, 172, 181, 188, 190
Ward, T.J. 163, 169
Warner, J.T. 51
Weaver, P.A. 222
Weber, S. 146
Weighting, cost-benefit analysis 254
Weston, J.F. 100
Westvlaams Ekonomisch Studiebureau
  146
Wheatcroft 204
Wheeller, B. 234
Williams, A. 257
Williamson, O.E. 4, 40
Willig, R. 210
Willingness to accept (WTA) 252, 253,
  258
Willingness to pay (WTP) 252, 253, 258
Willis, K.G. 251, 253
Wilson, D. 259
Wilson, P. 25, 26
Witt, C.A. 49
Witt, S.F. 31, 49, 53–4, 55–6, 151, 253
  World Bank projects 259, 261
World Commission on Environment
  and Development (WCED) 233, 234
World Tourism Organisation (WTO) 240
Wright, A.U. 12

Yield management 68
  package holiday pricing 201, 206–7
  programs 227

Zammit, A. 45

Index compiled by Liz Granger